LANDSCAPE DESIGN THAT SAVES ENERGY

LANDSCAPE DESIGN THAT SAVES ENERGY

by Anne Simon Moffat and Marc Schiler

Drawings by Dianne Zampino

WILLIAM MORROW AND COMPANY, INC.
NEW YORK   1981

Library of Congress Catalog Card Number
80-85098

ISBN 0-688-00031-2
ISBN 0-688-00395-8 (pbk.)

Printed in the United States of America

FIRST MORROW QUILL PAPERBACK EDITION
1 2 3 4 5 6 7 8 9 10

Designed by Bernard Schleifer

This book is dedicated to J.K.M.
who offered a proper mix of encouragement and criticism
    and to
Dianne, Jonathan and Karen,
and all other future stewards of the planet.

ACKNOWLEDGMENTS

MANY FRIENDS, PROFESSIONAL COL-leagues, and librarians contributed encouragement and expert advice to this book. Special gratitude is due to the Laboratory of Computer Graphics at Cornell University and to Professor Donald Greenberg for providing the resources needed to complete some of the research referred to in this book. Thanks are also due to Professors Arthur S. Lieberman, Robert G. Mower, and to the late Harold E. Moore, Jr., and to Bruce K. Forbes, for reviewing segments of the text, and to Drs. Robert Hunt and Lee Kass for reviewing the plant lists.

We are also indebted to Carolyn Schiff whose work on the Appendix did nothing to advance her medical studies; to Coraleen Rooney, who transformed our scrawl into clean typewritten copy; and to our artist, Dianne Zampino, a valuable contributor to this collaborative effort.

We extend special thanks to our editor, Robert Bender, who contributed sterling advice and support.

CONTENTS

Acknowledgments   7

Introduction   11

1 THE RATIONALE FOR LANDSCAPING TO SAVE ENERGY   13

2 HUMAN COMFORT AND CLIMATIC FORCES   23

3 ENERGY-EFFICIENT LANDSCAPE DESIGN FOR COOL
   CLIMATES   61

4 ENERGY-EFFICIENT LANDSCAPE DESIGN FOR HOT, ARID
   CLIMATES   77

5 ENERGY-EFFICIENT LANDSCAPE DESIGN FOR HOT, HUMID
   CLIMATES   93

6 ENERGY-EFFICIENT LANDSCAPE DESIGN FOR TEMPERATE
   CLIMATES   111

7 SOLVING SPECIAL PROBLEMS WITH PLANTS   137

8 LOOKING AHEAD   155

   APPENDICES   165

A MAP: THE ZONES OF PLANT HARDINESS   167

B MAP: THE LATITUDES OF NORTH AMERICA   169

C TABLE OF SOLAR ANGLES FOR U.S.   171

D TABLE OF TANGENTS   177

E TABLE OF TREE DENSITIES   181

F LISTS OF PLANTS ACCORDING TO SIZE AND FORM   183

   Bibliography   213

   Index   219

INTRODUCTION

Recent fuel shortages have forced us to reconsider life-styles, to redesign dwellings and modes of transport, and to eliminate wasteful habits. Many of the schemes to compensate for the dwindling supplies of fossil fuels stress the need for personal sacrifice and for acceptance of exotic, expensive, new systems for generating energy.

In contrast, landscaping, the practice of sculpting the earth and the plants that grow on it, offers a strategy for extending the availability of existing energy supplies.

Landscaping to save energy is a powerful tool for conservation: it controls wind, solar radiation, and precipitation, tempers extremes of climate, and can save up to 30 percent of a home's total energy requirements for space heating and cooling. Moreover, it uses common trees, shrubs, and ground covers to achieve its goals, is aesthetically pleasing, requires a relatively modest financial investment (unlike the installation of solar water heaters or heat exchangers), and is enjoyable to implement. This last benefit distinguishes landscaping to save energy from most other conservation techniques.

Plants were first valued for their productivity. They fed us, their fibers clothed us, and they provided shelter. We soon learned to love their beauty and make use of their medicinal powers. The goal of this book is to show that landscaping offers another strategy for energy conservation and, at the same time, enriches the environment. Year-round it can bring physical comfort into our homes and offices and aesthetic pleasures into our lives.

This book is written primarily for

11

homeowners: You are the people who decide what happens to your house and land and are, in fact, the designers for most of the landscapes in the country. Everything is explained, assuming no previous expertise. Landscape designers, architects, and planners will find it valuable as well because much of the information is new and extensive appendices and bibliographies have been included. It offers advice appropriate for urban, suburban, or rural settings. Apartment dwellers who have access to roof gardens, modest backyards, or balconies will find our suggestions useful. Landscaping ideas are offered for both the limited and the lavish budget.

The first part of this book explains the economic benefits of using a well-designed landscape to save energy, the historic origins of this strategy, and the scientific principles required to understand and plant an energy-efficient landscape. Readers with limited technical training will find this information challenging. Professional designers may use these first chapters as a helpful review. Chapters three through six present landscape models for each of the four main climatic zones in the United States: cool, hot-arid, hot-humid, and temperate regions. Each zone has different needs and therefore requires different landscape techniques for climate amelioration. The closing chapters show how landscape can also offer a great variety of other environmental benefits by controlling pollution, erosion, brush fires, and noise.

Throughout the book, plant species are described by both their common and proper scientific name as indicated by *Hortus Third*. If only one name is listed when the plant is first mentioned, it is because the common and Latin names are the same. Cultivars, referring to cultivated varieties, are indicated by the abbreviation "cv."

We want to demonstrate to you that landscape design is an appropriate technique for conservation and that planning to conserve our energy resources is not always synonymous with sacrifice.

ANNE SIMON MOFFAT
MARC SCHILER
Ithaca, New York

1

THE RATIONALE FOR LANDSCAPING TO SAVE ENERGY

THE EARLIEST HOUSE BUILDERS recognized the many uses of plants. They valued their usefulness as structural materials and as elements of the landscape that offered shelter from sun, snow, wind, and rain.

Builders knew that in the daytime the ground temperature in a forest was much cooler than at the top of the tree canopy, and that at midday a vine-covered wall was always cooler than a bare wall. A home sheltered on its upwind side by an evergreen windbreak used less fuel in winter, and a mature, deciduous tree shading a roof and southern wall offered great comfort to the building's residents during summer.

Knowledge of and respect for the local climate and a remarkable understanding of the performance characteristics of building materials and the landscape contributed to the exceptional success of early architecture. Despite meager resources, primitive societies designed habitats that successfully met the severest problems offered by hostile climates. House builders frequently used the landscape to improve microclimate, that is, the local climate on a small site.

For example, natives of the hot, humid South Pacific constructed extremely open homes of bamboo and palm leaves to take advantage of available, cooling breezes. Eighteenth-century Parisians planned the grand boulevards to promote commerce and military defense, but they also lined their avenues with trees, which reduced heat buildup along the paved highways.

In North America, early home builders used the natural landscape to their advantage. The Powhattan confederation of Indians in Virginia always put their buildings under trees to help shed snow and rain, and the nomadic Omaha Indians of the Plains abandoned their wooden abodes in the winter for tents set up in wooded ravines, which offered better protection from chilling winds.

American colonists considered the landscape in their building plans, as well. Captain John Smith describes an early seventeenth-century Virginia church that is far different from the splendid buildings in which Williamsburg worshipped a century later:

"When I first went to Virginia, I well remember we did make awnings of three or four trees to shade us from the sun; our walls were rails of wood, our seats, unhewn trees til we cut planks, our pulpit a bar of wood nailed to two neighboring trees. . . ."

In the cold Northeast, the early settlers built snug houses, well oriented to the sun, with strategically placed windbreaks of evergreens. In the Southwest, thick-walled haciendas with protected, internal patios were landscaped externally with cacti and other drought-resistant succulents, and internally with leafier species, which offered some shade and retained valuable moisture.

The pre-industrial architects of Colonial and early nineteenth-century America produced designs of wonderful climatic awareness and fitness. But this respect for the natural environment waned in Western societies with industrialization and the invention of mechanical home heating and cooling systems, dependent on oil, gas, and electricity. Fortified against the excesses of nature by faith in the new technology, builders ignored the impact and complexity of the natural environment.

Contemporary architecture for the most part is removed from climatic cause and effect and, for about a century, its inefficiencies were masked by cheap fuel. Prior to the 1970s, energy conservation was not a design criterion in most construction. The controlling factor in building design was construction cost; operating and life-cycle costs were not a major concern.

Fuel shortages, which increased the cost of maintaining human comfort, have forced us to recognize our failure to understand the environmental forces that play upon structures, and the inadequacies of modern building design. The public bemoans the inefficiencies of the automobile, but the impact of poor housing is more enduring. Gas-guzzling cars will have vanished from the roads long before our current housing is replaced by more energy-efficient structures.

Unfortunately, Americans have often limited their response to the challenge of building better structures to the application of more and more technology. Whole new industries manufacturing insulation, solar hot-water heaters, modular windmills, and other novel devices have emerged in recent years. We have failed to realize the benefits of using the simpler energy-saving techniques of our ancestors such as use of the landscape. Too often outdoor plants are still selected for their ability to impress neighbors and passersby, and not for their potential to improve a home's energy efficiency.

We must reexamine the house-building traditions of earlier, less wasteful societies, recognize the constraints imposed on energy-conscious architecture by the environment, and alter existing structures to become more responsive to local climate. We must learn to enlist nature as an ally in the design and construction of acceptable dwellings, rather than to regard it as an adversary. Landscaping can help to achieve this goal. It remains one of the most basic but neglected methods for conserving energy.

Landscaping to minimize heat loss or excessive heat gain is no substitute for proper insulation, storm windows, and tight construction. But for a modest additional sum it offers more energy efficiency than many of the exotic devices now on the market.

Slowly, awareness of the nation's energy shortage and knowledge of the power of plants to save energy are altering our attitudes toward the value of thoughtful landscape design. What distinguishes modern endeavors from earlier efforts to use the landscape to save energy is the availability of new methods for quantifying the energy-saving potential of landscaping. Modern architectural, engineering, and horticultural research are developing and refining techniques that precisely measure the ability of various planting schemes to protect buildings from extremes of temperature. (Numerical results of some of this research are in Appendix E.) The practice of landscaping to save energy is now evolving from an imprecise, "common sense" art into an exact science.

The most compelling reason for using energy-efficient landscape design is cost. Landscaping offers one of the most inexpensive, flexible forms of investing in energy efficiency and differs from most other conservation strategies by requiring no large initial financial investment. The residential landscape can be developed gradually as funds are available. Also, a single general strategy can conserve heat in the winter and simultaneously reduce the need for air conditioning during warmer periods. In contrast, most mechanical systems require separate sets of equipment for heating and cooling, which demand two financial commitments and two maintenance routines. Landscaping is one of the very few general strategies to offer some climate control year-round.

The economic merits of designing the landscape can be illustrated by contrasting two different planting strategies used to solve the simple climatic problem of too much heat. One requires a large financial investment and the second, a minimal one.

Trees are an excellent defense against excessive heat buildup, especially when they shade southern or western facades. They can transform an unbearably hot patio or inside liv-

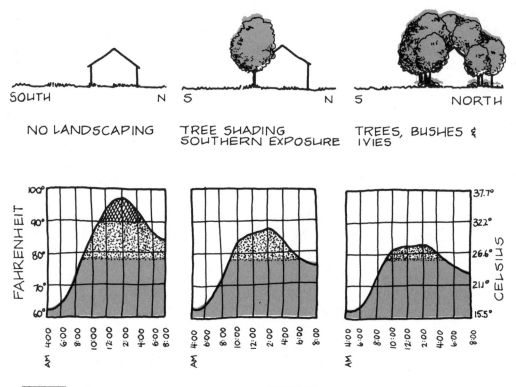

OVER 90°–INTOLERABLE   OVER 78°–DISCOMFORT

LANDSCAPING EFFECTS ON SUMMER TEMPERATURES OF
A HOUSE IN A TEMPERATE CLIMATE

ing area into a pleasant refuge. A tree with a light leaf canopy such as honey locust *(Gleditsia triacanthos)*, larch *(Larix decidua)*, or eucalyptus, can control the sun's heat inside a home better than a lightly colored plastic coating on a glass window or a white Venetian blind, fully drawn. A dense tree such as oak *(Quercus* species) or maple *(Acer* species), which throws a heavy shade, will temper heat buildup better than a heavy, reflective coating on glass. An average full-sized deciduous tree evaporates 100 gallons of water during a sunny summer day, which uses up about 660,000 British thermal units (Btus) of energy, and gives a cooling effect outside a home equal to five average (10,000 Btu) air-conditioners. Shading by foliage can lower the interior temperature of a lightly constructed building such as a garage by as much as 20 degrees Fahrenheit. It can also reduce, by one half, the length of time the building has an uncomfortable internal environment. However, the effects of shading by foliage inside a heavier, better insulated structure are less dramatic and vary significantly from home to home depending on construction materials.

A rapid solution to a hot room with

a southern or western exposure can be provided by the installation of a single, fifteen-foot deciduous shade tree such as red maple *(Acer rubrum)* at a total cost of about $500.* This tree has a four-inch trunk and rootball forty inches in diameter, weighs more than 1,000 pounds and usually requires professional moving and planting. If your needs are not that pressing or your budget not that generous, buy an inexpensive five- to six-foot shade tree for $25, three or four specimens of a fast-growing vine for $20, and materials to build a trellis. The installation of these plants is not difficult and a fast-growing vine such as select clematis species or Virginia creeper *(Parthenocissus quinquefolia)* will provide almost immediate shade. After about six years the smaller tree will have caught up with the fifteen-footer and offer the same benefits.

*Prices of plant materials vary considerably, depending on location.

The mechanical alternatives that provide the same climate control as the planting of a single tree are varied, and most are more expensive. None is as aesthetically pleasing. They include Venetian blinds, a specially fitted thermal window, lined drapes fitted on a mechanical rod, a fan or air-conditioner. Absorption refrigeration solar systems are devices that offer air conditioning by using a solar collector. Currently, their costs are prohibitive, and their reliability is questioned.

Similar arguments can be presented for the economic benefits of using landscape design to conserve heat in cold climates. Heat loss at a building's surface is proportional to the square of the wind velocity rushing past it. For example, if wind speed doubles, heat loss quadruples; if wind speed increases five times, heat loss is multiplied twenty-five times. Wind increases the heat load on a building by increasing the heat loss from the structure to the environment and by blow-

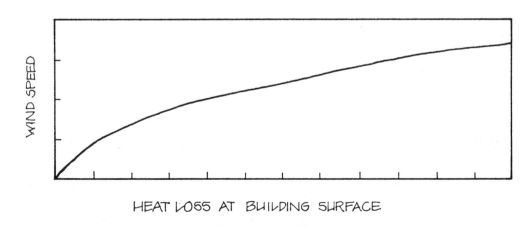

HEAT LOSS AT BUILDING SURFACE

WIND SPEED VS. HEAT LOSS

ing cold air into the building, which needs to be heated. Windbreaks, consisting of dense rows of trees such as evergreens, deflect wind over the structure and decrease its heat loss. Recent studies of identical buildings on similar sites in the temperate region have shown that the proper placement of a shelterbelt for one home reduced its winter fuel consumption by 33 percent.

A forty-foot-high mature windbreak, seventy to one hundred feet in length, protecting a moderately insulated house of average construction in a cooler, temperate zone can save about 3,900 kilowatt hours (kwh) in a winter, costing $330 if a kilowatt hour costs 8.5¢ (estimated mid-1980s cost).* Unfortunately, transplanting forty-foot mature trees is expensive and difficult. However, six immature, ten-foot trees, which you can install, cost about $300. The energy savings the year of their planting would be minimal but would increase with each year. Five years after transplanting, this windbreak would have paid for itself, saving the homeowner 2,000 kwh or about $170 during the fifth year alone. In another ten years the windbreak would offer the benefits of a full-size windbreak.

In certain situations, plants must be removed from grounds to achieve an energy-efficient design. For example, low-growing trees and shrubs that block desirable, winter sunshine or poorly placed windbreaks that cause heat-dissipating wind turbulence should be cut down.

Cost is not always the preeminent factor when considering systems that save energy. Any evaluation of the landscape as an energy-control system must also consider its desirable, passive regulating qualities. Unlike mechanical temperature-control systems such as heat pumps and solar heating devices, plant systems require little annual upkeep. The dynamics of seasonal foliage variation provide the constant resetting that in mechanical devices must be provided by human attention or thermostatic control devices.

In temperate climates, buildings tend to require the addition of heat in the winter and the removal of heat in the summer. The appropriate placement of a deciduous tree as a sun block will reduce or eliminate radiant energy in the overheated period and permit desirable sunshine to reach the home in winter. The time of full bloom of many trees coincides with the shading requirements of the season. Plants cooperate elastically with human needs in their yearly variations. In cold springs the leaves arrive later, and in Indian summers they last longer. Different shapes and densities of trees have different shading effects, from the delicate honey locust (*Gleditsia triacanthos*) to the dense Norway maple (*Acer platanoides*), and a

*Energy costs vary dramatically from region to region. They are usually cheapest in areas with hydropower and most expensive in urban areas supplied by recently constructed generators. These savings are calculated on the basis of a national average of energy costs and projected increases. Your exact savings will depend on your local energy situation.

range of form from a columnar sentry ginkgo *(Ginkgo biloba)* to the low, wide Carmine crab apple *(Malus X atro-sanguinea)*.

Even allowing for occasional pruning, spraying, and other care, passive plant systems used for temperature control require nowhere near the attention that mechanical devices do. Landscape maintenance rarely requires the skilled, expensive care of mechanical systems. Plant designs have few moving parts, add no thermal pollution, are self-regulating, dependable, and predictable, and have the added benefit of being beautiful. And unlike whatever technology may offer, a well-designed landscape doesn't wear out with increasing age.

Another advantage of using the landscape to save energy is that we have domestic production of all the resources needed to implement this conservation strategy. Both native plants and introduced species can contribute to energy-efficient design. Too often, inviting wildflowers and rugged native cacti are neglected as possible landscape materials. Ask your local nursery for native plants. If enough requests are made, nurseries will stock them.

We caution you that well-landscaped grounds are planned in some detail before a single plant is bought or a brick laid. The need for such an overall concept of the landscape is often ignored, because many people think first in terms of specific shrubs or trees. They fall in love with a windbreak of blue spruce *(Picea pungens)* or a shading flowering cherry *(Prunus cerasifera)*, rush out to buy them and get them into the ground without considering how they might be used in the total landscape. The result of this approach is a hodgepodge of nursery plants, hard to manage, disappointing to look at, and uncomfortable to live with.

Obviously, the size of your building site and aesthetic considerations determine the number of energy-saving landscape strategies you may use. Few can apply all of our suggestions for a particular climate, but everyone can select landscape suggestions most appropriate for his or her situation.

Landscaping to save energy offers the planner a new set of guidelines to consider when designing grounds.

2

HUMAN COMFORT
AND CLIMATIC FORCES

THE GOAL OF ALL contemporary building design, whether it falls under the heading of architecture, landscape planning, or interior decoration, is to increase human comfort and reduce energy needs for space heating and cooling. The physical strength and mental activity of all people are improved within a specific range of climatic conditions. Outside this comfort zone, efficiency plummets; discomfort, stress, and the threat of disease increase.

There is a slight variation in the perception of comfort, either because of inherited or cultural characteristics. Most women choose a temperature a few degrees warmer than do men, young people prefer a temperature a few degrees cooler than do the elderly, and Eskimos thrive in a cooler climate than do Africans. But there are accepted, worldwide standards for human comfort.

This chapter analyzes the sensation of comfort and describes how the great climatic forces—sun, wind, and precipitation—affect it. It also demonstrates how plants may enhance comfort while reducing energy consumption.

THE PHYSICAL CHARACTERISTICS OF COMFORT

The four factors that affect human comfort are: the energy contained in objects that radiate heat, the temperature of air, its movement, and humidity. Precise definitions of each are needed to understand how they influence comfort.

Heat, which is a form of energy, is distinguished from temperature, which is a measure of how much energy is stored. For example, two freshly poured cups of tea, one half-full and the other filled to the brim, are at the same temperature. But the full one contains more heat energy. Different materials require different amounts of energy to be raised to the same temperature. "Specific heat" refers to the energy needed to raise a given weight of a substance by one degree Fahrenheit. The higher a material's specific heat, the more energy it takes to reach a certain temperature, the more heat it holds, and the longer it takes to cool down. For example, air has an extremely low specific heat and heats up rapidly; metals such as gold and lead have higher specific heats. Water has a very high specific heat; it takes a lot of energy to reach a certain temperature, acts as an excellent reservoir of heat, and releases a lot of heat when cooling down. This is why large bodies of water such as lakes and oceans have a pronounced effect on climate. They heat up and cool down slowly, and moderate extremes of temperature.

Heat energy itself can be transferred by four methods: radiation, conduction, convection, and changes of state. Heat always travels from warmer to cooler substances, attempting to remove temperature differences.

Radiation transfers heat in space from object to object. It requires no contact between the object emanating

RADIATION

the heat and the receiving substance and may take place in a complete vacuum. Radiation is responsible for the heat you feel when you stand in front of a fireplace or lie on a beach and soak up the sun's energy. Radiant heat can be collected from the sun independent of the air temperature. A sun-filled room collects radiant heat and warmth through a window, even in midwinter. Conversely, at night heat energy that has been absorbed during the day will be reradiated back into the sky and lost, if it is not blocked. In arid regions that have cloudless nights there is the potential for enormous radiational cooling at night. In cities, however, the low overhead smog often prevents night-time radiational cooling. Radiation can be blocked by opaque barriers such as walls, heavy drapes, and plants with dense foliage, or it can be filtered by translucent objects such as clouds, light shades, or vines on trellises.

In contrast, conduction transfers heat by direct contact. It is responsible for the heat you feel when you touch a hot iron or press a hot-water bottle to an aching part of your body. Con-

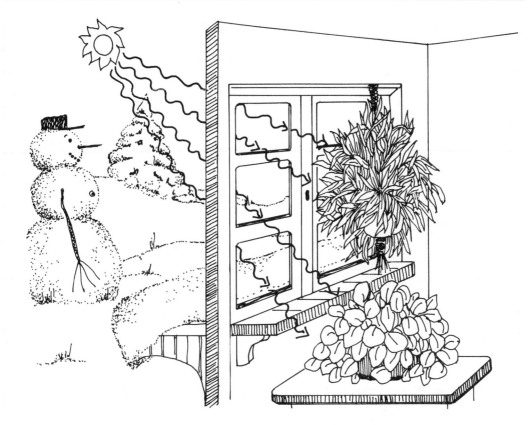

RADIANT SOLAR ENERGY WARMING ROOM IN WINTER

duction of heat away from the body produces the shivering sensation following a plunge into a cool swimming pool. Blocking conduction is more dif-

CONDUCTION

ficult than blocking radiation and requires specialized insulating materials with air cells that inhibit heat transfer such as wood, wool, polystyrene foam, rock wool, or thermopane windows.

Convection is similar to conduction, but it conveys heat in movable, fluid media, including air and water. It is a form of mixing and occurs simply because most materials expand and rise when heated. For example, warmed air rises, which is why smoke from fires drifts skyward. If you stand over a gravity-feed hot-air grate, the warm air currents transfer

CONVECTION

heat to your feet via convection. This mode of heat transfer can be blocked by physical barriers that inhibit the movement of air and other fluids.

Finally, heat can be transferred through a change of state, also called latent heat. It refers to the amount of heat taken up when a substance melts from a solid to a liquid or evaporates from a liquid to a gas. Changes of state consume vast quantities of energy. For example, it takes 180 British thermal units of heat energy to heat one pound of water from freezing to boiling.* One thousand additional Btus are required to evaporate the same pound of water into steam, without increasing the temperature of the steam at all. The enormous capacity of water for latent heat explains why a filled teapot cooking over a red-hot burner doesn't explode. The energy of the flame is used to convert water into steam. This principle also explains an

*The definition of a British thermal unit is the amount of heat energy needed to heat one pound of water one degree Fahrenheit. Therefore, it takes (212-32) or 180 Btus to heat a pound of water from freezing (32°F) to boiling (212°F).

important aspect of the human body's system for temperature regulation. The body releases excess heat by sweating, and the evaporation of this fluid uses up and draws away from the body large amounts of heat energy. Latent heat is also responsible for the air-conditioning influence of plants. Plants evaporate huge amounts of water by drawing heat from the air. This heat is stored as latent heat in gaseous water vapor. This process lowers the ambient air temperature and increases humidity. In a single sunny summer day an acre of turf can transfer more than 45,375,000 Btus of energy, enough to evaporate about 5,430 gallons of water. Ten square feet of grass can return half a ton of water to the atmosphere in the course of a growing season, transferring tremendous amounts of energy. Temperatures over grassy surfaces are about 10 to 14 degrees Fahrenheit cooler than temperatures over exposed soil because grass evaporates water and transfers heat energy of the air into the latent heat of water vapor. Obviously, plants must draw upon vast supplies of water to produce this dramatic cooling effect.

LATENT HEAT TRANSFER

If you have a good understanding of heat, temperature, and heat transfer, the other factors contributing to comfort—humidity and air movement are easier to understand.

Relative humidity is the ratio of the actual amount of moisture in the air to the maximum amount it could hold at a given temperature. As humidity increases it approaches the saturation point, the point at which air can hold no more moisture, and precipitation as snow or rain occurs.

With increasing humidity, it becomes harder to add more water to the air. It is more difficult to evaporate sweat in humid environments because the air is already approaching its saturation point. That is why you feel more uncomfortable in humid environments; it is more difficult to unload excess body heat by sweating and evaporation. When a relative humidity of 60 percent or more accompanies a temperature above 80°F., it feels uncomfortable, muggy, and humid. In an arid, desert climate, the same temperature would not be uncomfortable because body heat could be easily transferred into the air by sweating and evaporation. On the other hand, high humidity at low temperatures accentuates the impact of cold because it speeds heat loss and gives an unpleasant, raw feeling. When the air temperature is much lower than body temperature, conduction takes over. The air's specific heat is higher when moist, and it rapidly draws heat away from the body.

Air movements also contribute significantly to comfort and are measured by recording their velocity and direction. They have their greatest impact on comfort by increasing heat transfer. In hot, humid climates air movements are desirable because they increase evaporation and heat loss, but in hot, arid climates winds may be undesirable because they carry away precious water. Air movements in cold weather are undesirable and even dangerous because they carry away heat. The notorious "wind-chill" factor describes how air movements accelerate heat loss. For example, at zero degrees a casual well-clothed hiker need not worry about frostbite if the air is still. But at 20°, if a gusty 40-mile-per-hour wind is blowing, cautions should be taken to guard against excessive heat loss from the body's extremities, which may lead to frostbite.

WIND-CHILL FACTOR

To some extent, human comfort is determined by the body's physiological capacity to adapt to the stresses caused by heat, air movements, and humidity. In the above example of wind-chill, the body would first respond by contracting blood vessels on the body's surface, dropping the surface temperature to limit heat loss. Goose bumps may also appear, a residual response more appropriate for our hairier ancestors. Goose bumps are a sign that the hair shafts are erect, which produces a thicker, better insulating layer of fur for those mam-

WIND-CHILL FACTOR

	Actual Temperature (°F)											
	50	40	30	20	10	0	-10	-20	-30	-40	-50	-60
Wind Speed, mph	Perceived Air Temperature (°F)											
Calm	50	40	30	20	10	0	-10	-20	-30	-40	-50	-60
5	48	37	27	16	6	-5	-15	-26	-36	-47	-57	-68
10	40	28	16	4	-9	-21	-33	-46	-58	-70	-83	-95
15	36	22	9	-5	-18	-36	-45	-58	-72	-85	-99	-112
20	32	18	4	-10	-25	-39	-53	-67	-82	-96	-110	-124
25	30	16	0	-15	-29	-44	-59	-74	-88	-104	-118	-133
30	28	13	-2	-18	-33	-48	-63	-79	-94	-109	-125	-140
35	27	11	-4	-20	-35	-49	-67	-82	-98	-113	-129	-145
40	26	10	-6	-21	-37	-53	-69	-85	-100	-116	-132	-148

Wind speeds in excess of 40 mph have little additional chilling effect.

mals so endowed. They also indicate that skin pores are tightly closed, which reduces evaporative heat loss. Human response to cold may also involve shivering or running. Running may generate as much as 2,000 Btus per hour.

In warmer situations, the body responds by dilating the surface blood vessels to increase the transfer of heat from the blood to the skin surface. This increases heat loss from the body by convection, conduction, and radiation. At progressively higher temperatures, the body sweats to increase heat loss by evaporation. At air temperatures greater than body temperature, 98.6°F., convection and radiation can no longer transfer heat away from the body and latent heat loss by evaporation becomes the only method of energy transfer. At extremely high temperatures, even humans begin to pant, which promotes further heat loss by the evaporation of internal body moisture.

However, the ability of humans to adapt their physiology to extremes of climate is limited. Our ability to survive depends on our aptitude for manipulating our environment, and building shelters that adapt to the local climate. The following sections analyze the great forces that generate climate—sun, wind, and precipitation in its various forms—and indicate how our homes and offices can be designed to minimize the impact of adverse weather. We emphasize the value of using the landscape to temper extremes of climate and to promote human comfort.

THE SUN

The sun commands the daily genesis of weather and is the greatest single force affecting climate. Its radiant energy drives the machinery of climate all over the world. Annually, the earth makes a 600-million-mile orbit around the sun in an elliptical path and, at the same time, rotates on its own axis from west to east, making the sun appear to move from east to west. Knowledge of these two types of motion enables us to predict the sun's "position" in the earth's celestial dome. This permits some manipulation of the environment to utilize the sun's energy to best advantage. During warmer periods, the goal is to block the sun's radiant energy from entering living areas. But at other times, all available radiation should come into the home.

Acquiring an understanding of the sun's path, the arc it travels in the sky, is the first step to planning energy-efficient design. The solar path has two components: its absolute height in the sky, measured by the altitude angle; and the distance it travels on its path between the eastern sunrise and the western sunset, called the bearing angle. All positions in the solar hemisphere can be described by these two measurements. The bearing angle in this book is defined in reference to due north because most people learn to read maps from this perspective. (However, in some disciplines, including architecture and some branches of engineering, it is customary to measure bearing angles from due south.)

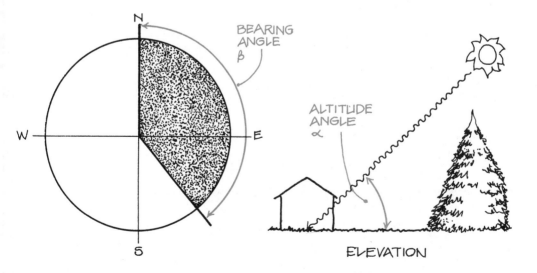

EXPLANATION OF BEARING AND ALTITUDE ANGLES

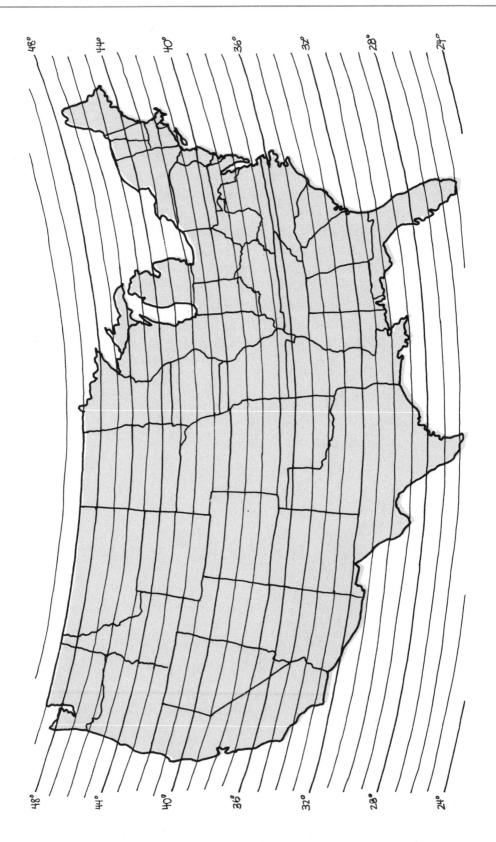

THE LATITUDES OF NORTH AMERICA

40° N. Latitude

	June 22			March 21, September 24			December 22	
time	altitude angle	bearing angle	time	altitude angle	bearing angle	time	altitude angle	bearing angle
5:00 am	4.23	62.69						
6:00 am	14.82	71.62	6:00 am	0	90.00			
7:00 am	25.95	80.25	7:00 am	11.17	100.08			
8:00 am	37.38	89.28	8:00 am	22.24	110.67	8:00 am	5.48	127.04
9:00 am	48.82	99.81	9:00 am	32.48	123.04	9:00 am	13.95	138.05
10:00 am	59.81	114.17	10:00 am	41.21	138.34	10:00 am	20.66	150.64
11:00 am	69.16	138.11	11:00 am	47.34	157.54	11:00 am	25.03	164.80
12:00 noon	73.44	180.00	12:00 noon	49.59	180.00	12:00 noon	26.55	180.00
1:00 pm	69.16	221.88	1:00 pm	47.34	202.45	1:00 pm	25.03	195.19
2:00 pm	59.81	245.82	2:00 pm	41.21	221.65	2:00 pm	20.66	209.35
3:00 pm	48.82	260.19	3:00 pm	32.48	236.95	3:00 pm	13.95	221.94
4:00 pm	37.38	270.71	4:00 pm	22.24	249.32	4:00 pm	5.48	232.95
5:00 pm	25.95	279.74	5:00 pm	11.17	259.91			
6:00 pm	14.82	288.37	6:00 pm	0	270.00			
7:00 pm	4.23	297.30						

To determine the solar path and its variation with changing seasons in your locality, first find the approximate latitude for your region on the map of the United States on the adjacent page. Then, turn to pages 171–175 in Appendix C for the charts on solar position and study the figures on the table for your approximate latitude. They chart the path of the sun over different latitudes at each of the four seasons. The data for June, March/September, and December are indicated because they represent the periods of the sun's longest, highest arc (summer solstice), the midpoint of its travels (fall and spring equinox), and its shortest, lowest arc (winter solstice).

The following example shows how the solar path charts are read for 40 degrees, North Latitude, a line which traverses the North American Continent across areas near New York City; Philadelphia; Pittsburgh; Columbus; Indianapolis; Springfield, Illinois; Denver; Salt Lake City; and Mendocino, California.

The first column under the monthly headings refers to daylight time, from the approximate time of sunrise for that season to the time of sunset.

The second column describes the altitude angle, or height of the sun in the sky, at a given time. The sun is always highest at noon.

The third column indicates the angle of the sun with respect to due north at different times of day. Notice the sun is always due south (180° away from north) at noon.

Note that daylight savings time artificially shifts the clock by one hour.

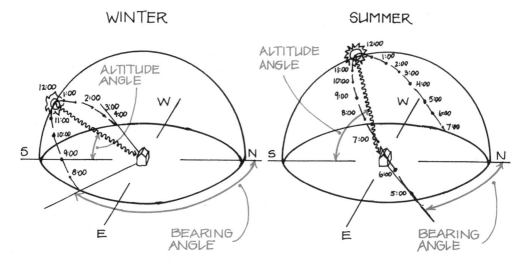

SUN'S PATH ACROSS THE SKY AT 40° LATITUDE

The sun rises one hour "later" than the value in the table, reaches its zenith at 1:00 P.M., and sets one hour later than the value in the table.

At latitude 40°N., in June, the sun rises at a bearing angle of 62.69° (northeast), sets at 297.30° (northwest), and reaches a maximum altitude angle of 73.44°; in March and September the sun rises at an angle of 90° (due east), sets at 270° (due west), and reaches a maximum altitude angle of 49.59°; in December the sun rises at 127.04° (southeast), sets at 232.95° (southwest) and creeps across the sky to reach only the low altitude angle of 26.55°.

Notice the change in the length and height of the sun's arc through the seasons. The sun's longest, highest arc is on the first day of summer, June 22, when the sun rises north of east and sets north of west. The lowest, shortest arc is on the first day of winter, December 22, when the sun rises south of east and sets south of west.

Use the tables in Appendix C to compare the solar path charts for different latitudes. You will notice that the seasonal changes in the sun's arc are most striking as you travel away from the equator. As you travel north, the period of daylength increases dramatically in the summer, until you reach the extreme of midnight sun in the arctic. In northern regions in the summertime, the sun rises farther to the northeast and sets farther to the northwest. In the winter the sun's shorter path originates farther southeast and sets farther southwest and barely rises over the horizon.

But in the extreme north, no matter

the length of the sun's arc, it never climbs very high into the sky. One must travel south, toward the equator and into the tropics, to witness the sun directly overhead.

Solar projection maps such as the one below observe the earth from a point in the sky vault and offer an excellent method for studying the sun's altitude and bearing angle during daylight throughout the year.

The ability of the sun to add radiant heat to a building depends both on its position in the sky and on the intensity of sunlight. The intensity of radiant energy reaching the earth depends on a number of variables, including the presence of clouds, smog,

and, most importantly, the density and thickness of the atmosphere. During winter the sun is lower in the sky than it is during the summer, and radiant heat must pass through a larger slice of the atmosphere to reach the earth than it does during summer. The longer trip through the atmosphere diminishes the sun's intensity. That is why the winter sun is generally weaker than the summer sun. However, if we use proper building design the winter sun can still contribute valuable radiant energy, despite its diminished intensity.

As light and heat in the form of solar radiation penetrate the atmosphere to the earth, a variety of

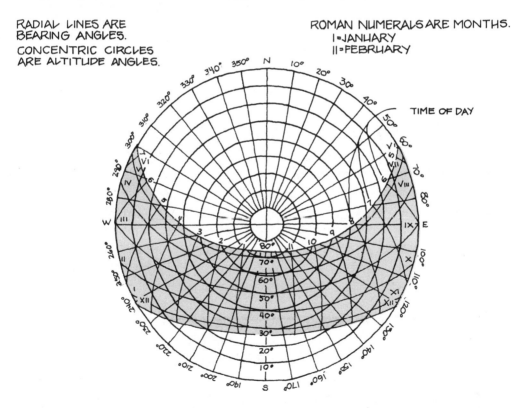

RADIAL LINES ARE BEARING ANGLES.
CONCENTRIC CIRCLES ARE ALTITUDE ANGLES.

ROMAN NUMERALS ARE MONTHS.
I = JANUARY
II = FEBRUARY

TIME OF DAY

SHADING MASK/SOLAR PROJECTION FOR 40° N LATITUDE

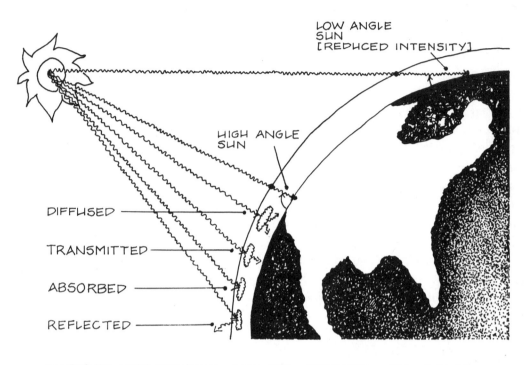

EARTH'S ATMOSPHERE AND ITS EFFECTS ON SOLAR INTENSITY

effects may occur. A fraction is reflected back into space from high clouds; part is scattered into the sky vault as it strikes small particles in the atmosphere; and part is absorbed and reradiated by the gases in the atmosphere. The remaining radiation penetrates to the earth's surface where it is either absorbed or reflected by the ground, buildings, plants, and animals. Absorbed radiation heats the objects, which can then reradiate the heat. Reflected radiation is not absorbed and is bounced back into the immediate atmosphere. In nature, most surfaces absorb some radiation and reflect another portion.

CONTROL OF RADIATION BY PLANTS

Control of both absorbed and reflected radiation is necessary to maintain human comfort, and this can be achieved by complete obstruction or filtration of direct radiation, or by the reduction of reflected radiation. Trees, shrubs, grasses, and other ground covers are among the best materials for the control of solar radiation. They offer climate control in tropical regions, where solar radiation is almost always oppressive, and in temperate regions, where solar radiation requires only seasonal control. Plants interact with solar radiation to influence microclimates in two ways. First, plants absorb solar radiation and cast shade. Second, most of this captured, radiant energy is used to evaporate water from plants. This converts most of the captured sunlight into latent heat, and relative humidity is increased instead of air temperature. In particularly dry air, plants may actually lower ambient air temperature if they have sufficient water to evaporate. The remaining captured radiation is used for photosynthesis and to heat the plants.

Selected plants can almost completely block the sun's rays. The chart on pages 181–182 in Appendix E describes the effectiveness of various trees at intercepting sun. Species such as Norway maple *(Acer platanoides)*, red ash *(Fraxinus pennsylvanica)* and the small-leafed European linden *(Tilia cordata)*, which have dense foliage, multiple leaf layers, or a dense canopy, can absorb and block at least 95 percent of the sun's energy in the visible spectrum and 75 percent across the full spectrum. A more modest filtration of solar energy occurs when plants with open, loose foliage, including vines and trees such as honey locust *(Gleditsia triacanthos)* and pin oak *(Quercus palustris)* are used. One advantage of vines is that they offer shade soon after planting while trees take longer to mature.

In temperate climates deciduous plants in full leaf are generally the best

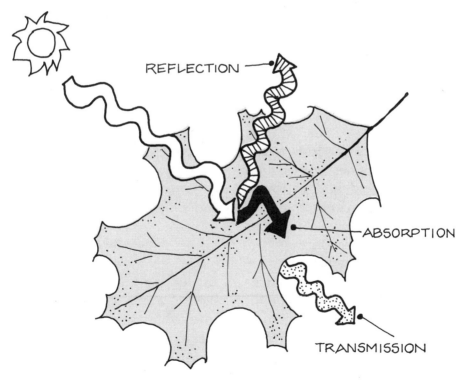

REFLECTION, ABSORPTION   AND   TRANSMISSION

interceptors of direct solar radiation. They offer their strongest sun-blocking potential in summer, and in winter, when their leaves have been shed, they permit desirable sunshine to penetrate. The dynamics of seasonal foliage variation provide natural sun control. When evaluating plants as sun filters, the species' shape must be considered along with its density. Each plant casts a distinctive shadow, which may be round, oval, pyramidal, or columnar in form. Pages 183–212 in Appendix F describe tree shape in the "Comments" column. Consider the form of the area to be protected before selecting plants to cast shade.

Reflected radiation from the sun is best controlled by plants with coarse surfaces. The multi-faceted surfaces of leaves are much better at reducing reflection than the light, smooth surfaces of man-made pavements or architectural materials. Dark plants with smaller leaf surfaces such as conifers (*Pinus* species, for example), or plants with pubescent, fuzzy surfaces, such as select elm (*Ulmus* species), greatly reduce reflection. Vines growing up walls or trellises and ground covers such as grass, pachysandra, or ice plant (*Mesembryanthemum*) also buffer against unwanted reflection.

By blocking or filtering direct or reflected sunlight, plants can temper local climates in a powerful fashion. In the daytime, the ground temperature in a forest may be as much as 25°F. cooler than the top of the tree canopy. At night the foliage mass prevents reradiation into the sky, and the temperature at the forest floor will be warmer than the temperature at the canopy. At midday, a vine-covered wall is always cooler than a bare wall. Dramatic proof of how plants cast shade and relieve the sun's impact was gathered by researchers in California's Imperial Valley, who found that bare-surface ground temperatures ranging from 136° to 152°F. cooled an average of 36°F. only five minutes after the arrival of the shadow line from overhead foliage.

WIND

The sun provides the energy that drives atmospheric motion or winds. They start blowing when warm air, expanding, rises and cooled air, contracting, sinks. From this simple beginning the behavior of winds grows almost inconceivably complex. Air movements, if at low velocity, are usually pleasant and desirable. However, when the velocity increases, they are capable of causing great discomfort and destruction to life and property.

Winds are grouped into three categories: local and regional persistent winds; global persistent winds such as the trade winds of the tropics; and maverick winds such as cyclones, tornadoes, and hurricanes. Local persistent winds are almost invariably small-scale convection winds—the sea breeze, the land breeze, the mountain wind, and the valley wind. They are of great importance in influencing human comfort, and they can be controlled with careful landscape design.

Air flows in much the same way as water. Cold air settles to the lowest level and hot air rises. It will flow over, under, and around anything that is sturdily engineered, and will be bent, bounced, and resisted by obstructions such as buildings, fences, hills, valleys and other earth forms, and plants. Air movements, again like water, exert pressure against any surface that inhibits their flow. Whenever the wind flows over a solid barrier there is increased pressure upwind (where the wind blows from) and a protected, low pressure area immediately downwind or to leeward (where the wind blows to). However,

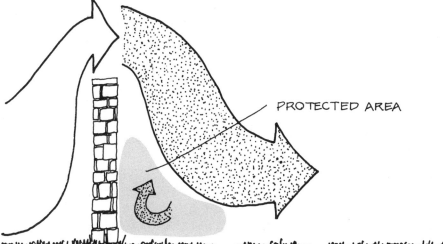

PROTECTED AREA

SOLID WINDBREAK

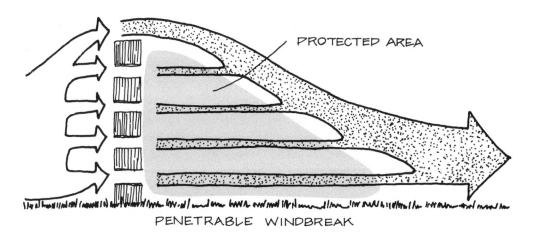

PROTECTED AREA

PENETRABLE WINDBREAK

THE EFFECT OF SOLID AND PENETRABLE WINDBREAKS ON AIRFLOW

the low pressure area pulls the boundary layer of air flowing over the barrier into it. Thus, the lee side of a slope receives protection and contains a pocket of relatively still, quiet air. But this protected region has a limited range because the low pressure region sucks wind back into place.

In contrast, a pierced barrier allows some wind to penetrate through it and creates less pressure differential between the upwind and the downwind side. This penetrable windbreak has less wind reduction near it, but the overall calming effect extends farther beyond it. The suction immediately behind this penetrable windbreak is less than that produced by a solid barrier, and the acceleration of wind back to its original speed is more gradual.

A windbreak of trees acts as such a penetrable barrier. These windbreaks are most effective when placed perpendicular to the prevailing wind.

WIND CONTROL BY PLANTS

As we have seen, heat loss from a building's surface is proportional to the square of the wind velocity. Wind increases heat loss by convection and by adding to the volume of cool air blown into a building, which subsequently may need to be heated. Therefore, a carefully situated windbreak of trees and shrubs can be a powerful energy saver in climates with periods of cool weather.

Because the quality of wind protection depends on the penetrability, height, and width of the plants used, recommendations for certain species as windbreaks are difficult to make. The more penetrable the windbreak, the more modest wind reduction to leeward, but the farther behind the windbreak this modest protection extends. Dense, coniferous evergreens that branch to the ground provide the most effective plants for year-round wind control, and deciduous trees and shrubs in full leaf are the most effective in summer.

In general, wind speed is reduced for a distance of two to five times the height of the barrier upwind of an obstruction, and up to fifteen times the height downwind. The maximum shelter from wind is obtained from three to five times the height of the barrier, downwind. Wind velocity is cut up to 80 percent directly downwind of a dense screen planting such as spruce (*Picea* species) or fir (*Abies* species) trees. For example, a windbreak of dense, twenty-foot Austrian pine (*Pinus nigra*) cuts a 12-mile-per-hour wind velocity to 3 miles per hour. A loose barrier of Lombardy poplar trees (*Populus nigra* cv. 'Italica') in full foliage reduces leeward wind velocity by only 40 percent. In general, a leafless deciduous tree has only 60 percent of the wind-blocking ability of its full, "leafed" potential. Irregular windbreaks that have some foliage density throughout their height are most effective at breaking up the airstream over it. Therefore, a mixture of species and sizes of plants makes a better wind control.

The lower wind velocities on both sides of windbreaks encourage precipitation to fall out of the air. This means that small snowdrifts may be formed upwind and large snowdrifts downwind of a windbreak. The rules that explain how plant barriers influence air movements also explain how such barriers affect snowdrifts. The downwind drifts near a solid barrier are deep and do not extend a great distance from the barrier. In contrast, the downwind drifts near a penetrable windbreak are shallow, extending to a greater distance from the barrier. Solid barriers produce drifts on both sides, and more open plantings keep the drift to the downwind side. The greater the velocity of the wind, the closer the drift to the barrier itself. A well-designed windbreak will slow the velocity of the wind and cause snow to be deposited before it reaches a path or driveway. In snowy climates, windbreaks should not be put immediately upwind of driveways or walkways, but rather a considerable distance upwind.

Plants that provide protection from wind to leeward may also produce a pocket of cold beneath them. Plant designs that group trees for wind control, and permit the accumulation of snow and undisturbed litter beneath them, insulate the ground. This means the ground warms slowly on a sunny day, which ensures that snow thaws later and more evenly in the spring. Spring perennials, such as early flowering bulbs, planted beneath such windbreaks will be well insulated against wind and extreme temperatures, but will bloom later in the spring.

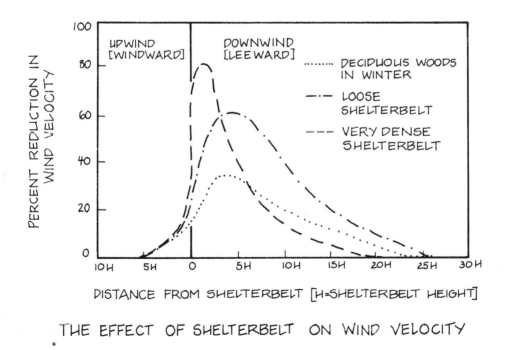

THE EFFECT OF SHELTERBELT ON WIND VELOCITY

It is also important to recognize that at a break in a wind barrier high pressure is released and the wind velocity increases above its open field velocity. This is known as the Venturi effect. For example, just past the edge of a moderately dense shelterbelt, wind speed is increased 10 percent above open field velocity. Also, because the foliage mass of a tree serves as a direct block to the passage of air, air movements directly beneath the

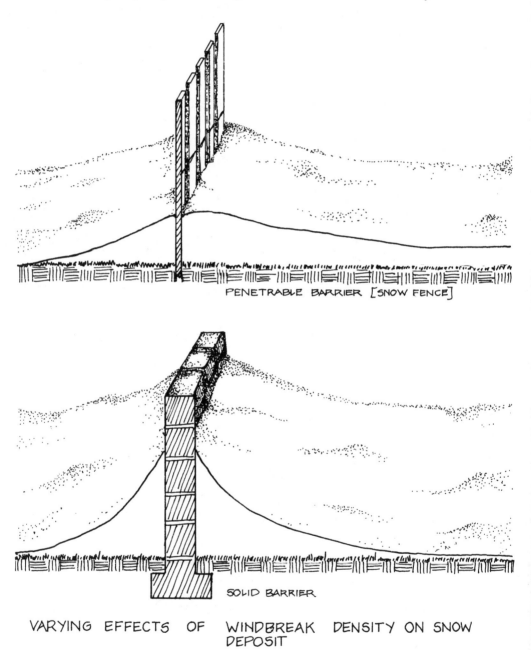

PENETRABLE BARRIER [SNOW FENCE]

SOLID BARRIER

VARYING EFFECTS OF WINDBREAK DENSITY ON SNOW DEPOSIT

leaf canopy may be accelerated. Therefore, careful placement of a windbreak is essential, and poorly placed windbreaks should be removed. Their growth should be carefully monitored to prevent the development of scrawny bare spots near the ground that encourage the acceleration of wind. If trees with high canopies are desired for a windbreak, fill in the bare spots beneath them with shrubs and bushes.

The Venturi effect may also be used to blow areas clear of snow and to provide snow-free parking areas, walkways, or roadways. Alternatively, plantings may be designed to channel winds and cause desirable snowdrifts and deposits on ski trails and toboggan runs.

Plants that block wind may also prevent heat loss by adding a layer of insulating air around a building. A hedge of yew (*Taxus* species) or privet (*Ligustrum* species) adjacent to a wall will provide a pocket of dead-air space, insulating against heat loss.

In addition to obstructing, filtering, and deflecting winds, plant barriers may channel and accelerate beneficial breezes into defined areas. This strategy is desirable in warm climates when cooling breezes are needed. A funnel of trees or tall hedges that guides the prevailing winds can provide constant, natural "air conditioning." Because of the Venturi effect, as the funnel narrows, wind velocity increases, making the arrangement more effective. A large scoop that contracts in breadth can increase the velocity of prevailing winds that are light but steady and would otherwise be ineffectual. If the narrowest end of the funnel is covered by a breezeway or a tree with a high

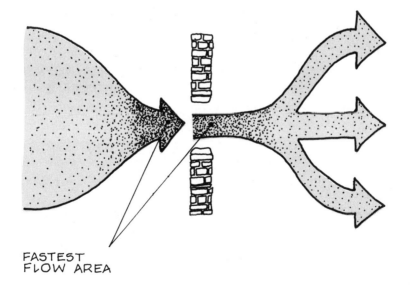

FASTEST
FLOW AREA

VENTURI EFFECT

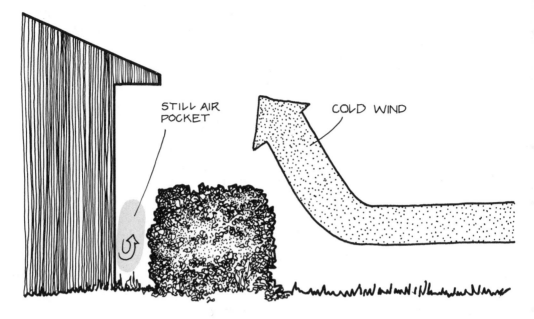

STILL AIR POCKET

COLD WIND

AN INSULATING HEDGE

canopy, the effect improves. Also, since cooler winds flow downhill, dense evergreens planted on a slope may trap and hold cold air, creating cool spaces, upwind of the barrier.

Thus, the advantageous use of plants to control wind can reduce the costs of both interior heating and cooling.

Effective wind controls demand careful analysis of the direction and strength of the prevailing winds at different seasons. Don't try to predict the wind situation around your home from information your neighbor has collected. Identical homes on adjacent lots can experience very different air movements. In addition to the prevailing winds there will be odd pockets of erratic wind in courtyards and between buildings.

To learn the direction of all air movements, tie strips of cloth on several posts, five or six feet tall. Anchor them securely at all compass points, plus any suspected odd wind pockets. Study the wind movements for at least several weeks each season and chart them. This information will guide landscaping plans. In more northern areas, wind patterns around buildings may also be traced by watching the way snow is deposited. Make your first observation after a fresh snow on a calm day. Later, observe the shift in snow patterns when the wind has blown channels and paths. Note where the ground is bare, and where the snow has piled in drifts. A third method for determining wind patterns is to study smoke released from a chimney, campfire, or barbecue.

Before planting trees or shrubs to control wind, check whether your selected species can withstand the region's strongest storm forces. Trees may fall onto buildings, causing injury or damage. Deadwood and weak or unbalanced branches are vulnerable to strong winds. It is prudent to plant soft-wooded trees a safe distance from outdoor living areas and buildings, if possible. Generally, the fast-growing trees such as pine (*Pinus* species) and larch (*Larix* species) have soft woods and are weaker. Silver maples (*Acer saccharinum)*, cottonwoods and poplars (*Populus* species), and willows (*Salix* species), are especially susceptible to breakage.

WATER

The third basic feature that establishes microclimate, after solar radiation and air circulation (wind), is moisture. Water is the best reservoir of heat energy and is the great equalizer. As we have noted, it has a high specific heat, warming up and cooling off slowly, and consumes large amounts of energy when it evaporates

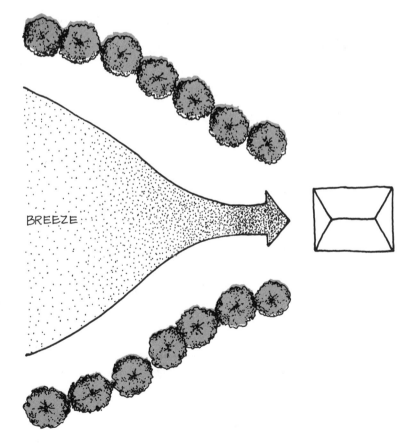

CHANNELLING OF COOL BREEZES IN WARM CLIMATES

into a gaseous state. These properties enable water to mollify extremes of climate by a variety of techniques.

When sunlight strikes water at a low angle, the light is reflected. However, when the sun's rays strike water at high solar angles, a large part of the radiant energy is captured and stored by the water. Therefore, large bodies of water act as giant solar storage tanks, retaining valuable energy, and releasing it slowly. The ameliorating effect of water helps to give ocean and lake properties their prime value. Conversely, the absence of water in the Great Plains and desert regions explains their extreme temperature fluctuations.

Large surfaces of water also temper extremes of climate by encouraging evaporation, and the transfer of radiant energy into latent heat. As evaporation takes place, energy is drawn from the surrounding air and temperature drops. At the same time, the humidity increases. Even small amounts of water, including ponds, pools, and fountains, can offer climate control by providing a base for evaporation. In general, the greater the total volume and surface area of a body of water, the greater its influence on climate.

Temperature differences between water and ground also generate convection air currents, resulting in the familiar offshore breezes which provide relief in hot climates. During

REFLECTION   ABSORPTION

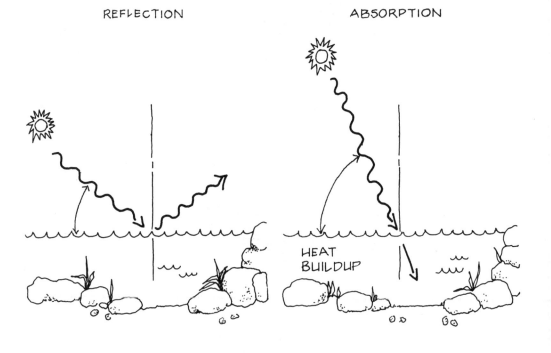

SOLAR RADIATION BEING CAPTURED AND STORED BY
WATER BODY

the day, the sun warms the land and the land warms the air over it. This warm air rises, and cool, heavier air rushes in off the sea to take its place. During night, if the land cools down sufficiently, the process is reversed: the sea, retaining much of its daytime warmth, heats the air over it, which rises and is replaced by heavier, cooler air blowing off the land. Thus, breezes flow from over a body of water onto shore during the day and evening, and off the land and onto water late at night and early morning.

The sea breeze and its nocturnal equivalent appear with clocklike regularity along coastlines. It is a dependable, valuable friend, especially in the tropics and subtropics, and carries picturesque, poetic names: the virazón of Chile, the datoo of Gibraltar, the imbat of Morocco, the ponente of Italy, the kapalilua of Hawaii, or the "doctor" of various English-speaking tropical regions. In temperate regions, sea breezes tend to be seasonal, appearing in the warmer weather of late spring and summer. The well-known San Francisco summer fog is brought in by such a breeze. Thanks to these refreshing winds off the Pacific, San Franciscans may work and sleep in the comfortable 60s°F. in July while ninety miles northeast and inland, in the breezeless oven of the Sacramento Valley, temperatures soar to 110°F. Seasonal sea breezes spring up habitually between ten and eleven o'clock in the morning and start to subside at about four o'clock in the afternoon. By seven or eight o'clock at night they

have died out. Then the land breeze freshens, and the time sequence is repeated.

This natural airflow pattern over large bodies of water may be used for natural ventilation and energy conservation.

Water in the form of snow is also a good insulator. Snow piled on a roof prevents heat loss by convection and reduces heating costs. Similarly, when snow is piled against a northern or windy wall, it protects against wind chill, reducing residential heat loss. Shrubbery helps to trap snow in preferred locations.

Water in the guise of clouds has an impact on climate, too. The sun's radiant energy, which is absorbed by the earth during the day, is easily reradiated back into space on a clear night. Cloud cover inhibits this reradiation loss. Therefore, temperatures are generally higher on overcast nights than on clear ones.

PLANTS AND WATER

It is no coincidence that classic gardens incorporate pools, fountains, or other bodies of water in their design. The various ways in which energy is exchanged between water, plants, and air can be manipulated to improve microclimates. All plants, especially trees, harness the water evaporation-energy exchange cycle. They cool by casting shade and by evaporating water. The energy required for this process is taken from warm air. Lower

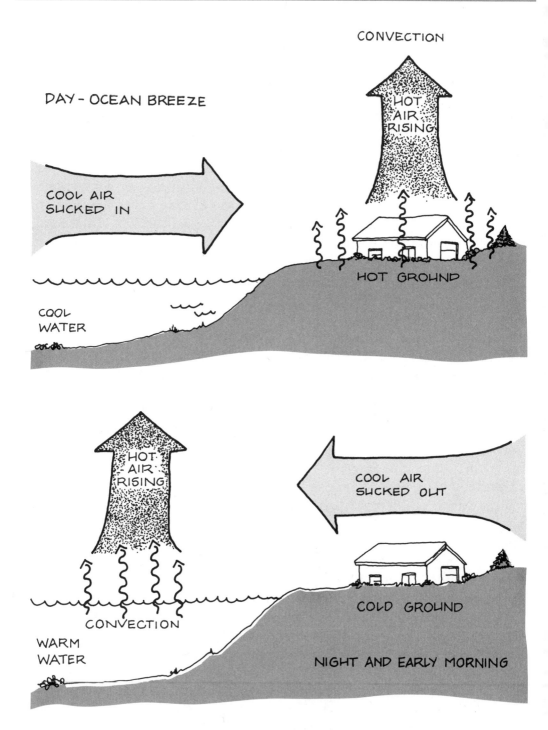

OFFSHORE AND ONSHORE BREEZES GENERATED BY
CONVECTION

ambient temperatures and increased humidity are the result.

Obviously, if plants cool the microclimate by evaporation, they must have access to water and numerous leaves. Desert plants expose a minimum of leaf surface to protect themselves from excessive evaporation and water loss. Such plants still offer the benefit of shade, but they can't be used to temper extreme heat by evaporating water. There is little water available, in any case.

Plants may alter microclimates by intercepting precipitation. Only 60 percent of the rain falling on a pine forest canopy and 80 percent of the rain falling on a hardwood forest reaches the ground. In general, softwoods (conifers) are more effective precipitation barriers than hardwoods.

Softwoods have leaves with a great number of sharp angles, and trap water droplets in their numerous cavities. Because trees intercept and slow down water movement, they also help to control surface water runoff and soil erosion.

Trees, vines, and shrubs can also be used to control moisture retention and humidity. Plants with high canopies lose water to the air. But because these same plants filter solar radiation and inhibit windflow, they also reduce evaporation from the vegetation and earth beneath. This results in an environment of controlled humidity and temperature on the forest floor. The relatively high humidity and low evaporation rate stabilize temperature, keeping it lower than the surrounding air during summer days and prevent-

HOW FORESTS INTERCEPT RAINFALL

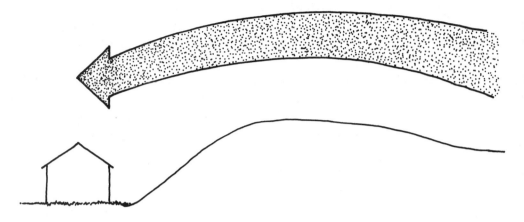

BERM DEFLECTING BREEZES

ing it from dropping greatly at night. A vine-covered trellis, gazebo, or pavilion in the garden will produce a similarly controlled environment.

LANDFORMS

Landforms, including hills, valleys, and deserts, influence climate and comfort by altering the swirling flow of the atmosphere. Mountain ranges are among the most dynamic determinants of local and regional weather. At the very largest scale, continental mountain ranges divert air masses, affect the flow of moisture-laden air, assist in trapping and condensing moisture, and block or accentuate the effects of sun.

Landforms need not be of majestic proportions to affect climate in a particular area. Berms, which are small, man-made mounds of earth, can block low sun, provide a better orientation for utilization of solar radiation,

obstruct or channel winds, or offer insulation. They also offer the added benefits of privacy and noise control. Negative landforms, which are small hollows in the earth's natural form, can also shape microclimate. Berms and hollows are especially valuable for enhancing the comfort of outdoor living areas.

LANDFORMS WITH PLANTS

It is much easier to enhance the comfort of outdoor living spaces by adding vegetation to the basic landform itself. Plants must be carefully selected for the artificial warm and cool pockets created by man-made landforms. They may have to withstand climatic conditions that are atypical for the area. A berm that is well designed and planted with trees, shrubs, and ground covers can become an important attraction. A carefully located berm can modify extremes of climate, provide privacy, and, in certain cases, reduce noise levels by as much as 80 percent.

Berms have another important power to control climate. Because soil retains heat and changes temperature gradually, it can be used against concrete and stone walls as the cheapest insulating material. Six inches of earth will provide "insulation" from wide daily swings in air temperature; this is why basements are protected from temperature extremes on sultry summer days or especially frigid winter nights. At greater depths, soil temperatures respond only to seasonal changes, and this change occurs after a considerable delay. The magnitude of the seasonal temperature changes decreases rapidly with increasing soil depth. For example, in the Minneapolis-St. Paul area, where there are frigid winters and warm summers, the temperature of soil fifteen to twenty-four feet below the surface remains near 50°F. year-round, only 18°F. less than comfortable room temperature.

The soil layer on berms used for insulation must be thick and kept dry, since wet soil drains energy. Earth banked against a wall can be attractive when landscaped with ground covers, flowers, and shrubbery. Because the tops of berms tend to be dry, species must be carefully selected. Another option is to mold small water-holding pockets into the soil around each specimen.

The use of berms to insulate against extremes of temperature within a building does have drawbacks. They must never be used adjacent to wood because underground wood provides a breeding site for termites, carpenter ants, and other insects that cause structural damage. If the sides of berms are too steep, they erode or wash away. They can also be hazardous to small children.

Despite these objections, berms are being incorporated into more landscaping plans. When taken to the extreme, they result in underground homes. Such structures are most practical in areas of extreme daily or seasonal temperature change. The Navajos and Chinese constructed such practical earth-sheltered homes for several centuries.

BUILDING MATERIALS FOR COMFORTABLE LIVING

Earth, masonry, concrete, metals, wood and wood products, and glass are among the favored building materials of architects and landscape designers. All such materials can be grouped into three classifications: natural, organic materials; natural, inorganic materials; and artificial (synthetic) materials. Each of these groups responds to heat energy differently. An understanding of their special qualities will improve building and landscape design.

Natural, organic materials are or once were alive. They include wood, thatch, all plants, fur pelts and wool, and they tend to resist the passage of heat. That is, they are good insulators, have low mass, and do not store much heat. They also tend to be biodegradable, and require special upkeep.

Natural, inorganic building materials are found in the natural environment but were never alive. They include substances such as earth, clay brick, and stone. They are good conductors of heat, have a high mass, store great quantities of heat, and are generally moderate or poor insulators.

Artificial building materials are manufactured for a specific purpose. They include polystyrene foam, glass wool, glass, plastics, and many others. Their insulating and conducting abilities cover the full range. They may be designed to be good insulators such as polystyrene foam or good conductors such as steel. Since air is a good insulator, insulators usually have a large number of air cells in their construction; good conductors are characterized by solid mass.

Color also influences a material's response to radiant energy. Light colors tend to reflect heat and reduce an object's heat gain; dark materials absorb energy and get hot. For example, summer air temperatures immediately above paved blacktop can be 20°F. or more higher than nearby shaded areas of grass. On the other hand, blacktop is preferred in areas that have snow because it easily absorbs the sun's radiant energy and snow melts and evaporates on it.

Until the Middle Ages, builders worked only with natural building materials, often in their natural colors. Most natural materials are opaque to solar radiation, which put further constraints on early building design, especially in colder climates. Energy-efficient design involved the placement of a high-mass, energy-storing core within an insulating, nonconducting shell. A centrally located brick fireplace within a wood house typifies this design scheme.

The development of window glass, one of the earlier synthetic building materials, revolutionized house design. Its greatest value is its ability to admit warming shortwave radiation and to block the longwave radiation that is reradiated by human bodies and other heated objects in a building. That is, glass has the ability to admit desirable radiation and insulate somewhat against unwanted heat loss. This is known as the greenhouse effect. It is based on the fact that the wavelength of radiation is inversely proportional to the temperature of the radiating object. That is, the hotter the object, the shorter the wavelength of emitted radiation. The sun, which is extremely hot, radiates energy of very short wavelengths. People and building materials, even when they feel hot, are really quite cold compared with the sun and radiate energy at long wavelengths. Thus, glass lets shorter wavelengths (sunlight) into the building, but doesn't let longer wavelengths (body and radiant building heat) out. This was something that none of the old, natural building materials could do. However, window glass must be appropriately placed to promote energy efficiency. A single, unaided pane of glass will usually result in a total energy-deficit for a building if it is not positioned carefully. Multiple layers of glass in nonconducting window frames, such as those found in Thermopane windows, make very effective construction materials. Heat loss by conduction is significantly reduced, but heat gain by radiation is maintained. Sheets of clear plastic perform in a manner similar to glass panes. They admit shortwave radiation and resist the passage of longwave radiation, and thus permit the greenhouse effect. Plastics may also be used to construct storm windows and greenhouses.

Today, the list of available synthetic building materials is long and varied. It includes cellulose, glass fibers, polystyrene, polyurethane, mineral fiberboard, asbestos, asphaltic coatings, gypsum board, tile, and many others. Synthetic building materials have the advantage of being designed to fit a particular building need. Novel materials are continually being developed for special con-

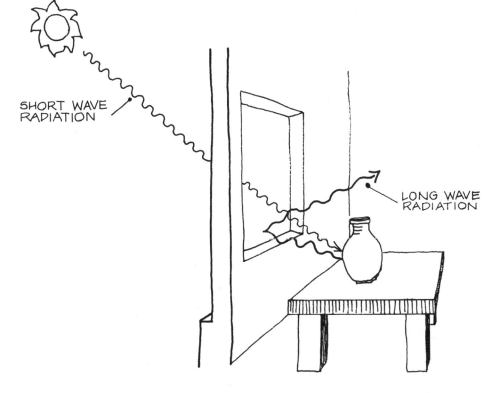

GLASS PASSING SHORTWAVE AND BLOCKING LONGWAVE
[GREENHOUSE EFFECT]

struction needs. But the model for energy-efficient building design remains the same: an insulating, non-conducting shell is built around a conducting, heat-storing core.

Unfortunately, many man-made materials share the disadvantage of being annoying to the human body. Some break up easily into fine, particulate matter and enter and irritate the human respiratory system. Glass fibers and asbestos are particular offenders. Workers who use these materials must protect themselves with gloves and face masks.

None of the synthetic materials has the desirable self-regulating qualities of natural live materials—plants. When it gets too hot, a plant evaporates water and tempers its own and the ambient air temperature. Some synthetic materials just continue to absorb the heat. For example, in Davis, California, during midday in October, the temperature above a rye grass lawn mowed at four inches was 67°F.; mowed at two inches, 79°F.; and mowed at half an inch, 83°F. In striking contrast, the temperature above Astroturf, the artificial "plastic grass" of athletic fields, was 125°F. Another study at Chicago's Comiskey Park in mid-August showed that although the temperatures of artificial turf, clay, and living grass were all about 80°F. in early morning, by 1:00 P.M. the grass temperature had risen to 85°F., the clay was 95°F., and the artificial turf had reached about 160°F. Selection of proper building and landscape mate-

rials can have a strong influence on comfort!

HOME DESIGN

Architects use their knowledge of climate and construction materials to plan energy-efficient buildings. Good building and landscape design and careful selection of building materials alone can compensate for many inadequacies in the most challenging climates. Long before high-technology environmental controls such as air-conditioners, electric heat, and dehumidifiers came into existence, primitive peoples maintained comfort in the harshest of climates. The Indians of the American Southwest thrived in underground hogans or cliff dwellings, the inhabitants of Alaska lived in earthen or ice structures, and natives of the subtropics built open-air dwellings perched on stilts. All relied on careful choice of materials and good design. If possible, landscaping always complemented a carefully planned structure.

Most Americans don't have the luxury of designing and building a home from scratch. But many do modify their housing to meet new needs. Energy conservation is a goal that prompts many to reevaluate the design of their homes or offices. This section describes the characteristics of four house designs, each a suitable model for one of the nation's four climatic zones: cool, temperate, hot-humid, and hot-arid. It offers the final preparation to understanding how landscaping can complement energy efficiency.

Cool. Reducing heat loss is the main goal of design in cool climates. This is accomplished by reducing the surface area enclosing the structure, thereby reducing heat loss by radiation, conduction, and convection.

Hemispheres are an ideal form for conserving heat, which explains why igloos take that shape. Igloos also have the advantage of being constructed of snow, an excellent insulator, and ice, which seals out the wind and reflects inward much of the heat radiated by internal sources such as humans, cooking fires, or oil lamps. Hemispheres are not popular shapes for buildings on the mainland of the United States because the most common building material, wood, does not lend itself easily to curved structures. The second-best structural shape for minimizing heat loss is the cube, which provides the model for Cape Cod-style homes often found in New England. Other desirable features for homes in cool climates are south-facing windows, dark-colored building materials, and a situation on a south-facing slope, preferably on the lee side of the wind direction. These features increase the structure's ability to capture and retain all available heat. The building may also have a flat or shallow-pitched, well-constructed roof to collect and hold snow for insulation. Outbuildings such as garages or barns should be positioned to break the prevailing cold winds. Communities of buildings in cold climates are clustered together to conserve heat.

Temperate. Homes in temperate climates should retain heat in winter and capitalize on the use of shade and natural cooling breezes in the summer. The ideal building shape is rectangular, oriented with an axis from slightly north of east to south of west, with most of the windows facing south-southeast. This situation gives the house all possible desirable heat and protects it from the unfavorable, late afternoon western sun, which generates unwanted heat in the summer and reflected glare from snow in the winter. The internal layout of the rooms should be planned to orient active living spaces to the south for winter warmth. Areas that generate a lot of heat such as workshops and laundry rooms should be placed to the north or northeast where the sun rarely appears. Outbuildings, including garages and storage sheds, should be placed to the north to break cold winds, depending on wind direction. Overhangs on a roof, trellises, and other structures that cast limited shade on the south face are desirable. They shade the hot summer sun, which is high in the sky, and permit the radiant energy of the low winter sun to enter unobstructed. Attics and crawl spaces must be provided with adequate ventilation. During the winter months this allows unwanted

VERNACULAR HOME IN COOL CLIMATE

VERNACULAR HOME IN TEMPERATE CLIMATE

VERNACULAR HOME IN HOT, HUMID CLIMATE

VERNACULAR HOME IN HOT, ARID CLIMATE

moisture to escape before it condenses and damages ceilings and walls. During the summer, ventilation releases excess heat which has risen to the roof peak.

Hot, humid. In hot, humid regions homes should become more elongated, or even irregular in shape, to increase surface area and encourage the dissipation of heat. The goals of energy-efficient house design in these areas are to reduce the penetration of solar radiation to living areas, to remove inside heat generated by people, lights, and other devices, and to improve evaporative cooling conditions by encouraging and directing cooling breezes. These goals are accomplished by designing homes with window openings oriented to the prevailing summer breezes, situating a home with an east-west lengthwise axis, providing escape for excess heat through a roof ridge vent, and selecting a light-colored, well-insulated roof that reflects solar radiation back into the atmosphere. It is also desirable to provide vertical shading devices on the eastern and western sides to shade against the low early morning and late afternoon sun, and to elevate floors and open walls to permit air circulation wherever possible. Communities in hot, humid regions are planned to encourage and direct cooling breezes. Houses are well spaced from one another to dissipate heat back into the atmosphere and promote cooling.

Hot, arid. Ideally, in hot, arid regions the elongated house form wraps around itself to create a rectangular structure with a central, open space. The purpose of this structure and its open core is to keep cool during daytime and warm at night in a climate characterized by extreme diurnal temperature variations (arid regions are usually cloudless and permit re-radiation of heat into the sky at night). Another important objective is the conservation of moisture. Buildings should be designed with small east, west, and south windows, and larger glass surfaces facing the internal courtyard. External windows should be high, to release heated air that has risen. Courtyard windows may be lower, to take advantage of the cooler, heavier air within the courtyard.

Generally, ventilation is not desirable because of the need to conserve moisture. Plants and fountains in the courtyard can create a defined, enclosed space with a higher, more comfortable humidity. The building walls and roof should be constructed of massive materials such as adobe and stone that have a high specific heat and, therefore, store heat slowly. Storing heat at a slow rate delays the impact of solar radiation. This effect offers protection from overheating in daytime and provides warmth throughout the night.

The ideal situation for such homes is in valleys or on the lower slopes of hillsides, where they benefit from the downward flow of cooler air.

Urban structures in these regions are clustered together in the manner of oasis villages to cast shade on each other and conserve their most valuable resource, water.

A common error in planning and zoning ordinances in hot, arid regions is the assumption that the more space there is between buildings and the greater the distance back from the street, the better. In urban, arid areas, two- and three-story homes clustered together and situated on narrow streets are ideal. They cast shade on one another and protect paved streets, which have the potential for absorbing great amounts of radiant energy. In rural areas, earth-sheltered homes are best. Features common to buildings in hot, arid areas include shaded windows, light-colored roofs and walls which are built partially underground with massive construction materials. All of these features are keys to energy conservation that are still applicable in the age of the air-conditioner.

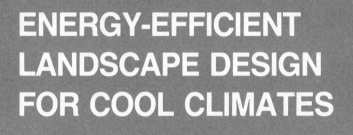

3

ENERGY-EFFICIENT
LANDSCAPE DESIGN
FOR COOL CLIMATES

THE COOL REGIONS OF the United States, including the northern reaches of New England and the north-central states along the Canadian border, are known for delightfully cool summers and roaring winter storms that blanket everything with snow. Residents of the area observe nature's signs of transition—the migrations of birds and the onset of colorful autumn foliage—with great care. They signify the beginning of prolonged, severe winters and help residents prepare for extended periods of biting cold, with temperatures plummeting below 0°F. for days and weeks at a time, often accompanied by accumulations of snow drifting to extraordinary depths. Harsh winters extending from October to late April or early May are relieved by comfortable summers with cool mornings, warm afternoons, and occasional periods of

extreme heat that are broken by thunderstorms.

In cool regions, average winter-morning minimum temperatures range from 0–20°F. and average winter-afternoon maximum temperatures range from freezing to 40°F. During the summer months, average morning minimum temperatures are in the chilly range of 50–60°F., and average afternoon maximum temperatures range from 70–85°F.

Evening and early morning humidity tend to be high, especially during summer and autumn. In general, the area receives ample precipitation as snow, rain, and hail.

Sunshine is available at least one half of all possible daylight hours, a small amount when compared with the nation's other regions. There is also tremendous seasonal variation in

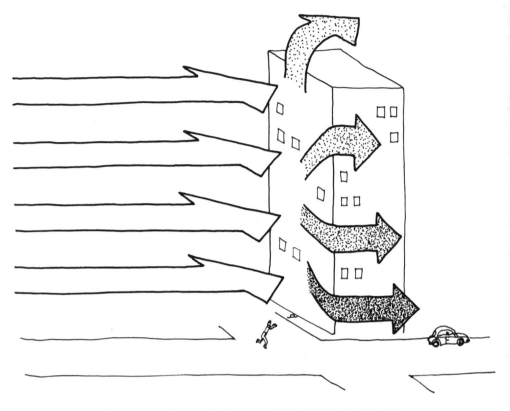

AIRFLOWS IN URBAN ENVIRONMENT

the availability of sunshine. In winter, the sun skirts the horizon for only eight hours; in midsummer there are fourteen hours of daylight.

Winds are a serious liability since they speed heat loss and can be enhanced by the area's many hills, valleys, lakes, and coastal influences. Northern cities with skyscrapers are especially affected by brisk winds. The canyonlike architecture of urban centers promotes adverse wind turbulence. When wind strikes the surface of a building its velocity is transformed into pressure, and about one half of this wind pressure flows down the building to the bottom of the structure. When an escape route is found, such as the corner of a tall building, the pressure is transformed back into wind velocity which accelerates heat transfer. These air movements account for the biting cold winds along Chicago's Lake Shore Drive in winter and the tremendous heating costs of the area's buildings. Skyscrapers help to funnel the wintry blasts traveling south over Lake Michigan into Chicago's business district.

Cool regions have a severe climate which was recognized by our nation's colonial settlers. The New England region abounds with historical examples of residential designs attuned to its unusual climatic demands, such as the saltbox and Cape Cod structures. These two designs set a standard for climatic awareness that should be copied by modern architecture.

The goals of the early builders were to keep inside the heat generated by human activities and the sun, and to keep the cold outside. Colonial structures, built as tightly as whaling ships, avoided infiltration and convective heat losses caused by winds and had windows only where they would let in sunlight.

Modern home-builders can copy these exemplary design goals by constructing well-insulated, weather-stripped, compact homes that are clustered together to minimize exposure to winds and heat loss. Windows should face south whenever possible, be minimized to the east or west, and avoided to the north. Double- or triple-glazed windows are required. Air locks and vestibules for doors are also desirable. Building sites should be carefully selected for maximum solar exposure and protection from winter winds. In drier areas of the cool region, home builders can evade excessive cold and wind by copying the conservation strategy used by North Dakota Indians, and building living areas underground.

Landscaping, including windbreaks and plant-covered berms, was recognized by our ancestors as an important contributor to energy-efficient design in the rugged, cool region. It can reduce heating needs by as much as 30 percent.

THE SUN

The simple, chilly climate of the northern regions of the United States has the virtue of being relatively easy to design for. The need to minimize heating loads outweighs all other considerations and streamlines the design process. Simply stated, all efforts should be made to welcome the sun into living areas.

This can be achieved by carving out a swathe from the southeast to the southwest face of a structure that is clear of all sun-blocking obstructions. In midwinter, about 85 percent of the total solar energy is collected between the hours of 9:00 A.M. and 3:00 P.M., when the sun travels from a bearing angle of about 150° (southeast) to 210° (southwest). During this six-hour period the sun traverses a short, low arc in the sky, going from an altitude angle at 9:00 A.M. of about 15° to a "high" noon altitude angle of only 20°. This crescent of sky is kept free of all tall-growing plant life. When the sun is low in the sky, its warming impact is highest (although still modest) on vertical south-facing wall surfaces and through vertical south-facing windows. For this reason, these walls and windows should have unobstructed access to the sun. Be cautioned that because the low winter sun casts especially long shadows, moderately distant objects that are due south may partially shade a structure and prevent all the sun's radiant energy from reaching the structure.

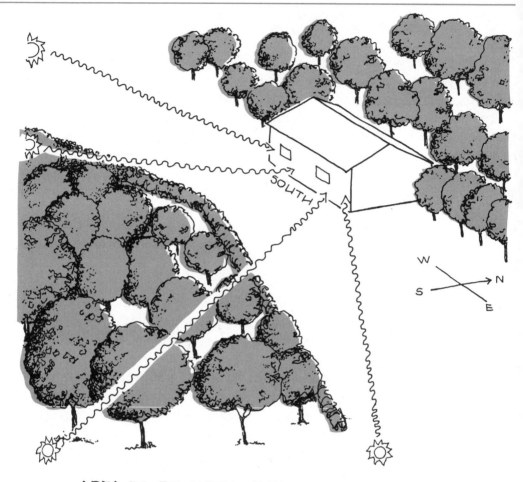

AREA TO BE KEPT CLEAR OF VEGETATION

To the east, north, and west—that is, outside of the winter sun's arc—landscape with thick plantings of trees, shrubs, and hedges. During winter, the early morning and late afternoon sun is so low in the sky that it offers no appreciable radiant heat, and therefore there is no harm in blocking the sun. During midsummer, when the sun rises at about 5:00 A.M., the plants will screen the sun and hinder premature, early morning awakenings.

If you live in a cool region that has occasional summer heat spells and would benefit from shade, plant a high-crowned deciduous tree close to the south face of a home. It will not screen the low winter sun but will offer desirable summer shade.

WIND

Landscapers in the cool region will get the greatest energy-saving return by investing in plant designs that deflect cold winds. If you have a limited budget, focus your resources on wind control. Cold blasts of air sweeping south from Canada or off the Great Lakes are a menace. Winds use convection currents to blow away a home's precious heat without even entering the structure. In addition, cold air seeps into a home via cracks and ill-fitting doors and windows and needs to be warmed up, putting further demands on the building's heating plant. The prevailing direction of such harmful air movements must be determined before any plans are made to divert them up and over a structure. Use the techniques described in Chapter 2 to check wind direction.

Rows of tall trees planted in stands that are wider than the mature height of the trees offer excellent shields from unwanted winds. These windbreaks offer the greatest protection if they are planted perpendicular to the direction of the wind. Single trees scattered loosely on grounds are useless as windbreaks and may even impair home energy conservation, since they can cause local air turbulence as wind blows through a maze of slim obstructions.

Recall from Chapter 2 that a solid screen barrier offers impressive protection from wind immediately downwind of the barrier, but the protection falls off rapidly and is lost beyond five times the height of the solid barrier. This is because a pocket of negative pressure is created downwind, and it draws winds back down and into place. On the other hand, a loose barrier offers more modest protection downwind, but its effectiveness extends a greater distance downwind, up to fifteen times the height of the barrier.

Therefore, if you want to cut winter winds dramatically over a short distance, plant windbreaks of dense evergreens such as pine (*Pinus* species) and spruce (*Picea* species)

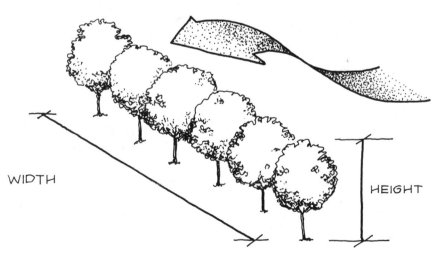

WINDBREAK: WIDER THAN TALL

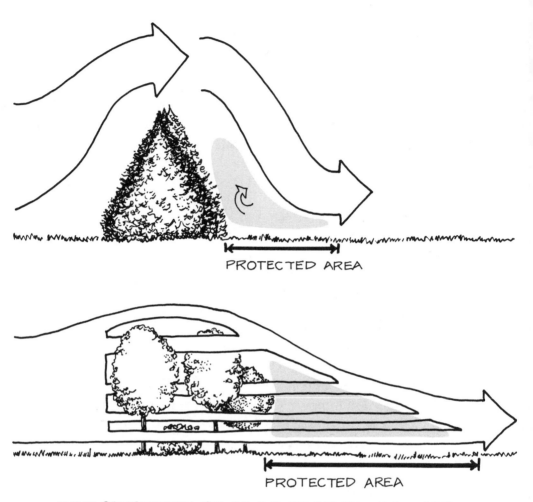

PROTECTED AREA

PROTECTED AREA

WIND PROTECTION DOWNWIND OF DENSE AND LOOSE SHELTERBELTS

close to the home. They offer excellent shelter from strong winds for a distance of up to five tree-lengths downwind of the barrier, with maximum protection at a distance of two to three tree-lengths. However, this strategy for blocking winter winds also blocks sun and is appropriate only if the winds blow from the northeast, north, or northwest, where there is no fear of obstructing the sun's precious radiant heat.

If you need to calm winds over a distance greater than five times the height of the windbreak, or if you require wind protection from the south, plant a loose barrier of conifers or deciduous trees some distance south of the home. It will protect from wind and allow exposure to sun.

Before planting a windbreak to the south, determine the maximum height of such a windbreak or the distance it should be placed from a structure.

This added calculation will prevent you from creating a windbreak that is too tall and blocks the winter sun. First, look up the altitude angle of the sun during the winter solstice (December 22) in your area, and its tangent from the tables in Appendices C and D on pages 171–179. The variables can be determined by the equation:

$$\text{Tangent of altitude angle of sun during midwinter solstice} = \frac{\text{maximum height of windbreak}}{\text{distance of windbreak from house}}$$

For example, if you live in Butte, Montana (latitude 46°N.), where the

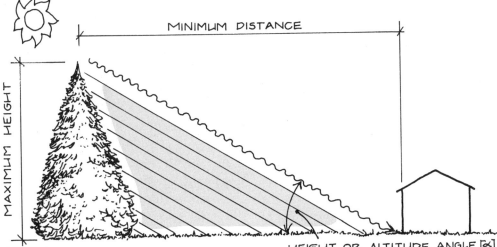

MINIMUM DISTANCE

MAXIMUM HEIGHT

SOUTH

HEIGHT OR ALTITUDE ANGLE [∝]
OF MIDWINTER SUN

CALCULATION OF TREE PLACEMENT TO ALLOW WINTER SUN TO REACH HOUSE

NOON WINTER SUN ANGLE FOR BUTTE, MONTANA [FROM TABLE FOR 46° N. LATITUDE] ∝ = 20.55° [β = 180° OR DUE SOUTH]

$$\text{TAN} \propto = \frac{\text{HEIGHT OF BARRIER}}{\text{DISTANCE TO HOUSE}}$$

TAN ∝ = .374 [FROM TRIGONOMETRIC TABLES OR FROM A CALCULATOR]

$$\frac{\text{HEIGHT OF BARRIER}}{\text{DISTANCE TO HOUSE}} = .374 \text{ OR ABOUT } \tfrac{1}{3}$$

THEREFORE:
CHOOSE A TREE THAT WILL NOT GROW TALLER THAN ⅓ THE DISTANCE TO THE HOUSE,
    OR CONVERSELY,
PLANT THE TREE THREE TIMES AS FAR FROM THE HOUSE AS THE EXPECTED MATURE TREE HEIGHT.
E.G.   A 37' TREE SHOULD BE AT LEAST 100' SOUTH OF THE HOUSE

midwinter sun rises to a maximum altitude angle of 20.55°, and you want to plant a windbreak 100 feet from the south face of your home, the trees selected should grow *no taller* than thirty-seven feet. Or:

$$\tan(20.55) = \frac{x}{100}$$

$$.37 = \frac{x}{100}$$

$$x = 37 \text{ ft.}$$

For example, a loose windbreak of American mountain ash *(Sorbus americana)* or tree lilac *(Syringa reticulata* var. *japonica)* planted 100 feet from the south face and growing to a maximum height of thirty feet, will offer reasonably good wind protection to the building and modest protection up to fifteen times its height. Yet the same windbreak will not obstruct the low winter sun.

The following summarizes the guidelines for planting windbreaks. Tall, *dense* barriers of evergreens and deciduous trees offer profound but short-ranging protection from winds and should be placed close to the home along its northern hemisphere. Most homes derive great benefit from generous landscaping to the north, and all energy-saving landscape designs in cool regions should begin with windbreaks planted to the north. *Loose* barriers of evergreens or deciduous trees offer more modest wind protection over a distance of up to fifteen times the height of the windbreak and should be placed 100 to 300 feet from the home. This type of barrier can be positioned anywhere without fear of totally blocking the sun.

Fast-growing trees such as white pine *(Pinus strobus)* are appropriate for starting windbreaks, but they have the drawbacks of being relatively soft woods and vulnerable to breakage in high winds. However, they do provide an environment appropriate for later, secondary hardwood growth. Patience and stability in your housing situation are required to witness the transition of a forestation pattern from soft to hardwoods.

The virtues of each of these growth types are combined by planting a double shelterbelt, a windbreak of fast-growing softwoods some distance from the home that will slow down winds, and a second of slower-growing hardwoods within their shadow. Eventually, the hardwoods will replace the softwoods.

WATER

As discussed in Chapter 2, water has a high specific heat and, therefore, lakes and other large bodies of water change temperature slowly. They also absorb and retain some of the sun's energy, acting as giant solar storage tanks. As winter approaches, the temperatures of large lakes remain higher than the ambient air temperature. On the other hand, shoreline areas are cooler in summer than inland areas. This explains in part why northern communities near large bodies of water such as Duluth, Minnesota, have milder climates than inland areas at comparable latitudes such as Bemidji, Minnesota.

Unfortunately, small pools and ponds that can be easily added to a landscape plan do not offer an appreciable ameliorating effect on climate. They simply do not hold enough heat to alter significantly the microclimate around a home. In fact, certain cautions should be taken so that they do not make the homesite less comfortable. For example, never construct a pond that is upwind of living areas. This situation will bring raw winds into the home, especially in spring, when the water temperature is colder than the air. Unshielded bodies of water to the west are also undesirable because they reflect glare into the home during the winter months, when the sun is low in the sky. Low-growing deciduous shrubs planted between the water and the structure can filter light reflected off ponds.

LANDFORMS

Artificially built-up landforms can be a major design asset in cool regions because they can divert unwanted winds away from buildings and, when placed close to a home, can insulate against sharp temperature drops. If possible, it is preferable to place berms immediately next to a structure to gain the full insulation value of the earth. However, a berm separated from a structure by a small air pocket will also provide for the deflection of wind. In cool regions of the United States, the most energy-efficient home designs take advantage of landforms by building underground and landscaping on the "roof" or along a "wall" of the structure.

The only area in the cool region where building underground is an inappropriate strategy is in regions of permafrost such as Alaska. An attempt at an underground home in this

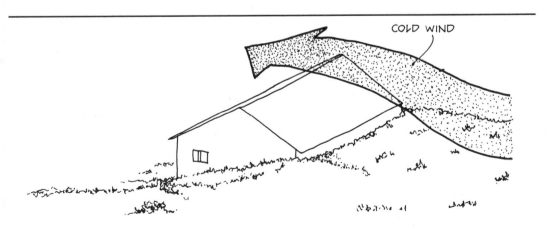

COLD WIND

BERM AGAINST HOME

region will yield disastrous results. Once you have made the extraordinary effort of cutting through the ground for construction, the heat generated within the structure would melt the permafrost, settling the home farther into the ground, usually unevenly.

If you build a conventional home in the cool region that is fully above ground, don't site it in a valley bottom. Cold air runs downhill and forms a pool in the valley. Similarly, don't place berms around a structure on the downhill side, as this catches cold air flowing downslope and creates a pocket of cool air.

SPECIAL LANDSCAPING STRATEGIES

An old adage says that wood warms you three times: once when you cut it, again when you carry it home, and, finally, when you burn it. In cool regions we have identified a fourth use: windbreaks of trees and wooden fences provide valuable protection from heat-stealing winds. Woody shrubs that hold snow against a wall also insulate against heat loss by trapping heat inside the structure and discouraging convective heat losses. Hardy vines such as American bittersweet (Celastrus scandens) or Virginia creeper (Parthenocissus quinquefolia) will offer modest insulation against convective heat losses as well, by pocketing a still layer of air between the wall and the vine.

Evergreen vines that also grow as ground covers, such as English ivy (Hedera Helix), are especially valuable landscape materials because they offer a splash of green during prolonged winters. Bricks, slate, and pavement are also appropriate ground covers on the south side because they absorb the sun's heat, giving an extra measure of warmth to an outdoor living area and making it comfortable for a few more weeks in the spring and autumn. This is especially valuable in cool regions where summers are brief and where there is a tradition of enjoying the outdoors whenever the weather permits.

Low-growing shrubs and ground covers are favored landscape materials in cool regions because ice and wind often ruin species that aspire to large stature; most species that thrive in the colder regions have learned to huddle together in a low profile.

In the northern regions of the United States, the use of Alpine plants in rock gardens results in attractive and colorful settings, especially to the south of a structure, where there is the need to use low-growing species. Delicate-looking Alpine plants can withstand the harsh stresses of the cool region, even in the rocky screes above the treeline. Successful rock gardens capture the character and feel of a mountain scene, with spots of delicate flowers, including select primrose (Primula species), anemone and phlox species, and ground covers set among boulders and less massive rocks. Never underestimate the attractive-

ROCK GARDEN

ness and value of select native wild-flowers and grasses in the development of a garden.

Design expertise is needed to create an artistic, natural rock garden. Haphazard planning has produced too many rock piles that masquerade as rock gardens. Always prepare a planting plan before purchasing a single species and locate plants in a pleasing arrangement according to their culture requirements and blossoming schedules. The first step in creating such a design is to become familiar with a plant's color, time of bloom, size, and growth habit. In a naturalistic garden, planting in formal rows or geometrical patterns should be avoided. Irregular plant groupings strengthen the desired natural effect. Rugged trees that withstand subzero temperatures, including jack pine *(Pinus Banksiana)*, red pine *(Pinus resinosa)*, Scots pine

(Pinus sylvestris), and Norway spruce *(Picea Abies)*, can offer an ideal backdrop to the delicate-looking rock gardens. Select birch *(Betula* species) and the eastern sycamore *(Platanus occidentalis)*, even when leafless, offer interesting color and form. There is an ample choice of deciduous and evergreen species that furnish constant color and mass, providing individual ornaments and privacy screens to northern landscapes throughout the year, while protecting homes by guiding cold winds away from living areas.

The following are suggestions for plant species that survive in the cooler regions of the United States. Not all of the species grow throughout the region. Check with your local Extension agent or nursery to determine a plant's growing pattern in your area. Please note that some species grow quite slowly here.

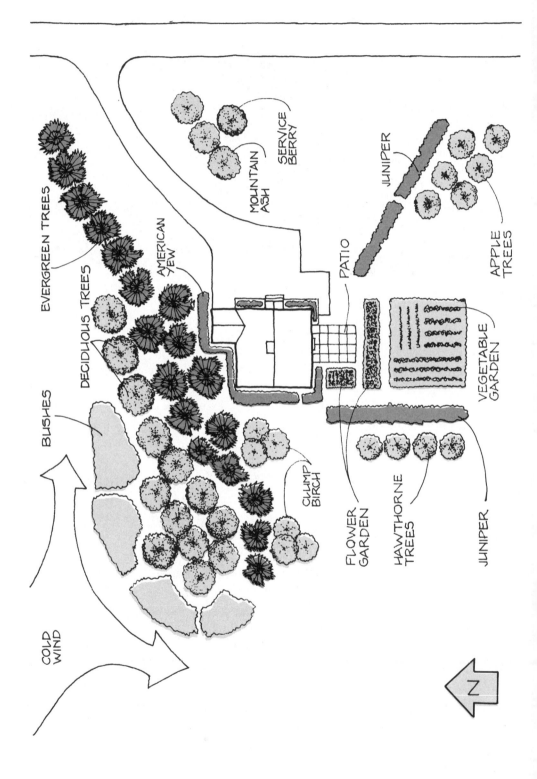

EVERGREEN TREES

DECIDUOUS TREES

AMERICAN YEW

BUSHES

CLUMP BIRCH

COLD WIND

MOUNTAIN ASH

SERVICE BERRY

JUNIPER

APPLE TREES

PATIO

VEGETABLE GARDEN

FLOWER GARDEN

HAWTHORNE TREES

JUNIPER

N

Tall Deciduous Trees (growing to a height greater than thirty-five feet)

Acer platanoides cultivars (Norway maple)
Acer rubrum (red maple, scarlet maple, swamp maple)
Acer saccharinum (silver maple)
Acer saccharum (sugar maple, rock maple)
Aesculus X carnea cv. 'Briotti' (ruby horse chestnut)
Betula papyrifera (canoe birch, paper birch, white birch)
Betula pendula cultivars (European white birch)
Cladrastis lutea (American yellowwood)
Fraxinus pennsylvanica lanceolata (green ash)
Gleditsia triacanthos (honey locust)
Nyssa sylvatica (black tupelo, black gum, sour gum, pepperidge)
Platanus occidentalis (eastern sycamore)
Quercus alba (white oak)
Quercus rubra (northern red oak)
Quercus coccinea (scarlet oak)
Salix alba var. *tristis* (golden weeping willow)
Tilia americana (American linden, basswood)
Tilia cordata (little leaf linden)
Tilia tomentosa (silver linden)

Short and Medium Deciduous Trees (growing to a height less than thirty-five feet)

Acer ginnala (Amur maple)
Amelanchier canadensis (shadblow, downy serviceberry)
Amelanchier grandiflora (apple serviceberry)
Crataegus mollis (downy hawthorn)
Elaeagnus angustifolia (Russian olive, oleaster)
Malus species (crab apple)
Morus alba (white mulberry)
Phellodendron amurense (Amur cork tree)

Prunus X blireiana (Blireiana plum, purpleleaf plum)
Prunus cerasifera (cherry plum)
Sorbus americana (American mountain ash)
Sorbus aucuparia (European mountain ash, rowan tree)
Sorbus decora (showy mountain ash)
Syringa reticulata var. *japonica* (Japanese tree lilac)
Ulmus pumila (Siberian elm)

Tall Evergreen Trees (growing to a height greater than thirty-five feet)

Abies balsamea (balsam fir)
Abies concolor (white fir, concolor fir)
Picea Abies, also called *Picea excelsa* and cultivars (Norway spruce)
Picea glauca cv. 'Densata' (Black Hills spruce)
Picea pungens (Colorado spruce)
Pinus Banksiana (jackpine, gray pine, scrub pine)
Pinus resinosa (red pine, Norway pine)
Pinus strobus (eastern white pine)
Pinus sylvestris (Scotch pine, Scots pine)
Pseudotsuga Menziesii, also called *Pseudotsuga taxifolia, Pseudotsuga Douglasii* (Douglas fir)
Tsuga canadensis cultivars (Canada hemlock)

Short and Medium Evergreen Trees (growing to a height of less than thirty-five feet)

Picea Abies cultivars (Norway spruce)
Tsuga canadensis cultivars (Canada hemlock)

Deciduous Windbreaks, Hedges, and Borders

Berberis Thunbergii cultivars (Japanese barberry)
Caragana arborescens (Siberian pea tree)

Elaeagnus angustifolia (wild olive, Russian olive, silverberry)
Elaeagnus commutata (silverberry)
Ligustrum amurense (Amur privet)
Lonicera species (honeysuckle)
Prunus tomentosa (Manchu or Nanking cherry)
Symphoricarpos albus var. *laevigatus,* also called *Symphoricarpos racemosis* (snowberry)
Syringa vulgaris hybrids (French hybrid lilacs)

Evergreen Windbreaks, Hedges, and Borders

Juniperus chinensis cultivars (Chinese juniper)
Juniperus virginiana cultivars (eastern red cedar)
Thuja occidentalis (American arborvitae)

Deciduous Shrubs

Cornus alba cv. 'Sibirica' (Siberian dogwood)
Potentilla fruticosa (bush cinquefoil)
Spiraea latifolia (meadowsweet)
Viburnum trilobum, also called *Viburnum americanum* (American cranberry bush)

Evergreen Shrubs

Chamaecyparis pisifera cultivars (Sawara false cypress)
Euonymus Fortunei cultivars (winter creeper)
Juniperus communis cultivars (common juniper)
Pinus aristata (bristlecone pine, hickory pine)
Pinus cembra (Swiss stone pine)

Pinus Mugo, also called *Pinus montana* (mugo pine, Swiss mountain pine)
Rhododendron maximum (rosebay rhododendron, great laurel)

Deciduous Vines

Celastrus scandens (American bittersweet)
Clematis hybrids (hybrid clematis)
Humulus japonicus, also called *Humulus scandens* (Japanese hop)
Parthenocissus quinquefolia (Virginia creeper)
Parthenocissus tricuspidata (Boston Ivy)
Polygonum Aubertii (silver-fleece vine, silver-lace vine)
Vitis riparia (riverbank grape)

Evergreen Vines

Hedera Helix cultivars (English Ivy)

Ground Covers

Aegopodium Podagraria cv. 'variegatum' (silver-edge bishop's weed, silver-edge goutweed)
Ajuga reptans cultivars (bugleweed, carpet bugle)
Androsace sarmentosa (rock jasmine)
Antennaria dioica (everlasting, pussy's toes)
Arctostaphylos uva-ursi (bearberry, kinnikinnick)
Hedera Helix cultivars (English ivy)
Juniperus horizontalis cv. 'Wiltonii' (Wilton carpet juniper)
Saxifraga species (rock foils)
Sedum species (stonecrop, live-forever)
Thymus praecox subsp. *arcticus* (mother-of-thyme)
Vinca minor (common periwinkle, trailing myrtle, creeping myrtle)

4

ENERGY-EFFICIENT LANDSCAPE DESIGN FOR HOT, ARID CLIMATES

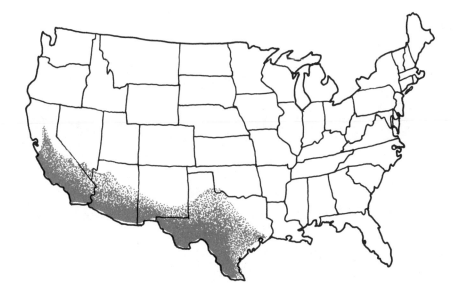

WIDE DAILY FLUCTUATIONS in temperature characterize the climate of hot, arid regions. During the day, the hot sun parches the earth of all available moisture. At night, a clear, cloudless sky permits heat to reradiate into space, and the ground temperature plummets. A daytime temperature of more than 100°F. can drop to 65°F. within hours.

The cool season lasts from November to March or April. Minimum January temperatures range from 30° to 40°F., and maximum January temperatures range from 60° to 70°F. The summers are extremely hot; average maximum temperatures above 100°F. are common, and minimum temperatures during this season average 70° to 80°F. The region is one of the sunniest in the United States and has a small amount of precipitation, usually between one and ten inches per year.

Hot winds are regarded as plagues. They carry away precious moisture and bring dust and sand. Furnacelike blasts add a hard edge to arid environments and dehydrate skin and scorch eyes. The winds of drought are often given proper names, like personal enemies, an example being Southern California's Santana. Cool winds, though rarely available, are treasured, and are funneled into living areas.

Keeping cool during the day and warm at night are the goals of energy-efficient home planning. Successful home and landscape designs in hot, arid regions temper and equalize extremes of temperature by discouraging hot winds and retaining any available moisture. Economical use of plants and water can help to accomplish these goals.

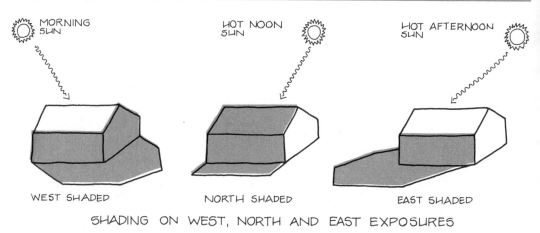

SHADING ON WEST, NORTH AND EAST EXPOSURES

As indicated in Chapter 2, day-to-night temperature fluctuations can be ameliorated within buildings by the use of heavy construction materials, which absorb and release heat slowly. Any external paved areas made of concrete or stone, which absorb and reradiate heat, should be minimized, shaded, and located downwind of and as far as possible from dwellings and related outdoor living areas. The ideal house design for arid climates has few doors and windows opening to the outside. Instead, most windows face an internal courtyard or patio, where care has been taken to reduce heat buildup, dehydration, and glare. The ideal house also offers protection from blowing dust. Any living areas that are outside the walls, including patios or balconies, should be located east or north of the house. An eastern location benefits from late afternoon shadows, and the northern from midday shadows. Unfortunately, this shading effect is minimal in the summer, when it is needed most, and maximized in the winter, when overheating and the need for shading is less severe.

The use of latent heat for temperature control depends on the local availability of water. Plants are preferred to fountains or pools for evaporative temperature control because plants also cast shade, control reflection, and usually provide usable space underneath. Plants, especially trees, may also tap hidden sources of moisture, producing masses of foliage and edible fruits. Certain trees have roots that can penetrate more than 100 feet into the subsoil and rocky substrata in their search for subterranean springs. Drought-resistant trees such as the almond (*Prunus dulcis*) can survive and flourish in apparently waterless conditions. Olives (*Olea europaea*) and carobs (*Ceratonia Siliqua*) can be planted in clefts of rocks where no soil is obvious; their roots will penetrate deep into a hillside, seeking water.

From an environmental perspective, plants are always superior to mechanical cooling devices for temperature control because they use no artificially generated energy and they create no mechanical heat which, in turn, must be dissipated.

DESERT LANDSCAPE

Residential and small business structures built according to guidelines for hot, arid climates, and using an energy-efficient landscape to complement the structure's design, can save more than 33 percent of the energy bill of similar structures not following such design principles. This reflects the sum spent on air conditioning.

SUN

In hot, arid regions, uncontrolled radiant energy during the hot months is the greatest liability to home energy consumption. Landscapes should be designed to subdue the effects of the summer sun, which arches high into the sky and is almost overhead during midday.

An investment in landscaping on the southern exposure will yield the maximum energy-saving benefits in this region. If you have a limited budget, focus your resources here. The goal is to block the rays of the sun as it reaches its zenith directly overhead. Tall, high-crowned trees planted close to the home are best. Palm trees are often chosen for this solar control. However, some palm species such as the Mexican Washington palm *(Washingtonia robusta)*, present a fire hazard in arid regions because they store dead leaves at the crown and along the trunk. These leaves should be removed regularly. Also, care must be given to retrieving the fruit borne by the palms. Tall, columnar Eucalyptus species that require little moisture such as the desert gum *(Eucalyptus rudis)* may also be used as sunscreens.

Another strategy for shading south-facing roofs, walls, or windows is the use of trellises. The slatwork on these structures can be angled to block summer sun and permit winter sun to

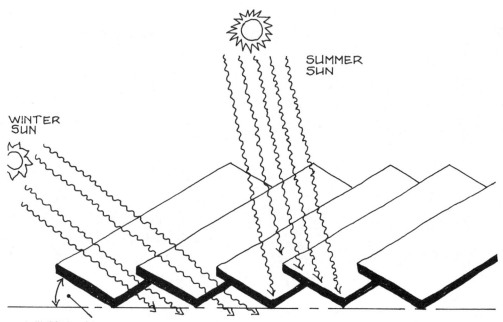

WINTER SUN

SUMMER SUN

WINTER ANGLE

TRELLIS WITH SLATS AT SOLAR CONTROL ANGLE

penetrate. Trellises covered with thick vines cast additional shade. Coral vine (*Antignon leptopus*) and cat's claw vine (*Macfadyena Unguis-cati*) are species that thrive with little moisture. Reflected glare on southern exposures can be controlled by planting drought-resistant ground covers, including Sprenger asparagus (*Asparagus Sprengeri*), select juniper, ceanothus, sedum species, and ground morning glory (*Convolvulus mauritanicus*). Grass is an extremely poor choice for ground cover because it requires more water per square foot than any other ordinary landscape material as well as large amounts of fertilizer. The ground covers mentioned above will cut glare as effectively as grass and require far less energy-intensive main-

tenance. On the other hand, if regular activity is planned for the area, few ground covers endure trampling as well as grass does.

On the eastern face of a structure, sun can be controlled by planting bushes or low trees such as honey mesquite (*Prosopis glandulosa*) or desert willow (*Chilopsis linearis*). In regions where water is rationed, many species of low-growing cactus such as prickly pear (*Opuntia littoralis*) planted close to the home are appropriate. In general, species with light foliage or a loose structure are desirable to the east. They hinder early morning heat buildup but permit the pleasant dawn light to filter in.

To the west, landscaping is needed for protection from low but torrid late afternoon sun. Low trees with dense foliage such as California live oak *(Quercus agrifolia)* and fan palms *(Palmaceae chamaerops)* or thick bushes, including thorny elaeagnus *(Elaeagnus pungens)* and sweet bay *(Laurus nobilis)*, will effectively block the sun if planted close to the home. Low-growing cacti, including prickly pear and organpipe *(Lemaireocereus Thurberi),* can accomplish the same goal if planted adjacent to the structure. Western exposures are also vulnerable to harsh glare and benefit from verdant expanses to cut reflection. Choose drought-resistant ground covers such as stonecrop *(Sedum species)*. If water is extremely short, divide the yard into sections of planted ground cover and nonreflecting natural materials such as wood chips. This design adds color and tex-

ture to a yard or patio, does not reflect heat or light, conserves moisture, and relieves the severity of a desert-like landscape.

Since sun rarely appears on the north face, landscaping along this quadrant has minimal value for controlling radiation. Bushes planted to the northwest and north may be desirable for blocking unwanted midsummer sun shortly before sunset, and reflected light or hot winds. If there are no hot winds from the north, short plantings such as California privet *(Ligustrum ovalifolium)* or tamarisk *(Tamarix parviflora)* at a distance of ten feet or more from the house are appropriate. They reduce glare and heat reflected from the ground, cut off the midsummer evening sun, but allow the house to reradiate heat toward the sky during the night.

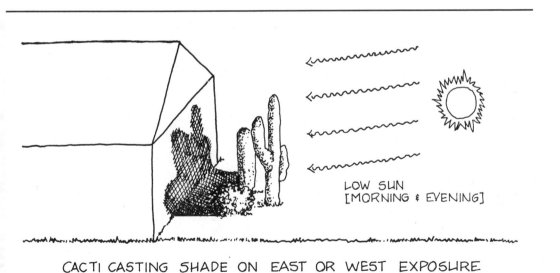

CACTI CASTING SHADE ON EAST OR WEST EXPOSURE

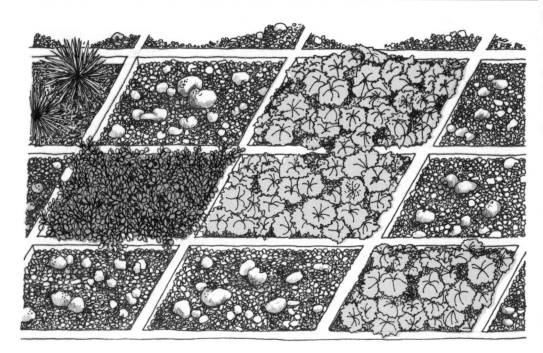

GROUND COVERS IN CHECKERBOARD PATTERN

WIND

The guidelines for controlling winds are simple. Hot, dry winds must be channeled away from living areas, using bushes, palms, cacti, or evergreen trees, or man-made screens or baffles. Windbreaks should be planted perpendicular to the prevailing winds. Entrances and windows should receive extra protection from hot blasts. If your site has the blessing of cool, moisture-laden breezes from some specific direction, landscape to funnel them into living areas. The Venturi effect (see Chapter 2) can enhance such breezes.

WATER

Evaporative cooling from plants, pools, or fountains can provide ideal air conditioning. But areas that suffer from drought should also have landscape designs that enclose the water source, prevent moisture loss, and provide natural recycling of water. This can be accomplished by limiting plantings to an internal atrium, a fully enclosed courtyard, or indoor plants, and making special efforts to envelop all sources of moisture outside a home. For example, exposed pools and fountains should be shaded, and walls or closed fences should be built

HOT
WIND

HEDGE PROTECTING HOME ENTRANCE FROM HOT WINDS

to contain and direct into living areas the cool air resulting from the evaporative process. Trellises or canopies can partially enclose or cover water sources and help to contain the valuable cool, moisture-laden air. Submersible electric pumps no bigger than a man's fist can recirculate the same water over and over without the need for costly pipe connections to house plumbing; they make shaded fountains a relatively inexpensive proposition. If it is impossible to enclose the source of water, at least place it up-

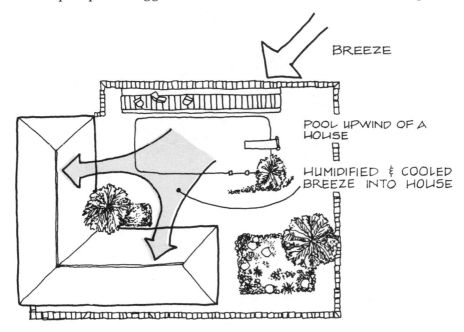

BREEZE

POOL UPWIND OF A
HOUSE

HUMIDIFIED & COOLED
BREEZE INTO HOUSE

BIRD'S EYE VIEW [PLAN] OF POOL UPWIND OF HOUSE

wind from the home so that humidified breezes pass through the living areas.

In this region, pools that contribute pleasantly to cooled, humidified air can also be the source of unwanted glare, especially when they are west of a living room. The low, late afternoon sun reflects off the water. This offensive reflection can be broken by a hedge or windbreak. (See Chapter 7 for techniques to cut reflected glare.)

SPECIAL PLANTING STRATEGIES

In arid regions, more than any other climate, houseplants improve the internal environment and can limit energy consumption. They are extremely effective humidifiers and air coolers and, with a minimum of care, are far more reliable than mechanical humidifiers and air-conditioners. Because the air is always arid, houseplants help to maintain a healthful climate year-round. (Houseplants do not get the same recommendation in hot, humid areas, where added moisture in the air is a liability.) Place houseplants in a sunny window to get the double benefit of shade and an added dose of humidity.

Outside a building, plants make the outdoors an inviting alternative to indoor, air-conditioned spaces. The most productive planting strategy for

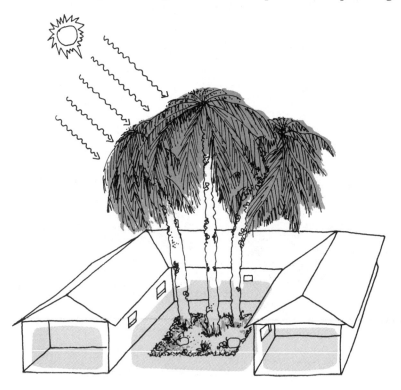

HIGH PALMS SHADING ATRIUM

hot, arid areas is the design of an enclosed garden or atrium. High-crowned trees such as palms cast shade immediately below during the summer. Low shrubs, flowers, and ground covers cool the air further by evaporating water. Because cooled air falls, this valuable commodity is retained and protected within the confines of the atrium. Enclosed atriums also offer protection from moisture-stealing hot winds and are the ideal location for fountains or man-made pools. Precious moisture is recycled in enclosed landscape designs.

If your home was not designed with the benefit of an enclosed court-yard, build an enclosure around a selected outdoor living area. Put walls around your swimming pool, fountains, or reflecting ponds and build trellises over at least part of the area. Minimize paved areas and landscape with drought-resistant species. Your reward is a protected, climate-controlled area that needs only a modest volume of water to replenish daily losses to evaporation. The atrium or courtyard may even support plant life not indigenous to hot, arid regions.

Outside the atrium walls, however, where species must withstand low humidity, limited irrigation, poor soils, and extremes of temperature, only native species endure. This is not a serious constraint for landscape designers. There is a great wealth of flowering and nonflowering materials; some of the most beautiful flowering plants thrive here, providing a display possible only under glass in cooler climates. Dry gardens can generate high drama with plantings of ocotillo (*Fouquieria splendens*), yucca, century plants (select *Agave* species), tamarisk, Jerusalem thorn (*Parkinsonia aculeata*), fan palms, cacti, and other succulents. But more important than the plant varieties is the way in which they are used. Restraint is the key. Use plenty of open space between plantings and don't crowd plants together. An uninhibited use of gray gravel, raked earth, and other materials that reflect little light should separate plants. Some plants can thrive in containers. This kind of landscape might look strange if each plant is a different species, but by keeping the palette simple and by planting in great drifts, the homeowner achieves a unified look in the garden.

Gardeners new to this region should be cautioned that most native species thrive with little moisture. Some novice landscapers have drowned their gardens with an overabundance of attention and water. Excessive irrigation wastes energy and some species such as the California live oak (*Quercus agrifolia*) succumb to excess watering.

Landscape design in arid regions should also attempt to provide shade for necessary paved areas, including parking bays and sidewalks. Asphalt and concrete retain enormous amounts of radiant energy and can easily reach 120°F. when the air temperature is 95°F. Moreover, pavements cool slowly because of their high specific heat. Carefully planted hedges, vines, and trees can transform an unbearably hot walkway or street into a cool, shaded passage.

The benefits of the planting strategies just described were documented in Davis, California, where researchers found that large trees could lower the temperature of a commercial shopping area by at least 10°F., making shoppers happier and reducing air conditioning bills. Air-conditioners should also be shaded. Their metal frames retain radiant energy, putting added pressures on the machinery. Trees, shrubs, and vines offer appropriate sunscreens.

Gardeners in arid regions must abandon the horticultural designs characteristic of the temperate regions if they wish to adhere to a plan of energy conservation. Economy in watering is usually necessary. Hand watering is best done at windless times—during night or early morning hours—to reduce evaporation. Drip irrigation, which involves delivering water to individual plants through a system of narrow tubes or porous tubing, may be one of the most efficient methods ever devised for watering flowers, trees, shrubs, vines, and commercial crops. It can cut water use by 20 to 50 percent. Mulching also helps hold soil water by reducing evaporation. To mulch, cover root areas with such materials as pine needles, composted manure or garden refuse, ground bark, leaves, sawdust, straw, or a dust mulch.

Transplanting demands watering. Most native plants should be set out in the fall to benefit from winter rains. If your area is suffering from any kind of unusual drought, postpone extensive planting.

THE RESULTS

The overall appearance of a landscaped site in an arid region differs radically from the manicured lawn and shrub settings found in other locales. It is naturalistic in appearance. The land is harsh and native plants are often sharp and jagged. There is a dramatic seasonal transition in color, from the lush colors of winter and spring, when water is adequate, to the golden browns of summer and fall. Landscaping with native plants recreates and preserves the best of natural desert ecosystems and, at the same time, conserves energy within the home and in the garden. However, landscaping inside a protected courtyard or atrium may produce a small paradise of lush greens, even during dry summers.

The following suggested plants survive in arid or semiarid regions. Not all of the species grow throughout the nation's hot, dry areas, and some species that are normally trees may grow only into squat shrubs in the more severe climates. Much depends on the immediate environment and on pruning. Check with your local Extension agent or nursery to determine a plant's growing pattern and whether it is appropriate for your location.

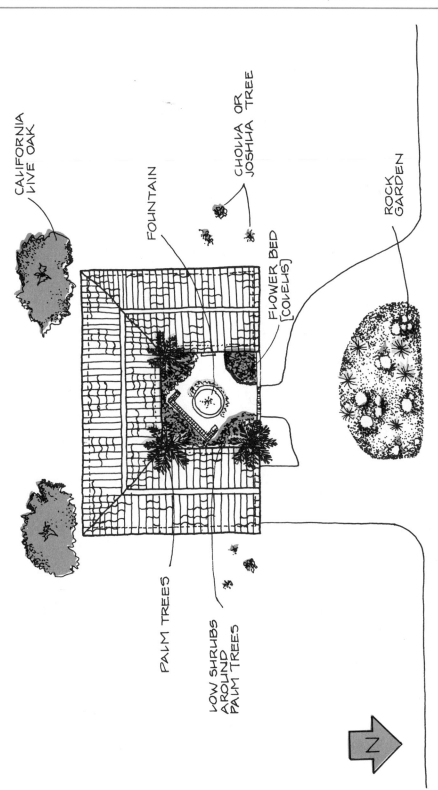

CALIFORNIA
LIVE OAK

CHOLLA OR
JOSHUA TREE

FOUNTAIN

FLOWER BED
[COLEUS]

ROCK
GARDEN

PALM TREES

LOW SHRUBS
AROUND
PALM TREES

Tall Deciduous Trees (growing to a height greater than thirty-five feet)

Acer macrophyllum (big-leafed maple, California maple)
Cercidiphyllum japonicum (katsura tree)
Cladrastis lutea (American yellowwood)
Fraxinus velutina var. *glabra* (Modesto ash)
Ginkgo biloba (ginkgo, maidenhair tree)
Gleditsia triacanthos var. *inermis* (thornless honey locust)
Koelreuteria paniculata (golden-rain tree, varnish tree)
Magnolia heptapeta (Yulan magnolia)
Morus alba (white mulberry)
Parkinsonia aculeata (Jerusalem thorn)
Paulownia tomentosa (empress tree, royal paulownia)
Pistacia chinensis (Chinese pistachio)
Platanus racemosa (California plane tree)
Pyrus Calleryana (Callery pear)
Sophora japonica (Japanese pagoda tree, Chinese scholar tree)
Ulmus parvifolia (Chinese elm)
Zelkova serrata (Japanese zelkova)

Short and Medium Deciduous Trees (growing to heights less than thirty-five feet)

Albizia julibrissin (silk tree)
Amelanchier X *grandiflora* (apple serviceberry)
Cercidium floridum (Palo Verde)
Cercis canadensis (eastern redbud)
Cornus florida (flowering dogwood)
Elaeagnus angustifolia (Russian olive)
Lagerstroemia indica (crape myrtle)
Malus baccata (crab apple)
Prosopis glandulosa, also called *Prolopsis juliflora* (honey mesquite)
Prunus dulcis (almond tree)

Tall Evergreen Trees (growing to heights greater than thirty-five feet)

Araucaria heterophylla (Norfolk Island pine)
Cedrus atlantica cv. 'Glauca' (blue Atlas cedar)
Ceratonia Siliqua (carob tree)
Cupressus arizonica (Arizona cypress)
Eucalyptus polyanthemos (red box gum, silver dollar tree, Australian beech)
Eucalyptus rudis (desert gum)
Magnolia virginiana, also called *Magnolia glauca* (sweet bay)
Pinus canariensis (Canary Island pine)
Pinus Thunbergiana (Japanese black pine)
Quercus agrifolia (California live oak, coast live oak)
Quercus suber (cork oak)
Quercus virginiana (live oak)

Short and Medium Evergreen Trees (growing to heights less than thirty-five feet)

Agonis flexuosa (willow myrtle, peppermint tree, Australia willow myrtle)
Chilopsis linearis (desert willow)
Olea Europaea (common olive)
Pinus halepensis (Aleppo pine)
Pittosporum phillyraeoides (weeping or willow pittosporum)
Pittosporum rhombifolium (diamond-leaf pittosporum, Queensland pittosporum)
Yucca brevifolia (Joshua tree)

Tall Palm Trees (growing to heights greater than thirty-five feet)

Arecastrum Romanzoffianum, also called *Cocos plumosa* (queen palm)
Washingtonia filifera (Washington palm, desert fan palm, petticoat palm)
Washingtonia robusta (Mexican Washington palm, thread palm)

Short and Medium Palm Trees (growing to heights less than thirty-five feet)

Brahea dulcis (rock palm)
Chamaerops humilis (European fan palm, Mediterranean fan palm)

Phoenix Roebelenii (dwarf date palm, pigmy date palm)

Trachycarpus Fortunei, also called *Trachycarpus excelsus, Chamaerops excelsa* (windmill palm)

Deciduous Windbreaks, Hedges, or Borders

Berberis Thunbergii (Japanese barberry)

Chaenomeles, also called *Cydonia,* species (flowering quince)

Cotoneaster divaricatus (spreading cotoneaster)

Kolkwitzia amabilis (beauty bush)

Ligustrum ovalifolium (California privet)

Lonicera species (honeysuckle)

Symphoricarpos orbiculatus (Indian currant, coralberry)

Tamarix parviflora (tamarisk, salt cedar)

Evergreen Windbreaks, Hedges, or Borders

Berberis Julianae (wintergreen barberry)

Berberis X mentorensis (Mentor barberry)

Elaeagnus pungens (thorny elaeagnus, silverberry)

Euonymus japonica (evergreen euonymus)

Ilex vomitoria (yaupon)

Juniperus chinensis cultivars (Chinese junipers)

Juniperus scopulorum cultivars (Rocky Mountain juniper, Colorado red cedar)

Juniperus virginiana cultivars (eastern red cedar)

Ligustrum japonicum (Japanese privet)

Lonicera nitida (box honeysuckle)

Opuntia littoralis (prickly pear, tuna cactus)

Osmanthus heterophyllus, also called *Osmanthus ilicifolius* (holly osmanthus)

Photinia serrulata (Chinese photinia)

Pyracantha coccinea (fire thorn)

Deciduous Shrubs

Buddleia Davidii (orange-eye butterfly bush)

Calycanthus floridus (strawberry shrub, Carolina allspice)

Deutzia species (deutzia)

Fouquieria splendens (Ocotillo, coach whip, vine cactus)

Hibiscus syriacus (rose of Sharon, shrub althea)

Parkinsonia aculeata (Jerusalem thorn, Mexican Palo Verde)

Philadelphus species (mock orange)

Spiraea species (spirea, bridal wreath)

Tamarix ramosissima, also known as *Tamarix pentandra* (Odessa tamarisk)

Evergreen shrubs

Abelia X grandiflora (glossy abelia)

Agave attenuata (fox tail agave)

Agave Vilmoriniana (century plant)

Aucuba japonica (Japanese aucuba, Japanese laurel)

Ceanothus species (ceanothus, California lilac, wild lilac)

Coccoloba uvifera (sea grape, shore grape)

Cotoneaster dammeri, also called *Cotoneaster humifusus* (bearberry cotoneaster)

Cotoneaster horizontalis (rock spray, rock cotoneaster)

Euonymus Fortunei (winter creeper)

Euphorbia pulcherrima (poinsettia)

Fatsia japonica, also called *Aralia japonica, Aralia sieboldii* (Japanese fatsia, Formosa rice tree, paper plant)

Ilex X altaclarensis cv. 'Wilsonii' (Wilson holly)

Ilex cornuta (Chinese holly)

Juniperus communis (common juniper)

Juniperus conferta (shore juniper)

Juniperus procumbens (Japanese garden juniper)

Juniperus sabina (savin juniper)

Laurus nobilis (sweet bay)
Lemaireocereus Thurberi (organpipe cactus)
Leptospermum scoparium (tea tree, New Zealand tea tree, manuka)
Myrtus communis (myrtle)
Nandina domestica (nandina, Chinese sacred bamboo)
Nerium Oleander (oleander, rosebay)
Nolina Parryi (beargrass)
Pinus aristata (bristlecone pine, hickory pine)
Yucca Whipplei (Candle of the Lord)

Deciduous Vines

Actinidia arguta (bower actinidia, tara vine)
Antigonon leptopus (coral vine)
Campsis X *Tagliabuana* cv. 'Madame Galen' (Madame Galen trumpet vine)
Celastrus scandens (Amrican bittersweet)
Clematis hybrids (hybrid clematis)
Hydrangea anomala, also called *Hydrangea petiolaris* (climbing hydrangea)
Macfadyena Unguis-cati, also known as *Bignonia tweediana* (cat's claw vine)
Polygonum aubertii (silver-fleece vine, silver-lace vine)
Wisteria floribunda cultivars (Japanese wisteria)
Wisteria sinensis, also called *Wisteria chinensis* (Chinese wisteria)

Evergreen Vines

Akebia quinata (five-leaf akebia)
Bignonia capreolata, also called *Anisostichus capreolatus*, or *Doxantha capreolata* (cross vine, trumpet flower)
Bougainvillea hybrids (bougainvillea)
Euonymus Fortunei (common winter creeper)
Jasminum species (jasmine)
Lonicera sempervirens (trumpet honeysuckle)

Ground covers

Aegopodium Podagraria (silver-edge bishop's weed, silver-edge goutweed)
Ajuga reptans (bugleweed, carpet bugle)
Arctostaphylos uva-ursi (bearberry, kinnikinnick)
Asparagus Sprengeri (Sprenger asparagus)
Baccharis pilularis (dwarf coyote bush)
Bougainvillea species (bougainvillea)
Ceanothus gloriosus (Point Reyes ceanothus)
Ceanothus griseus var. *horizontalis* (Carmel creeper)
Ceanothus thyrsiflorus var. *repens* (creeping blue blossom)
Convolvulus mauritanicus (ground morning glory)
Dichondra micrantha, also called *Dichondra repens* (dichondra)
Echinocereus Englemanii (hedgehog cactus)
Euonymus Fortunei winter creeper)
Juniperus horizontalis cv. 'Wiltonii' (Wilton creeping juniper)
Lantana montevidensis (weeping lantana)
Osteospermum fruticosum (trailing African daisy)
Pachysandra terminalis (Japanese pachysandra, Japanese spurge)
Rosmarinus officinalis cv. 'Prostratus' (dwarf rosemary)
Sedum species (stonecrop, live-forever)

5

ENERGY-EFFICIENT LANDSCAPE DESIGN FOR HOT, HUMID CLIMATES

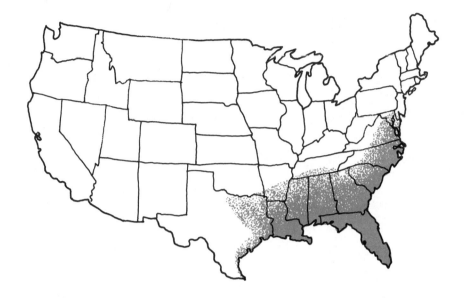

MARITIME TROPICAL AIR, heated by the sun, sweeps off the Caribbean and the Gulf of Mexico to shape the hot, humid climate of Florida and the coastal regions of Georgia, South Carolina, and the Gulf States. This air is heavy with the latent energy of evaporated water and occasionally explodes as the torrential downpours of a hurricane. But most often hot, humid climates are sultry and slow-changing. Moisture-laden, muggy air resists wide, daily fluctuations in temperature.

A hot, humid climate is especially challenging to manage if the goal is to keep within the comfort zone for as long as possible. The temperature can't be reduced by evaporation because additional water in the air only adds to the discomfort; long-term heat spells eliminate the possibility of using thick construction materials (as is done in hot, arid regions) to transform extremes of climate into a comfortable middle range within a building; and no construction material exists that filters humidity to a desirable level and still permits adequate airflow.

Despite these drawbacks, the hot, humid region offers a most congenial climate, without the extremes of cold, dryness, and temperature that plague other areas of the United States. This climate also nurtures the greatest profusion of exotic and colorful flora found anywhere in the country. Here, the sun shines on an average of two thirds of all possible daylight hours. Seventy-five percent of the average yearly temperatures fall within the range of 65–85°F., with temperatures seldom slipping into the 32–65°F. range, or exceeding 90°F.

However, an average annual rainfall of sixty inches or more coupled with the presence of undrained lowlands can produce unpleasantly high humidity during most of the year. This muggy atmosphere magnifies the oppressive effects of heat. For example, the limit of human tolerance (that is, the maximum air temperature at which extended work can be performed) approaches 150°F. in dry air but is reduced to only 90°F. in full humidity. This latter limit is completely within reach in hot, humid regions, especially from May through October.

Avoiding heat storage and promoting ventilation to dissipate humidity are the two key goals of energy-efficient design in hot, humid areas.

The best-planned buildings in this region use a two-stage or slotted roof, minimize interior walls, have elongated shapes with a high surface area, and raise floors off the ground, to maximize air movement and dissipate heat and humidity. Such designs draw in cooler, heavier air through the ground floor or basement and release warmer, lighter air via roof vents, creating a constant internal, light breeze. Galleries around a building, floor-to-ceiling windows, and jalousies can enhance air movement. Homes in the humid subtropics also have lightly constructed walls of pale shades, to lessen heat retention.

Landscaping can further reduce the retention of heat and humidity by shading windows, walls, roofs, and air-conditioners, and by channeling cool breezes into living areas. However, landscape materials must be carefully selected and placed since heavy plantings can have the undesirable effect of generating unwanted excess humidity or blocking desirable light winds. In fact, some established plantings may have to be removed to enhance comfort.

At its best, landscaping also increases comfort by expanding the use of outdoor living areas. Many designers in this region suggest planning grounds to increase time spent living in the landscape. Outdoor areas, if properly shaded, screened, and ventilated, can be comfortable year-round. The exotic and colorful plants that grow profusely in various parts of this region, including Chinese hibiscus (*Hibiscus rosa-sinensis*), the common camellia (*Camellia japonica*), southern magnolia (*Magnolia grandiflora*), the bird of paradise plant (*Strelitzia reginae*), and shrimp plant (*Justicia Brandegeana*), can shelter and decorate trellises, pergolas, patios, and gazebos and make outdoor living an attractive alternative to conventional indoor living. The creation of a climate-controlled outdoor living area will not only cut fuel bills for air conditioning and dehumidifiers, but will also provide a screen from neighbors and from the heat and noise of the street. It will offer an opportunity to enjoy more birds, butterflies, and other wildlife.

An energy-efficient landscape design for a suburban lot can reduce air temperatures about 7°F., or more i

LANDSCAPED PATIO WITH BARBEQUE

shade falls on paved surfaces. Anyone who has visited a well-designed nursery in a hot, humid area knows the value of landscaped grounds. They always offer a cool, colorful, and fragrant refuge.

In the hot, humid region, individual energy conservation goals can reap extra benefits if they are expanded beyond single sites to large-scale developments of single-family homes or small business structures. For example, valuable site-planning principles for this region include positioning traffic thoroughfares to channel desirable breezes, dispersion of structures to allow maximum wind circulation, and the planting of canopy shade trees along property lines. Also desirable are centrally located community facilities which may be reached via tree-shaded pedestrian walkways. Convenient and comfortable pedestrian access to such facilities can reduce unnecessary automobile use. Using plants to shade community activities was once a widespread practice. For example, in sixteenth century Oaxaca, Mexico, a 500-year-old Montezuma cypress *(Taxodium mucronatum)* was used as a meeting place because its leaves could purportedly shade 1,000 people. Today, unfortunately, the air-conditioner substitutes high technology for simple, careful design.

THE SUN

A home nestled in the midst of a grove of high-canopied palm trees uses the ideal technique for providing shade from oppressive sun. During the morning and evening hours, when the low sun casts long shadows, distant palms will shade the eastern and western walls. At midday, when the high tropical sun is immediately overhead, palms planted close to the home will shade the roof. Such high-crowned plants provide shade while allowing cooling breezes to reach the protected structure.

However, few are privileged to have access to this ideal natural site. In hot, humid regions, landscape designers are challenged to use plants to provide shade, but at the same time the number of these plants must be limited because of the undesirable effects of extra humidity produced by heavy plantings. Overly dense plantings block cooling breezes and trap humidity in a pocket of dead air.

Homeowners in this region who build solar energy panels on their roofs must weigh the advantage of building shade canopies, which diminish the cost of air conditioning, against the need for unobstructed solar collectors, which reduce the cost of heating water. If solar collectors are

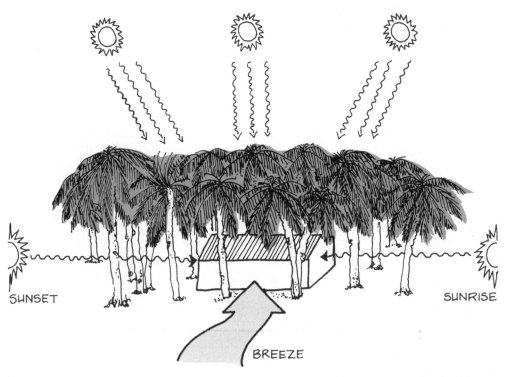

SUNSET

SUNRISE

BREEZE

VENTILATING BREEZES PASS UNOBSTRUCTED UNDER CANOPY

BENEFITS OF PLACING HOME IN PALM GROVE

NORTH

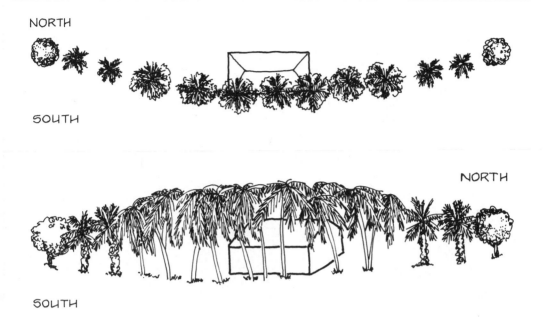

SOUTH

NORTH

SOUTH

PLAN OF TREE LAYOUT

considered, a good solution is to shade most of the roof and to place the collectors on the remaining unshaded area. However, the proper positioning of the collectors must not be abandoned. Sometimes it is wiser simply to place the solar collectors on the ground in an unshaded area, even though a pump may be required to recirculate water from the collectors.

Those who don't have the natural solar protection offered by a palm grove can plant a fast-growing light shade tree to the east. Species such as the silk oak (*Grevillea robusta*) or scrub palmetto (*Sabal palmetto*) will filter the early morning sun.

Protecting the home from the high midday sun is the single most important landscape strategy. If you have limited resources for a new landscape design, use them to solve this problem and protect the southern facade of the structure. On the south face, high-crowned palms such as *Veitchia winin* or Sagisi palm (*Heterospathe elata*) planted close to the home will shade the roof from the blazing summer sun during midday. When planting these and similar species, remember that the mature crowns of such palms can be up to twenty feet in diameter, and well-spaced plantings are needed for healthy growth. If several palms are planted some distance from the south face of the structure, they will block the lower winter sun during midday. Decide whether the winter sun is desirable before planting to screen it. Palms are ideal sunscreens but they do have some drawbacks: some have sparse root systems, which may cause them to topple during severe hurricanes; a few have heavy fruits such

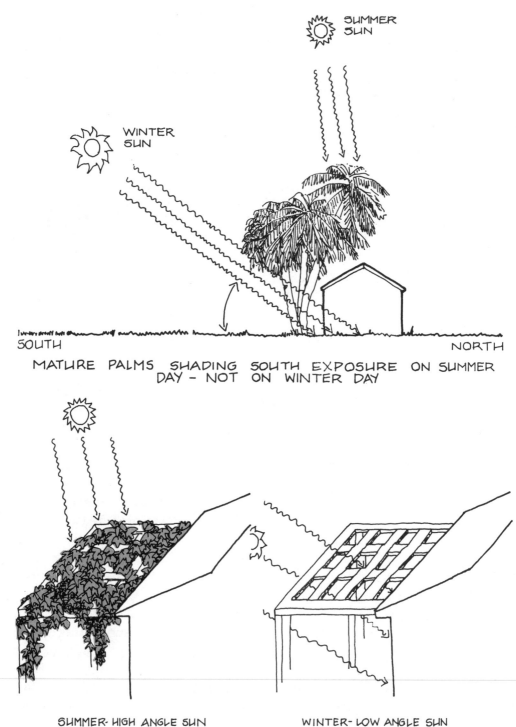

SOUTH

NORTH

MATURE PALMS SHADING SOUTH EXPOSURE ON SUMMER
DAY – NOT ON WINTER DAY

SUMMER- HIGH ANGLE SUN

WINTER- LOW ANGLE SUN

VINE COVERED TRELLIS SHADING SOUTHERN EXPOSURE

as coconuts that must be removed at frequent intervals lest they fall and injure passersby; and others develop a dry thatch that can be a fire hazard, especially in hot, humid regions where roofs may be lightweight and are, therefore, vulnerable to flames.

Another strategy for shading southern windows and walls, which also permits the installation of unobstructed solar collectors on roofs, is the construction of "eyebrow" trellises attached to the undersides of eaves and covered with deciduous vines such as Virginia creeper (*Parthenocissus quinquefolia*). In winter the leaves fall, allowing the sun's rays to penetrate to the home. Be careful in your selection of vines. Aggressive species with woody stems can invade and damage construction materials; for example, they can enter the cracks in roofing tiles and grow into a home.

To the west, a grove of distant, tall palm trees or shorter palms planted closer to the home, or a single large tree such as gumbo-limbo (*Bursera simaruba*), will shade walls and windows from the hot, late afternoon sun. A trellis covered with a vine such as skyflower (*Thunbergia grandiflora*), with its pendant clusters of large, light-blue flowers, will also accomplish this goal. Some people are reluctant to plant large shade trees or build trellises to the west because they block views of the sunset. Unfortunately, without some shading such views are extremely expensive to maintain. Air conditioning is needed to temper the effects of a blazing afternoon sun during the period before sunset. When the sun approaches the horizon it is perpendicular to the western facade, and the western wall absorbs much of the sun's radiant heat. In some areas, especially those close to the sea or with thin soils, it is customary to cover grounds with light-colored coral, stone chips, or other reflective materials. This is a very poor landscape strategy for a western facade because these materials reflect the light and heat of the low afternoon sun into the home. Ground covers such as artillery ferns (*Pilea microphylla*), asparagus fern (*Asparagus Sprengeri*), the yellow-flowering wedelia (*Wedelia trilobata*) or wandering Jew (*Zebrina pendula*), are far more desirable than coral or stone chips, even if you can only afford to plant them in artistically defined sections of your garden. Their greater cost will be compensated for, in part, by reduced air conditioning bills and lessened visual glare.

There is little reason to plant species to the north for sun shading, since the sun rarely appears on this facade in the United States. On occasion, however, low-growing species may be of value if planted to the extreme northwest, where they will block the early evening sun during several weeks of midsummer. Plantings on the north may also be useful for screening reflection and glare, but must not block any ventilating breezes.

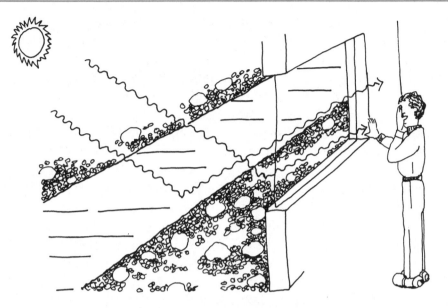

LIGHT GRAVEL/PAVEMENT REFLECTING SUNLIGHT INTO HOME

WIND

In hot, humid regions, cool winds that dispel moisture and promote the evaporation of sweat are treasured. Identify them, understand their behavior and direction, and learn to use them to your advantage.

Testing their flow can be a challenge since sluggish tropical air movements can be difficult to detect. Try to investigate their nature by observing a wind sock or piece of yarn nailed to a pole, or the pattern of water droplets falling from a fountain or lawn sprinkler. Make these observations over a period of days during each season. Offshore breezes will probably have a predictable, cyclical nature.

Breezes may be managed by designing the landscape to channel breezes into a home or an outdoor living area. Here, the Venturi effect can be used to advantage. A narrowing wind scoop that funnels air toward the home can accelerate and increase the cooling impact of a light breeze that would otherwise be ineffective. As we have seen, a trellis or other structure that offers a "roof" to the funnel can further enhance the cooling breeze.

In some hot, humid areas, occasional winter winds that blast out of the north can cause temperatures to plunge, perhaps even to freezing. If this is a problem in your area, the effects of these northern winds can be minimized by planting windbreaks of pines (*Pinus* species), Senegal date palms (*Phoenix reclinata*), or Spanish stopper (*Eugenia foetida*). Windbreaks should be planted perpendicular to the direction of the wind, and used only if really necessary.

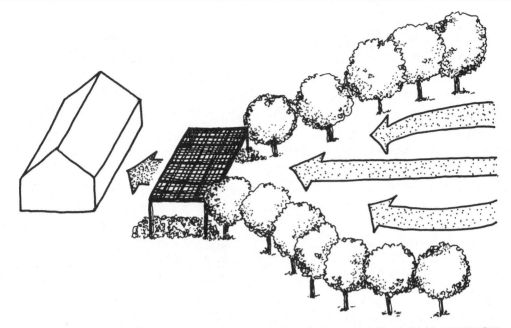

TREE FUNNEL WITH COVERED END FOR ENHANCING BREEZE

WATER

From a strictly physical viewpoint, the addition of pools, ponds, or water basins to a hot, humid climate is not a good idea. They add humidity, exacerbate the mugginess, attract insects, and cause glare, adding further discomfort. These disadvantages more than offset any slight drop in ambient temperature they offer. However, psychology offers its own arguments to support the addition of pools or ponds to the landscape. Water offers recreation opportunities and brings a garden alive with its reflections, sparkling movement, and soothing sound. The sight of cascading fountains or rippling pools projects a relaxing atmosphere and, for this reason, many gardeners in hot, humid regions choose to add bodies of water to gardens. However, a plan that incorporates ponds, pools, or fountains into the landscape should follow certain guidelines to minimize their potential unpleasant effects.

To reduce reflected glare into the home, build ponds as far away from the home as possible and never locate them to the south or west. If a body of water already exists at these compass points, low-growing shrubs or hedges can screen reflected light. Try not to place a body of water upwind from the home or patio, because it will only contribute more humidity to living areas. Again, if this situation is unavoidable, always shut windows facing the muggy breeze. Don't completely enclose fountains or pools with trellises or walls: they discourage breezes and contain the humid air.

Proper drainage is an important consideration when landscaping in hot, humid areas because still waters encourage the proliferation of mosquitoes and other insects. Mildew, fungus, and musty odors are also more likely to appear if drainage is improper. Use nonreflecting, permeable paving materials in the garden such as treated wood slabs or brick to prevent puddles. If irrigation is needed, subsurface or drip systems are preferable to sprinklers.

LANDFORMS

Modest-sized landforms are of little benefit in altering the microclimate in this region, but they shouldn't be ignored. Depressions in the earth may give rise to drainage problems since water puddles evaporate with difficulty in a hot, humid environment. Siting a new structure on a slight rise in the terrain is advantageous since it often increases the breeze and ventilation effects through the building.

SPECIAL LANDSCAPE STRATEGIES

Houseplants are unlikely to improve the indoor climate in this region because they release moisture into the air and may further increase unwanted humidity. If, in your judgment, the psychological advantages of having colorful plants at home outweigh the disadvantage of added mugginess, cultivate houseplants but remove them from direct sunlight to reduce excess evaporation.

Apartment or condominium dwellers who garden on small terraces have available a number of landscape techniques to control climate. For example, a woman in Houston, Texas, who lives in a small apartment facing north and opening onto a little balcony several floors above the street, has devised a high-rise, low-maintenance garden perfectly suited to meet her needs. On the east and west sides of the balcony she planted clematis vines (*Clematis* hybrids) that grow upward from tubs onto a wide-meshed net stretched from her balcony railing to the lower railing of her neighbor's

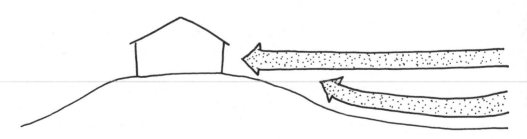

BENEFIT OF PLACING HOME ON A RISE

LANDSCAPED BALCONY

balcony above. In the morning, the big blue, pink, and purple clematis blooms welcome her with a dazzling display. When she returns from work, the handsome foliage screens her from the view of neighbors and reduces the heat and glare of the late afternoon sun. Vines can cool terraces and adjacent rooms with dappled shade in the heat of summer and—if deciduous types are used—will lose their leaves to admit welcome winter sun.

Vines are not the only plants which help control the microclimate of an urban aerial garden. Some woody plants, including holly (*Ilex* species) and fire thorn (*Pyracantha* species) grow well in containers and can be used to cast shade. Moreover, they have the advantage of being movable, and their position on a balcony may be changed several times during the year to correspond to the changing arc of the sun, and related shading needs. Even a common tomato plant (*Lycopersicon lycopersicum*), growing from a plastic tub and trained up a wooden stake, may offer valued shade

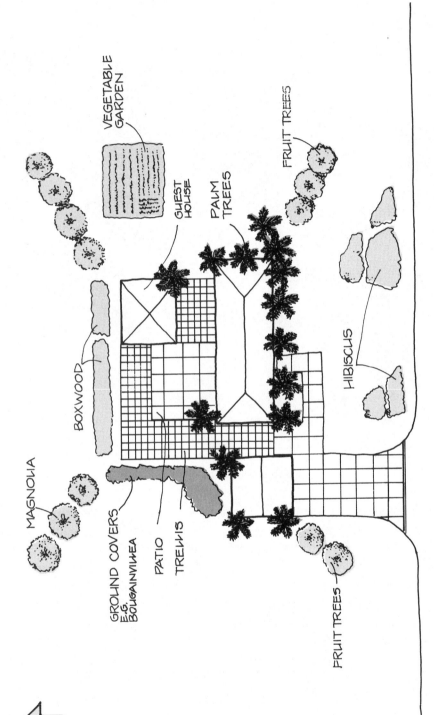

(as well as vegetables) to the urban gardener. However, before planning a roof or terrace garden, check with a building engineer to determine whether the structure can withstand the stress of the added weight of a garden.

THE RESULTS

The greatest benefit of landscaped grounds in hot, humid climates is the potential for transforming outdoor areas into usable, livable extensions of the home. A well-designed and properly used garden and patio removes heat- and humidity-generating activities such as cooking, cleaning, and eating from the confines of heat-retaining walls. It also maximizes freedom of choice in using outdoor spaces and offers a secluded retreat from everyday pressures.

A mark of good design in hot, humid regions is not only a house that invites you in, but also a garden that invites you out.

The following lists name representative landscape materials appropriate for the hot, humid region. The definitions of shrub, tree, hedge, and ground cover are not inflexible. Much depends on the environment and how the plant is pruned and fed. For example, some trees such as bottlebrush (*Callistemon citrinus*) can make fine shrubs. Down a step in size, some low-growing shrubs can be used as ground covers.

These lists should be used as helpful guides. Before making a final selection, check with a local nursery or your Extension agent to determine a plant's growth habit in your area.

Tall Deciduous Trees (greater than thirty-five feet in height)

Bursera simaruba (gumbo-limbo, West Indian birch)
Cercidiphyllum japonicum (katsura)
Cladrastis lutea (American yellowwood)
Fraxinus pennsylvanica (red ash, green ash)
Jacaranda mimosifolia (green ebony)
Liquidambar Styraciflua (sweet gum)
Liriodendron Tulipifera (tulip tree)
Nyssa sylvatica (black tupelo, black gum, sour gum, pepperidge)
Paulownia tomentosa (empress tree, royal paulownia)
Pistacia chinensis (Chinese pistachio)
Platanus X acerifolia (London plane tree)
Quercus nigra (water oak)
Quercus palustris (pin oak)
Quercus phellos (willow oak)
Taxodium mucronatum (Montezuma cypress)
Ulmus parvifolia (Chinese elm)

Short and Medium Deciduous Trees (less than thirty-five feet in height)

Albizia Julibrissin (silk tree)
Bauhinia variegata (Buddhist bauhinia, mountain ebony, orchid tree)
Cercis canadensis (Eastern redbud)
Chionanthus virginicus (fringe tree)
Cornus florida (flowering dogwood)
Cornus Kousa (Japanese dogwood)
Delonix regia (poinciana regia, poinciana tree, royal flame)
Halesia carolina (Carolina silverbell)
Koelreuteria elegans (Chinese flame tree)
Lagerstroemia indica (crape myrtle)

Magnolia heptapeta (Yulan magnolia)
Magnolia X *Loebneri* (Merrill magnolia)
Magnolia X *Soulangiana* (saucer magnolia)
Magnolia stellata (star magnolia)
Morus alba (white mulberry)
Parkinsonia aculeata (Jerusalem thorn)
Prunus X *blireiana* (blireiana plum, purple-leaf plum)
Prunus cerasifera cv. 'Thundercloud' (Thundercloud plum)
Sapium sebiferum (Chinese tallow tree)

Tall Evergreen Trees (greater than thirty-five feet in height)

Araucaria heterophylla (Norfolk Island Pine)
Calocedrus decurrens, also called *Libocedrus decurrens* (California incense cedar)
Casuarina equisetifolia (horsetail beefwood, Australian pine)
Cedrus Deodara (deodar cedar)
Cupressus sempervirens cv. 'Stricta' (Italian cypress)
Ficus benjamina (weeping fig, Java fig, weeping Chinese banyan, Benjamin fig)
Grevillea robusta (silk oak)
Magnolia grandiflora (Southern magnolia, bull bay)
Magnolia virginiana, also called *Magnolia glauca* (sweet bay)
Pinus canariensis (Canary Island Pine)
Pinus caribaea (slash pine, swamp pine, Cuban pine)
Quercus Suber (cork oak)
Quercus virginiana (live oak)
Ulmus parvifolia, also called *Ulmus sempervirens* (Chinese evergreen elm)

Short and Medium Evergreen Trees (less than thirty-five feet in height)

Bauhinia Blakeana (Hong Kong orchid tree)
Brassaia actinophylla, also called *Schefflera actinophylla* (Australia umbrella tree, Queensland umbrella tree, octopus tree)

Callistemon viminalis (weeping bottlebrush)
Cephalotaxus Harringtonia, also called *Cephalotaxus drupacea* (Japanese plum yew)
Cinnamomum Camphora (camphor tree)
Citrus species (orange, lemon, lime, and grapefruit trees)
Litchi chinensis (lychee, litchi nut)
Manilkara Zapota (sapodilla)
Podocarpus macrophyllus cultivars (yew podocarpus)
Psidium littorale (strawberry guava)
Pyrus Kawakamii (evergreen pear)
Schinus terebinthifolius (Brazilian pepper tree)

Tall Palm Trees (greater than thirty-five feet in height)

Arecastrum Romanzoffianum, also called *Cocos plumosa* (queen palm)
Heterospathe elata (Sagisi palm)
Veitchia Winin

Short Palm Trees (less than thirty-five feet in height)

Acoelorrhaphe Wrightii, also called *Paurotis Wrightii* (Everglade palm)
Chamaerops humilis (European fan palm, Mediterranean fan palm)
Chrysalidocarpus lutescens, also called *Areca lutescens* (butterfly palm, yellow palm, bamboo palm, Areca palm, cane palm)
Phoenix reclinata (Senegal date palm)
Phoenix Roebelenii, also miscalled *Phoenix loureirii* (dwarf date palm, pigmy date palm)
Ptychosperma Macarthurii (Macarthur palm)
Rhapidophyllum hystrix (needle palm, porcupine palm, blue palmetto)
Rhapis excelsa, also called *Rhapis flabelliformis* (lady palm)
Sabal Palmetto (cabbage palmetto)
Trachycarpus Fortunei, also called

Trachycarpus excelsus, Chamaerops excelsa (windmill palm)

Deciduous Windbreaks, Hedges, and Borders

Calycanthus floridus (strawberry shrub, Carolina allspice)

Chaenomeles species, also called *Cydonia* (flowering quince)

Hydrangea macrophylla, also called *Hydrangea hortensis* (common bigleaf hydrangea, house hydrangea)

Ligustrum amurense (Amur privet)

Ligustrum ovalifolium (California privet)

Spiraea species (spirea, bridal wreath)

Vitex Agnus-castus (chaste tree)

Evergreen Windbreaks, Hedges, and Borders

Buxus sempervirens (common boxwood)

Coccoloba uvifera, also called *Coccolobis uvifera* (sea grape, shore grape)

Codiaeum variegatum cultivars (croton)

Elaeagnus pungens cultivars (thorny elaeagnus, silverberry)

Eriobotrya japonica (loquat, Japanese plum)

Eugenia foetida (Spanish stopper)

Euonymus japonica cultivars (evergreen euonymous)

Feijoa Sellowiana (pineapple guava)

Gardenia jasminoides cultivars (gardenia, cape jasmine)

Ilex opaca cultivars (American holly)

Ilex vomitoria (yaupon)

Ixora coccinea (flame-of-the-woods, jungle geranium, ixora)

Jasminum humile cv. 'Revolutum' (Italian jasmine)

Juniperus virginiana cultivars (eastern red cedar)

Ligustrum japonicum cultivars (Japanese privet)

Lonicera nitida (box honeysuckle)

Myrtus communis cultivars (myrtle)

Nerium Oleander cultivars (oleander)

Osmanthus heterophyllus, also called *Osmanthus ilicifolius* (holly osmanthus)

Photinia serrulata (Chinese photinia)

Pittosporum Tobira (Japanese pittosporum)

Prunus caroliniana (Carolina cherry laurel)

Pyracantha coccinea cultivars (fire thorn)

Thevetia peruviana, also called *Thevetia nereifolia* (yellow oleander)

Viburnum odoratissimum (sweet viburnum)

Viburnum Tinus (laurustinus)

Deciduous Shrubs

Buddleia Davidii (orange-eye butterfly bush)

Cotoneaster divaricatus (spreading cotoneaster)

Deutzia species (deutzia)

Hibiscus Rosa-sinensis cultivars (Chinese hibiscus, rose of China)

Hibiscus syriacus (rose of Sharon, shrub Althea)

Evergreen Shrubs

Abelia X grandiflora (glossy abelia)

Aucuba japonica (Japanese aucuba)

Brunfelsia calycina cv. 'Floribunda' (yesterday, today, and tomorrow)

Callistemon citrinus, also called *Callistemon lanceolatus* (lemon bottlebrush)

Camellia japonica cultivars (common camellia)

Camellia sasanqua (sasanqua camellia)

Carissa grandiflora (Natal plum)

Cotoneaster dammeri, also called *Cotoneaster humifusus* (bearberry cotoneaster)

Cotoneaster horizontalis (rock spray, rock cotoneaster)

Cotoneaster lacteus (Parney's red clusterberry)

Euonymus Fortunei cultivars (winter creeper)

Euphorbia pulcherrima (poinsettia)

Fatsia japonica, also called *Aralia japonica, Aralia sieboldii* (Japanese fatsia)

Ilex X altaclarensis cv. 'Wilsonii' (Wilson holly)

Ilex aquifolium cultivars (English holly)

Ilex cassine (dahoon, dahoon holly)
Ilex cornuta cultivars (Chinese holly)
Ilex crenata cultivars (Japanese holly)
Juniperus chinensis cultivars (Chinese juniper)
Juniperus communis cultivars (common juniper)
Juniperus conferta (shore juniper)
Juniperus procumbens cultivars (Japanese garden juniper)
Juniperus sabina (savin juniper)
Justicia Brandegeana, also called *Beloperone guttata* (shrimp plant)
Nandina domestica (nandina, Chinese sacred bamboo)
Platycladus orientalis cultivars, also called *Thuya orientalis* (Oriental arborvitae)
Rhododendron evergreen hybrids (evergreen hybrid azalea)
Rhododendron indicum cultivars (Indian azalea)
Tetrapanax papyriferus, also called *Fatsia papyrifera* (ricepaper plant)
Tibouchina Urvilleana, also called *Tibouchina semicandra* and *Pleroma grandiflora* (glory bush)

Deciduous Vines

Actinidia arguta (tara vine, bower actinidia)
Campsis X *Tagliabuana* (trumpet vine)
Clematis hybrids (hybrid clematis)
Hydrangea anomala subsp. *petiolaris*, also called *Hydrangea petiolaris*, *Hydrangea scandens* (climbing hydrangea)
Parthenocissus quinquefolia, also called *Ampelopsis quinquefolia* (Virginia creeper, woodbine)

Parthenocissus tricuspidata, also called *Ampelopsis tricuspidata* (Boston ivy, Japanese creeper)
Polygonum Aubertii (silver-fleece vine, silver-lace vine)
Wisteria floribunda cultivars (Japanese wisteria)
Wisteria sinensis, also called *Wisteria chinensis* (Chinese wisteria)

Evergreen Vines

Akebia quinata (semievergreen) (five-leaf akebia)
Bignonia capreolata, also called *Anisostichus capreolatus*, *Doxantha capreolata* (cross vine, trumpet flower)
Bougainvillea hybrids (bougainvillea)
Ficus pumila (creeping fig)
Gelsemium sempervirens (Carolina jasmine)
Hedera canariensis (Algerian ivy)
Hedera Helix (English ivy)
Justicia Brandegeana, also known as *Beloperone guttata* (shrimp plant)
Lonicera sempervirens cultivars (trumpet honeysuckle)
Thunbergia grandiflora (skyflower, blue trumpet vine, clock vine)
Trachelospermum jasminoides, also called *Rhynchospermum jasminoides* (star jasmine, Confederate jasmine)

Ground Covers

Asparagus sprengeri (Sprenger asparagus)
Hedera Helix (English ivy)
Pilea microphylla (artillery fern)
Sedum species (stone crop, live-forever)
Wedelia trilobata (wedelia)
Zebrina pendula (wandering Jew)

6

ENERGY-EFFICIENT LANDSCAPE DESIGN FOR TEMPERATE CLIMATES

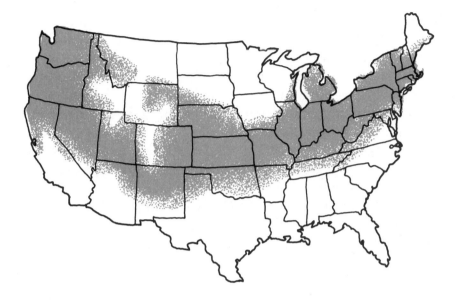

THE ESSENCE OF TEMPERATE ZONE weather is extreme change. Temperate regions are blessed with contrasting seasons, and each season provides weather for a variety of recreational activities and offers the enjoyment of a broad sampling of wildlife. But the word temperate can be a misnomer. Tropical and polar air masses meet and battle over these regions. The weather runs to extremes, from sub-zero icy to subtropical steamy. Cold snowy winters succeed hot, humid summers. Transitional periods can bring destructive storms, mercurial temperature changes, and winds, which can be persistent and irritating. These winds can accent discomfort by driving up the wind-chill factor in winter or they can take the form of cooling summer breezes.

Temperate regions receive 40 to 70 percent of total possible hours of sunshine and ample rainfall. Snowfall varies widely, from twenty inches or less annually in some southern and coastal regions to more than seventy inches annually in the snowbelt.

Energy-efficient design in temperate regions must meet two sets of objectives. During winter the goals are to keep heat inside and cold outside, offer protection from wind, and let all available sunlight penetrate. During summer the goals are to keep heat outside, offer shade from the sun, and open up living areas to cooling breezes. These two sets of guidelines may seem to contradict each other. However, a well-planned home can meet all these objectives.

Buildings in the temperate zone should be compact, well insulated, caulked and weatherstripped for winter comfort. Windows should be double- or triple-glazed, shuttered, kept to a minimum on the east and west, and avoided on north elevations. Construction materials should be selected for thermal efficiency. For example, wood construction gives good insulation and prevents conductive heat losses, but metals (sometimes found in window frames) can unpleasantly accentuate heat loss or gain. Air locks and vestibules can also cut heat loss and porches can contribute to cool, airy summer living.

If possible, a building site should be selected that permits exposure to winter sun and offers protection from undesirable winter winds. Unattached structures such as garages or tool sheds should be positioned to block unwanted winds.

Outdoor living areas with paved or stone surfaces are best located to the south, under a deciduous tree. There, they derive the benefits of shade in the summer. In early spring and late fall, when trees are bare, the same paved areas retain an extra measure of the sun's heat for additional days of comfortable outdoor living.

Energy-conscious early American settlers established this prototype by adapting traditional English houses and reducing living space and window areas, using wood as the building material (instead of the traditional stone or brick), and often placing a massive chimney in the center to store and radiate heat. Judicious design of open porches provided natural ventilation for passive cooling. They also used windbreaks to block brisk northerlies, and deciduous trees to offer summer shade.

The potential rewards for such careful planning are great. In temperate regions as much as 20 percent of a homeowner's heating and cooling costs can be saved by using landscaping to save energy. Proper planting coupled with routine care can moderate uncomfortable extremes of temperature twenty-four hours a day year-round.

Because of the changeable nature of temperate climates, landscaping to save energy in these regions is more challenging than in other climatic zones, where the planner deals with overheating or overcooling alone, and trees, shrubs, and ground cover are planted to accomplish a single goal. In temperate regions, landscape design must conquer both overheating and overcooling, or accomplish one goal without interfering with the other. Weatherwise landscaping calls for highly sophisticated planning.

SUN

The key factor in planning energy-efficient landscape design in temperate climates is learning to use the sun's radiant energy to advantage; it is the driving force of all weather systems and is the most important consideration in planning one's energy strategy. In temperate climates, sun-wise landscaping has two goals: to block or filter summer sun that causes overheating, and to permit all warming winter radiation to reach most living areas. Both goals can be met with knowledgeable selection of plants for height, foliage density, and growing patterns, and careful placement of these plants around the home. Dense trees such as Norway maple *(Acer platanoides)* can block as much as 95 percent of the sun's radiant light and 75 percent of its radiant heat. Even a leafless deciduous tree cuts out as much as 25 percent of the sun's energy.

The correct positioning of plants is achieved by planting species in harmony with the solar paths (as discussed in Chapter 2). For example, the sun strikes the east side of a home at a low angle throughout the year and transmits little radiant heat. The hours following sunrise are underheated in the winter and occasionally overheated in the summer. Therefore, plants such as low deciduous trees that block or filter the sun only in the summer are desirable on the east and north-

east. However, because sunlight often provides an early morning psychological boost, trees that filter rather than block summer sunlight are best. The appropriate model for this situation is a low-density, light and low-crowned deciduous tree such as dogwood *(Cornus florida)* or some cultivars of Japanese Maple *(Acer palmatum)* planted close to the home. An open deciduous shrub of medium height such as pussy willow *(Salix discolor)* or lilac *(Syringa vulgaris)* is also good for an eastern or northeastern location. Plants that cast light shade outside a window temper the sun's energy more effectively than a lightly colored plastic coating on windows or a fully drawn white Venetian blind.

If you live in the northern extremes of the temperate zone, where all radiant heat is usually desirable, or if you are working with a very limited budget, add no sun-blocking species on the east. Save landscaping additions for the western and southern facades,

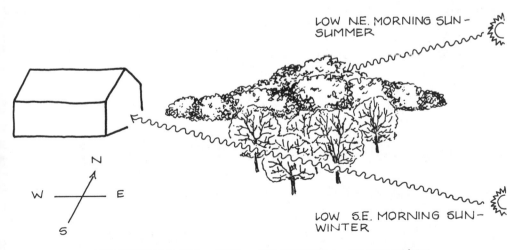

LOW N.E. MORNING SUN –
SUMMER

LOW S.E. MORNING SUN –
WINTER

N
W — E
S

VEGETATION FOR EASTERN EXPOSURE

BENEFITS OF TALL NARROW TREES VS. SHORT WIDE TREES

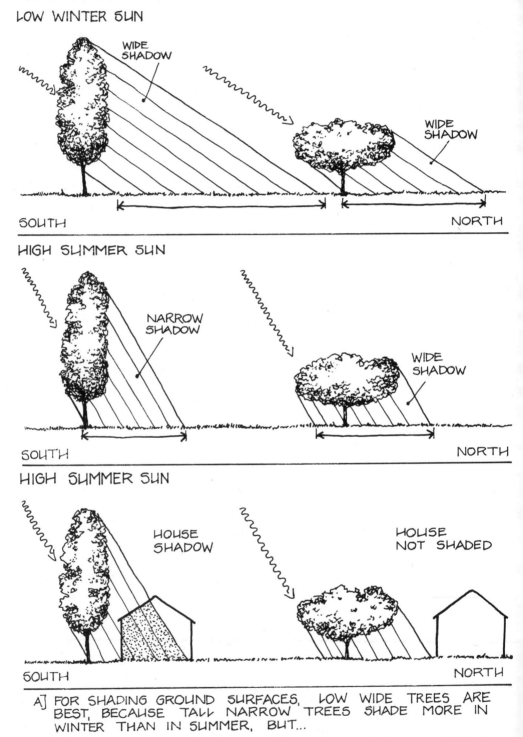

LOW WINTER SUN

WIDE SHADOW

WIDE SHADOW

SOUTH   NORTH

HIGH SUMMER SUN

NARROW SHADOW

WIDE SHADOW

SOUTH   NORTH

HIGH SUMMER SUN

HOUSE SHADOW

HOUSE NOT SHADED

SOUTH   NORTH

A] FOR SHADING GROUND SURFACES, LOW WIDE TREES ARE BEST, BECAUSE TALL NARROW TREES SHADE MORE IN WINTER THAN IN SUMMER, BUT...

B] FOR SHADING BUILDINGS, TALL TREES ARE NECESSARY.

where plantings have a greater impact on comfort and energy consumption.

On the south side of a house, the sun's angle varies greatly between summer and winter. The summer sun is very high in the sky at midday and can be cut off by planting a high-crowned, dense, tall, columnar tree very close to the house. If this tree is both high crowned and deciduous, it will not cut off the desirable winter sunlight and warmth. Red maple (*Acer rubrum*) or eastern sycamore (*Platanus occidentalis*) is a good species to plant adjacent to southern exposures. Such tree forms give the added benefit of a slight breeze under the tree. Dense trees evaporate great amounts of water vapor, "using up" latent heat energy, which makes the air cooler. The combination of shade, evaporation, and convection offered by a single mature tree gets rid of as much heat as five 10,000-Btu air-con-

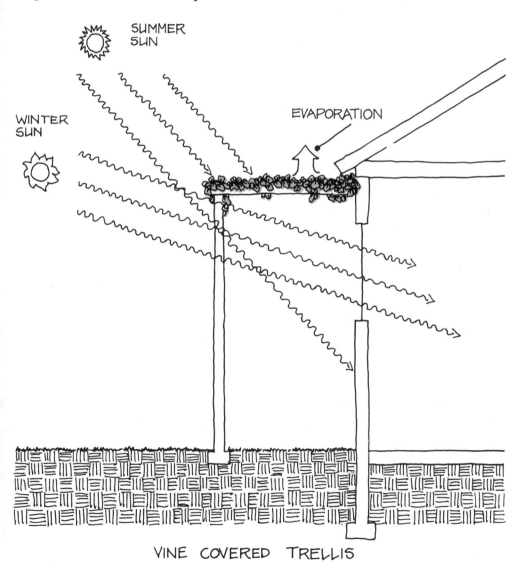

VINE COVERED TRELLIS

ditioners. A single, carefully selected tree is also much cheaper and easier to maintain, to say nothing of its natural beauty.

However, this planting strategy should not be used if solar collectors are mounted on the roof. If a solar collector is to be used in summer, then do not shade it, even at the expense of letting the temperature inside the house rise somewhat. Perhaps the best solution to the problem of overheating is to plant a tall tree close to the south face of the house to avoid excess heat gain, before purchasing a collector that will generate energy to cool the structure. If a collector is desired for domestic hot water heating, place it on an unshaded roof area, or on unshaded ground on the south side.

An overhang on a roof, an arbor, a trellis, or a pergola covered with deciduous vines such as wisteria or select clematis species can also effectively protect southern exposures from excessive summer sun, simultaneously providing both shade and the cooling effect of evaporation.

Dense trees or shrubs planted in southerly positions away from the structure are ineffective barriers to summer sun and may be harmful filters of winter solar radiation. Before planting trees to the south or deciding whether to remove existing specimens, determine the maximum height of such a hedge or the distance it should be placed from a structure. This added calculation will prevent you from creating a hedge, or living

with an existing one, that is too tall and blocks the winter sun.

Begin by looking up the altitude angle of the sun during the winter solstice (December 22) in your area and its tangent from Appendices C and D on pages 000 and 000. The variables can be determined by the equation:

$$\text{tangent of altitude angle of sun during midwinter solstice} = \frac{\text{maximum height of hedge of trees}}{\text{distance of trees from house}}$$

For example, New York City, Philadelphia, Pittsburgh, Columbus, and Denver all lie at about 40°N. latitude where the midwinter sun rises to a maximum altitude angle of about 26.50°. There, if you want to have a hedge of trees 100 feet from the south face of your home, the trees selected should grow no taller than fifty feet.

A hedge made of Norway maple (*Acer platanoides*) or most fruit trees planted 100 feet from the south face and growing to a maximum height of fifty feet will not block the low winter sun. In this situation, an existing hedge of trees taller than fifty feet should be trimmed.

Western exposures always receive sun at a low angle. The late afternoon hours are almost always too hot in the summer and, because the reflection from snow can unpleasantly accentuate sun, overheating and glare may occur in winter, too. In this situation the sun should certainly be cut off in the summer and, depending on local climate, may need tempering even in winter. A combination of short, low crowned evergreens and deciduous

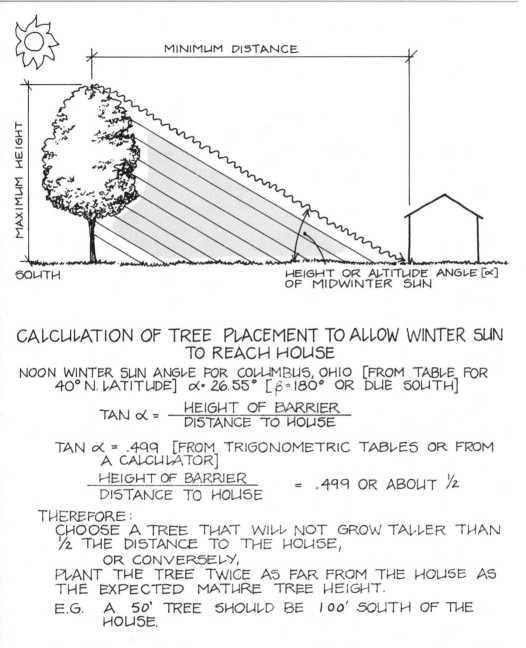

CALCULATION OF TREE PLACEMENT TO ALLOW WINTER SUN TO REACH HOUSE

NOON WINTER SUN ANGLE FOR COLUMBUS, OHIO [FROM TABLE FOR 40° N. LATITUDE] α = 26.55° [β = 180° OR DUE SOUTH]

$$TAN\ \alpha = \frac{HEIGHT\ OF\ BARRIER}{DISTANCE\ TO\ HOUSE}$$

TAN α = .499 [FROM TRIGONOMETRIC TABLES OR FROM A CALCULATOR]

$$\frac{HEIGHT\ OF\ BARRIER}{DISTANCE\ TO\ HOUSE} = .499\ OR\ ABOUT\ \frac{1}{2}$$

THEREFORE:
 CHOOSE A TREE THAT WILL NOT GROW TALLER THAN ½ THE DISTANCE TO THE HOUSE,
  OR CONVERSELY,
 PLANT THE TREE TWICE AS FAR FROM THE HOUSE AS THE EXPECTED MATURE TREE HEIGHT.
 E.G. A 50' TREE SHOULD BE 100' SOUTH OF THE HOUSE.

plants, placed close to the home on the west and northwest, will filter the late afternoon sun in the winter while providing complete screening in the summer. Yews (*Taxus* species), arborvitae (*Thuja occidentalis*), and apple (*Malus sylvestris*) or pear trees (*Pyrus communis*) are appropriate. When planting species close to the home, select those with root systems that don't invade and interfere with water pipes, foundations, and downspouts. Medium and tall trees such as horse chestnut (*Aesculus Hippocastanum*) and

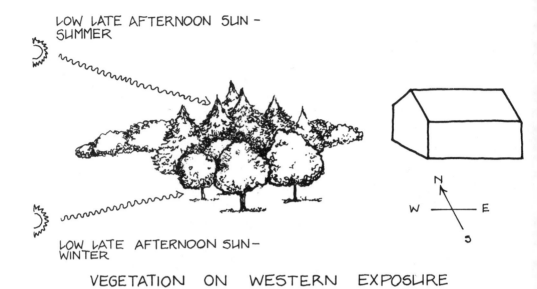

LOW LATE AFTERNOON SUN –
SUMMER

LOW LATE AFTERNOON SUN –
WINTER

VEGETATION   ON   WESTERN   EXPOSURE

mature pines, if planted a distance from the house, cast long shadows and screen late afternoon sun. In more northerly latitudes, trees of medium to low height may also be useful on the northwest exposure, because the midsummer sun sets at this compass point.

Sunscreening on the north side is seldom of concern, since the winter sun is, unfortunately, absent and the midsummer sun is either not present or (in extreme northerly latitudes) is at a very low angle. The majority of radiation available to northern exposures is reflected and refracted radiation. Energy-efficient design in general suggests a minimum area of glass on the northern exposure, which reduces the impact of any plantings. However, for house designs that demand large, northern window placements or for those people who simply enjoy uniform, northern light, appropriate plantings can be made. Loose,

open, low-crowned trees, including many fruit trees, or chest-high shrubs such as privet (Ligustrum species) are advised; the goal is to provide a slight windbreak without cutting off the desired light. Otherwise, windscreening is the most significant consideration.

WIND

Wind, which blows and redistributes the radiant heat created by the sun and drains off warmth generated by mechanical devices inside the home, is the second climatic factor considered in energy-efficient landscape design. A row of trees or shrubs can filter, divert, or obstruct up to 85 percent of the force of cold winds. Taming winds can dramatically diminish winter fuel needs up to 30 percent. Plant forms that block wind can also guide or trap drifting snow, intercept unwanted precipitation, and affect the depth of the frost line, as discussed in Chapter 2.

Clever use of landscaping also reduces the costs of interior cooling by accentuating and guiding cooling breezes in the summer months. Such wind funnels use the Venturi effect (see Chapter 2) to increase wind velocity at their narrowest point.

It is more challenging to design a landscape to control wind than to control sun because strategies to control wind must contend with plantings already established to use or screen sun. Managing both sun and wind is not impossible, but it requires thoughtful analysis and planning.

The first step in wind control is the determination of the direction(s) of the prevailing winds on your site throughout the year. Use the strategies suggested in Chapter II. Peculiarities of

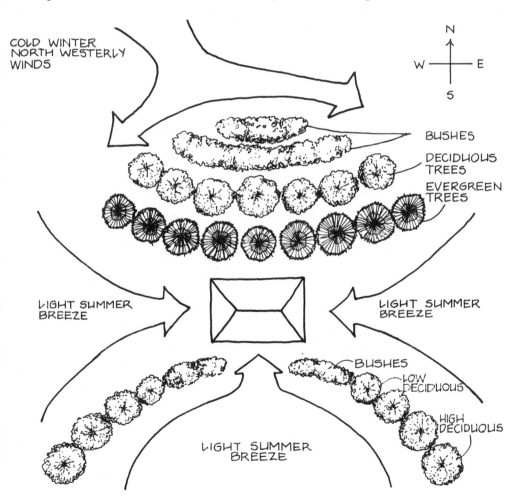

IDEAL WINDBREAKS - BLOCK WINTER WINDS AND FUNNEL SUMMER BREEZES

individual location, such as the slope of the land, existing vegetation, and the positions of neighboring buildings, influence the patterns of airflow.

If the summer and winter winds come from different directions, there is little problem in designing landscaping to manage both. However, if both come from the same direction, you must decide whether it is more energy-efficient to control one or the other. As a rule of thumb, if your winter heating bills are greater than summer air conditioning bills, landscape plans should focus on using plants for winter windbreaks and insulation. Different planting strategies are used to cut cold winds and to enhance the desirable, heat-dissipating breezes of summer. In general, frigid winter winds are prevented from reaching the home and cooling summer breezes are funneled toward the living area.

An all-purpose scheme for controlling cold winds is to establish a barrier of tall dense plantings close to and upwind of the building. This windbreak diverts winds over the structure. However, this landscaping also blocks available sunlight. If your goal is to permit sunlight to reach the home and to manage wind as well, distant, sparse windbreaks planted upwind of the structure to be protected are better. They will calm winds and not screen sun.

Trees and shrubs in rows are far more desirable than those planted in small clusters; trees planted singly are nearly useless for wind control. New trees for wind control should be selected to grow rapidly to a large height, such as black locust (*Robinia Pseudoacacia*). Windscreens are always oriented perpendicular to observed wind direction rather than to compass points. But because in temperate climates landscaping for wind control is usually secondary to landscaping for sun control, our approach to wind analysis follows the same format used to resolve sun management; that is, analysis by compass direction.

If the prevailing winter winds blow from the east, the goal is to block the heat-dissipating gusts without shutting out all solar radiation. This is done by placing tall trees with loose foliage such as larch (*Larix* species) and locust two to five tree lengths away from the house. Ideal plantings do not prevent the radiation of the low winter sun from reaching living areas, yet still temper wintry blasts. To reduce the impact of cold gusts further, well-maintained high-crowned trees such as Norway maple (*Acer platanoides*) are placed close to the house on the eastern side. These trees further deflect wind which has already been calmed by the distant, tall plants but they do not interfere with the radiation of the low morning sun.

Southern winter winds are trickier to control. Again, it is desirable to have a hedge of trees with sparse foliage some distance from the house to filter winds. They will buffer wind speeds for a distance up to fifteen times their height. But because the low winter afternoon sun is needed to

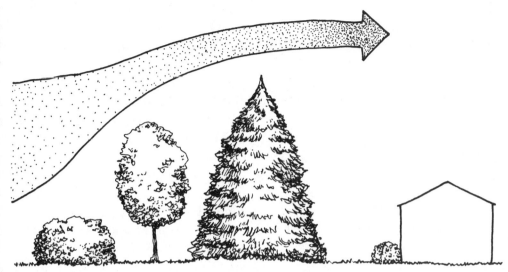

NORTH

WIND CONTROLS ON NORTH

upply warmth, wind blocks must not be so high that they obstruct sun. To determine the maximum height for such a southern windbreak on your property, use the same equation that was used to determine the maximum height for a hedge of trees that is a given distance south of the structure.

$$\text{tangent of the angle of sun at winter solstice} = \frac{\text{maximum height of barrier}}{\text{distance of wind barrier from house}}$$

The heights and densities of most common deciduous trees are such that they should be placed two to six times their mature height from the building to be protected.

A tree very close to the house on the southern side is also desirable for deflecting winds over the structure. But it must be a well-maintained, tall, high-crowned specimen or it will block the desirable winter sun.

On the western side, use a strategy to block wind similar to the one used on the eastern side; that is, plant tall trees with loose foliage some distance from the house or dense species up close. Thick plantings may be used anywhere north of west; thinner, higher-canopied plantings are preferred south of west (to retain use of the low winter sun).

Plantings to control wind on the northern side are easy to plan. Because there is no solar conflict, thick, coniferous trees close to the home are best. They give maximum shelter immediately downwind of the planting.

If cold winter winds are not a problem in your area but cooling summer breezes are needed, as in southern regions of the temperate zone, different strategies to control winds should be used. The goal here is to encourage breezes toward the building. A funnel of tall hedges that channels the prevailing winds uses the

Venturi effect to accelerate breezes, dissipate heat, and provide constant, natural "air conditioning." As the funnel narrows, wind velocity increases, making the arrangement more effective. This breeze enhancement alters perception of temperature. For example, at 70°F. an 18-mile-per-hour wind makes the air temperature feel like 58°F.

But a word of caution is needed. Elaborate wind funnels are complicated to design. Universities and other research organizations test plans by using expensive wind chambers, with tiny buildings carefully built to scale. For home analysis, a smoky fire in a garbage can on a windy day could be used. It provides a cheaper test ground, although it will not endear you to neighbors or the local fire chief.

A second word of caution on wind control is offered to those who live near the seashore. There, extra efforts to funnel summer winds toward the home are often unnecessary, since existing offshore breezes offer ample, periodic airflow. For example, in the San Francisco area, two out of every three days from May through September the winds exceed 20 miles per hour. In Seattle, almost every summer day has winds above 10 miles per hour. Prolonged buffeting from winds can be upsetting. The persistent, whistling Mistral wind of the Mediterranean is said to drive people mad, and the hot, sandy Sirocco wind out of the Sahara has similar notoriety. If these cyclical breezes are so strong that wind blocks are needed, but tall plant growth near the seashore is a problem, a well-anchored fence will serve as a windbreak. A louvered fence (one with slats) gives the largest area of protection downwind, even though some wind passes through it into the protected area. (See Chapter 2.)

Another landscaping strategy that controls wind is the use of berms. Such mounds of earth will deflect winds before plants grow to the height needed to produce a similar effect. However, berms must also be designed with attention to the prevailing winds and to outdoor living space. A poorly placed berm may improve a home's energy efficiency but create unwanted wind turbulence and gusts in outdoor play areas.

WATER

Ponds, pools, and lakes are powerful climate controllers because they store enormous amounts of heat energy. During the warmer months, they evaporate water, draw energy from the air, and reduce temperature. But along with this desirable cooling effect comes an increase in humidity, which is undesirable in most temperate regions.

Placid pools or ponds can also reflect unwanted heat and light into living areas and may attract insects. For these reasons, man-made water reservoirs are not always beneficial, energy-efficient additions to the landscape.

The decision about whether to include bodies of water in your landscaping plans should be based on broader principles than energy efficiency. Landscapes with ponds have many positive points: they store water, control runoff, offer recreation, and raise the water table. They also offer psychological benefits. A rippling pond or running water has a positive, restful effect.

Remember that climate control alone is not a good reason for constructing a pond. Rows of trees that funnel a breeze into a living area offer much the same cooling effect as a pond, but without some of the drawbacks just discussed. If, for aesthetic reasons, a pond is desirable, place it some distance from the house and position a few trees or shrubs to block reflected glare that may enter the home.

SPECIAL PLANTING STRATEGIES

Landscaping in temperate regions offers the greatest potential for using a wide variety of plant forms and landscaping schemes. After planning basic sun, wind, and water management with trees and large bushes, the next step for the energy-efficient designer is to use low-growing foliage or vegetation such as shrubs, vines, and ground covers. They are excellent at tempering extremes of hot and cold. These plant materials throw cooling shade, draw heat out and away from the earth and buildings, reduce heat

reflected from building materials, and insulate against excessive wind and cold. Plant species with low or small foliage such as honeysuckle (*Lonicera* species) or grapevines (*Vitis* species) often grow faster than trees and provide climate control before larger species establish themselves. They offer quick solutions to problems of excessive heat loss and buildup and can be used while grander landscaping matures. (However, along with the benefit of rapid growth comes the risk of invasive growth. Such plants must be carefully tended.)

Small-scale evergreen trees and shrubs are valuable when planted next to homes, because they create dead air spaces that insulate buildings from abrupt temperature changes. Yew species and the dwarf juniper (*Juniperus chinensis* cv. 'Sargentii') are ideal for this purpose.

Deciduous shrubs such as *Euonymus alata* cv. 'Compacta' can shade walls from a hot summer sun and in winter will permit the sun to warm walls through bare branches. This arrangement is especially effective for western exposures.

Both deciduous and evergreen bushes can hold snow around their low-growing branches, thus offering additional wall insulation. The wall and ground near the house under the snow's protective blanket will be warmer than frigid air temperatures. The heat inside the home is trapped by the snow. Heat loss from an exposed foundation can be significant in winter, and snow around the base of home-hugging shrubs cuts heating costs. Be sure the roots of the shrubs you select do not invade and destroy building foundations or drainage tiles. If fallen leaves are left under the plants in autumn, they provide even more insulation under the snow. When they decay, they return nutrients to the soil. However, they have one drawback that affects gardening plans: they remain wet and cold late into spring and will retard the growth of early blooms.

A particularly effective combination windbreak and insulator is a double-row plant screen, with a row of evergreens such as yew planted behind a row of deciduous shrubs. Shrubs are less expensive to plant than pine or spruce (*Picea* species) trees, and will outperform them for the first few years. Eventually, the evergreens grow taller, while the shrubs in front continue to provide depth and color. Shade-tolerant shrubs such as witch hazel (*Hamameli virginiana*) and Japanese barberr (*Berberis Thunbergii*) are tough enoug to survive as underplantings beneat taller plants, as long as they are wa tered and occasionally fertilized.

Because this planting strateg obstructs sunshine, it should be use only where sun is of little concer such as on the north face of a building

In temperate regions, deciduou vines such as Japanese wisteri (*Wisteria floribunda*), most clemati hybrids, concord grapes (*Vitis Con cord*), and goldflame honeysuckl (*Lonicera Heckrottii*) reflect sun an heat away from the home, provid dense shade and a layer of insulatin air between plant growth and th wall, and give a cooling effect in sum mer. They grow rapidly—ten to fift feet in a single season—and offer thei shading benefits almost immediately you have an outdoor living area or sun-struck wall. They give their coo ing effect by evaporating enormou

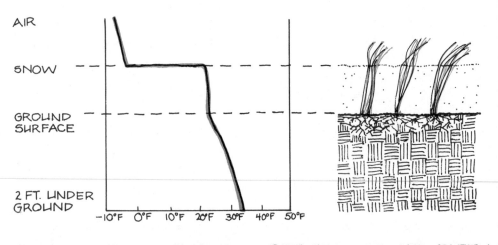

TEMPERATURE DIFFERENTIAL BETWEEN AIR AND EARTH
INSULATED UNDER SNOW

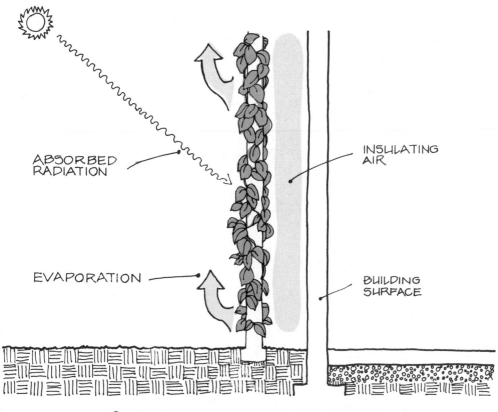

ABSORBED
RADIATION

INSULATING
AIR

EVAPORATION

BUILDING
SURFACE

PROTECTIVE EFFECT OF VINES

mounts of water from leaf surfaces. However, vines lower temperature at the expense of increasing humidity. Windows on walls covered by vines should be kept closed to keep unwanted excessive humidity outside. Vines are therefore not used in hot, humid regions or in temperate regions which lack breezes to blow away the excess moisture.

Vines have two other serious drawbacks. They can grow too rapidly, entangling adjacent trees and shrubs, even killing them, and they give a junglelike appearance to a garden. Some species such as Chinese actinidia *(Actinidia chinensis)*, Hall's honeysuckle *(Lonicera japonica* cv. 'Halliana'), kudzu vine *(Pueraria lobata)*, glory vine *(Vitis coignetiae)*, and select wisteria species sometimes grow fifty feet in a year. Some vines may also attack mortar, wood shingles, window frames, downspouts, and gutters with a vengeance. Such species must be managed carefully. If you don't have the time to devote to this sort of activity, avoid selecting these plantings.

Ground covers such as grasses, common periwinkle *(Vinca minor)*, ivy *(Hedera* species), Japanese spurge

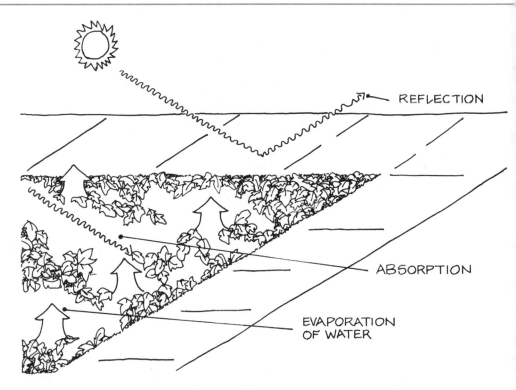

GROUND COVERS REDUCE REFLECTION AND INCREASE ABSORPTION OF RADIATION AND EVAPORATION OF WATER

(Pachysandra terminalis), mondo grass (Ophiopogon japonicus), and creeping thyme (Thymus praecox) are also effective controllers of microclimates in gardens. They reduce heat buildup by evaporating water, and they do not reflect or reradiate heat as walls and pavements do. Recall from Chapter 2 that the ability of ground covers to temper heat depends on the species and its height.

The ability of ground covers to moderate high temperatures is even more impressive when one considers that many natural and man-made materials such as artificial turf, asphalt, stone, and shingle accentuate heat accumulation. It is not uncommon for an asphalt surface to be 25°F. hotter than the air temperature.

Ground covers can be any height. A good bed of thickly planted one- to three-foot-high juniper such as carpet juniper (Juniperus horizontalis cv. 'Wiltonii') or creeping juniper (Juniperus chinensis cv. 'Procumbens') requires little maintenance and is much cooler in full sun than a paved area. Eventually, it grows taller than most weeds. Its initial cost is high but still less than paving.

In general, selection of ground covers often involves a tradeoff between increased initial investment to establish ground cover and a promise of reduced future maintenance. Inexpensive ground covers often need more maintenance. Thus, of all ground covers, grass lawns are among the least expensive to establish but require a high level of energy-intensive care. In temperate climates, ground covers are almost self-sustaining, if good soil and adequate water are available. However, many ground covers need a yearly weeding; otherwise, weeds and eventually shrubs and trees take over.

Successful use of low-growing foliage for climate control depends on careful selection and maintenance. Shrubs and hedges need regular clipping; vines demand conscientious pruning; and ground covers require weeding, feeding, and trimming.

The common practice of cutting bushes into flat tops or into little balls does not conform to their natural growth, and it makes extra work and expends unnecessary human and electrical energy. If you want low-growing shrubs, then you should plant low-growing varieties.

For example, yews must be selected with care. A poor choice, originally planted to frame a door or window, will soon block the door and obliterate the window.

Urban gardeners, even those with just a small balcony, can plant an energy-efficient garden. Terraces and rooftops come in assorted sizes, but several square feet is all you need for a lush container garden. Potted plants can screen sun, block unwanted wind, and deliver a welcome dose of green-

LANDSCAPED BALCONY

ery and color to the urban landscape.

Begin by measuring the area and drawing a simple diagram, noting its widest and narrowest dimensions and the locations of doors and windows. Then note the solar path over the planned garden. Check the sun's strength along with its position.

What you find will determine your horticultural purchases. Part shade or morning sun is fine for growing begonias (*Begonia* species), a flowering crabapple tree (*Malus* species), rhododendrons (*Rhododendron* species), or Japanese maple (*Acer palmatum*). But roses, dwarf fruit trees, and rosemary (*Rosmarinus officinalis*) prefer longer hours of stronger sunlight.

Wind sometimes presents a problem in the city, especially in areas with many tall buildings. The strength and location of these gusts can vary greatly, even for different tenants in the same apartment complex. Observe where they occur, and if they seem severe, consider planting a barrier of wind-tolerant trees or shrubs. Wind-resistant species include black pine (*Pinus nigra* subsp. *Laricio*), forsythia (although they may fail to blossom in the northern reaches of the temperate region), Russian olive (*Elaeagnus angustifolia*), and privet (*Ligustrum* species). Several plants that do not have a good tolerance for high winds are dogwoods, laurels (*Rhododendron maximum*), and fuchsia species. These will do better in a quiet corner.

Plan to place your tubs where the plants will be seen from inside, through windows or glass doors. Where space is tight, use the corners and ends of terraces and balconies for larger specimens. If the containers are arranged in groupings of three or four, a more interesting design and an illusion of more space will result.

City gardeners are sometimes surprised to discover there are many woody plants that will grow outside in containers all year long. These are winter-hardy trees and shrubs such as flowering cherry (*Prunus* species), fire thorn (*Pyracantha coccinea*), and winged euonymus (*Euonymus alata* cv. 'Compacta'). The key to successful maintenance of woody species is to provide them with as large a planter as possible. The roots of plants can use a generous amount of soil in which water and nutrients may be stored. The soil also insulates against the hazard of frost injury. Use common sense, however, and take care not to overload balconies with larger tubs. Check with the building engineer for structural considerations.

Another successful city-garden strategy is landscaping with climbing deciduous vines. When planted on a western facade, they screen harsh, late afternoon summer sun and offer a dazzling, colorful display. They can be planted in tubs and trained onto wide mesh netting that may be secured to stakes or balcony rails. They offer maximum vertical display without taking up much ground space. Japanese wisteria (*Wisteria floribunda*) and select rose varieties can be trained into an attractive aerial bower.

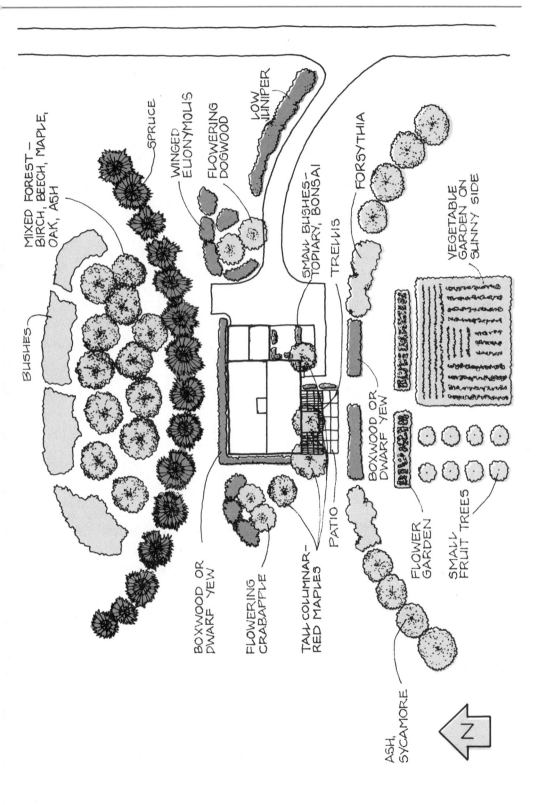

MIXED FOREST—
BIRCH, BEECH, MAPLE,
OAK, ASH

SPRUCE

WINGED
EUONYMOUS

FLOWERING
DOGWOOD

LOW
JUNIPER

BUSHES

SMALL BUSHES—
TOPIARY, BONSAI

TRELLIS

FORSYTHIA

VEGETABLE
GARDEN ON
SUNNY SIDE

BOXWOOD OR
DWARF YEW

BOXWOOD OR
DWARF YEW

FLOWER
GARDEN

SMALL
FRUIT TREES

FLOWERING
CRABAPPLE

TALL COLUMNAR—
RED MAPLES

PATIO

ASH,
SYCAMORE

N

THE RESULTS

In temperate regions, homes and gardens with energy-efficient design are appealing to the eye and are in harmony with the environment. The seasonal transitions in foliage patterns respond elastically to human energy needs: in summer they block excess radiation and in winter they allow the penetration of sunlight. Also, the availability of a great variety of plant materials provides for continual transitions of color and texture and year-round protection from extremes of heat and cold.

The following lists include a selection of plants appropriate to landscaping in temperate regions. Not all species can be grown throughout the temperate region. Ask your local Extension agent or a nursery if a species will thrive in your area and if its particular growth rate and form are appropriate.

Tall Deciduous Trees (growing to a height greater than thirty-five feet)

Acer platanoides (Norway maple)
Acer rubrum (red maple, scarlet maple, swamp maple)
Acer saccharinum (silver maple, soft maple)
Acer saccharum (sugar maple, rock maple)
Aesculus X carnea cv. 'Briotii' (ruby horse chestnut)
Aesculus Hippocastanum (horse chestnut)
Betula papyrifera (canoe birch, paper birch, white birch)
Betula pendula (European white birch)
Carya ovata (shagbark hickory)
Castanea mollissima (Chinese chestnut)
Cercidiphyllum japonicum (katsura tree)
Cladrastis lutea (American yellowwood)
Cornus Nuttallii (Pacific dogwood)
Fagus sylvatica (European beech)
Fraxinus pennsylvanica (green ash)
Ginkgo biloba (ginkgo, Chinese maidenhair tree)
Gleditsia triacanthos var. *inermis* (thornless honey locust)
Koelreuteria paniculata (golden-rain tree, varnish tree)
Larix decidua (European larch)
Liquidambar Styraciflua (sweet gum)
Liriodendron Tulipifera (tulip tree)
Magnolia heptapeta (Yulan magnolia)
Morus alba (white mulberry)
Nyssa sylvatica (black tupelo, black gum, sour gum, pepperidge)
Paulownia tomentosa (empress tree, paulownia)
Platanus X acerifolia (London plane tree)
Platanus occidentalis (eastern sycamore)
Pyrus calleryana (callery pear)
Quercus alba (white oak)
Quercus coccinea (scarlet oak)
Quercus macrocarpa (mossy-cup oak)
Quercus palustris (pin oak)
Quercus phellos (willow oak)

Quercus rubra (northern red oak)
Quercus virginiana (live oak)
Robinia Pseudoacacia (locust, false acacia)
Salix alba (golden weeping willow)
Sophora japonica (Japanese pagoda tree, Chinese scholar tree)
Sorbus Aucuparia (European mountain ash, rowan tree)
Stewartia Pseudocamellia (Japanese stewartia)
Tilia americana (American linden)
Tilia cordata (little-leaf linden)
Tilia tomentosa (silver linden)
Ulmus parvifolia (Chinese elm)
Ulmus procera (English elm)
Zelkova serrata (Japanese zelkova)

Short and Medium Deciduous Trees (growing to heights less than thirty-five feet)

Acer Ginnala (Amur maple)
Acer palmatum (Japanese maple)
Albizia Julibrissin (silk tree)
Amelanchier canadensis (shadblow or downy serviceberry)
Amelanchier X grandiflora (apple serviceberry)
Cercis canadensis (eastern redbud)
Chionanthus virginicus (fringe tree)
Cornus florida (flowering dogwood)
Cornus Kousa (Japanese dogwood)
Crataegus mollis (downy hawthorn)
Crataegus laevigata (English hawthorn)
Crataegus Phaenopyrum (Washington hawthorn)
Elaeagnus angustifolia (Russian olive, oleaster)
Halesia carolina (Carolina silverbell)
Laburnum X watereri, also called *Laburnum vossii* (golden chain tree)
Magnolia X soulangiana (saucer magnolia)
Magnolia stellata (star magnolia)
Malus X atrosanguinea (carmine crab apple)
Malus floribunda (showy crab apple)
Malus ioensis (prairie crab apple)

Malus X purpurea (purple crab apple)
Malus sylvestris, also known as *Pyrus malus* (apple)
Oxydendrum arboreum (sorrel tree)
Phellodendron amurense (Amur cork tree)
Prunus X blireiana (Blireiana plum, purple-leaf plum)
Prunus cerasifera (cherry plum)
Prunus serrulata (Oriental cherry)
Prunus subhirtella (Higan cherry)
Prunus virginiana (choke cherry)
Prunus yedoensis (Yoshino cherry)
Pyrus communis (pear)
Salix babylonica (Babylon weeping willow)
Sorbus decora (showy mountain ash)
Syringa reticulata var. *japonica* (Japanese tree lilac)

Tall Evergreen Trees (growing to a height greater than thirty-five feet)

Abies concolor (white fir, concolor fir)
Calocedrus decurrens (California incense cedar), also called *Libocedrus decurrens*
Cedrus atlantica cv. 'Glauca' (blue Atlas cedar)
Cedrus Deodara (deodar cedar)
Chamaecyparis Lawsoniana (Lawson false cypress, Port Orford cedar)
Cryptomeria japonica (cryptomeria, Japanese cedar)
Magnolia grandiflora (southern magnolia, bull bay)
Magnolia virginiana, also called *Magnolia glauca* (sweet bay)
Picea Abies, also called *Picea excelsa* (Norway spruce)
Picea glauca cv. 'Densata' (Black Hills spruce)
Picea pungens (Colorado spruce)
Pinus nigra subsp. *Laricio* (black pine)
Pinus ponderosa scopulorum (Rocky Mountain yellow pine)
Pinus Strobus (eastern white pine)

Pinus sylvestris (Scotch pine, Scots pine)
Pinus Thunbergiana (Japanese black pine)
Pseudotsuga Menziesii, also called *Pseudotsuga taxifolia, Pseudotsuga Douglasii* (Douglas fir)
Tsuga canadensis cultivars (Canada hemlock)

Short and Medium Evergreen Trees (growing to heights less than thirty-five feet)

Cephalotaxus Harringtonia, also called *Cephalotaxus drupacea* (Japanese plum yew)
Podocarpus macrophyllus (yew podocarpus)
Sciadopitys verticillata (umbrella pine)
Tsuga canadensis cultivars (Canada hemlock)
Tsuga caroliniana (Carolina hemlock)

Deciduous Windbreaks, Hedges, or Borders

Berberis Thunbergii (Japanese barberry)
Calycanthus floridus (strawberry shrub)
Caragana arborescens (Siberian pea tree)
Chaenomeles species, also called *Cydonia* (flowering quince)
Cotoneaster divaricatus (spreading cotoneaster)
Elaeagnus multiflora, also called *Elaeagnus longipes* (cherry elaeagnus)
Euonymus alata cv. 'Compacta' (dwarfed winged bush, dwarf burning bush)
Forsythia species (forsythia)
Kolkwitzia amabilis (beauty bush)
Ligustrum amurense (Amur privet)
Ligustrum ovalifolium (California privet)
Ligustrum vulgare (prim privet)
Lonicera species (honeysuckle)
Prunus tomentosa (Manchu or Nanking cherry)
Salix discolor (pussy willow)
Symphoricarpos albus var. *laevigatus*, also

called *Symphoricarpos racemosus* (snowberry)
Syringa vulgaris cultivars (lilacs)
Vitex Agnus-castus (chaste tree)
Weigela species (weigela)

Evergreen Windbreaks, Hedges, or Borders

Berberis Julianae (wintergreen barberry)
Buxus microphylla japonica (Japanese little-leaf boxwood)
Buxus sempervirens (common boxwood)
Camellia japonica (common camellia)
Camellia Sasanqua (sasanqua camellia)
Cotoneaster lacteus (Parney's red clusterberry)
Euonymus japonica (evergreen euonymus)
Ilex vomitoria (yaupon)
Juniperus chinensis cultivars (Chinese juniper)
Juniperus scopulorum cultivars (Rocky Mountain juniper, western red cedar)
Juniperus virginiana cultivars (eastern red cedar)
Kalmia latifolia (mountain laurel)
Ligustrum japonicum (Japanese privet)
Osmanthus heterophyllus, also called *Osmanthus ilicifolius* (holly osmanthus)
Photinia serrulata (Chinese photinia)
Pieris japonica (Japanese andromeda, lily-of-the-valley bush)
Prunus Laurocerasus (cherry laurel, English laurel)
Pyracantha coccinea (fire thorn)
Taxus cuspidata (Japanese yew)
Taxus X media (intermediate yew)
Thuja occidentalis (American arborvitae Douglas arborvitae)
Viburnum rhytidophyllum (leatherleaf viburnum)
Viburnum Tinus (laurestinus)

Deciduous Shrubs

Buddleia davidii (orange-eye butterfly bush)

Cornus alba cv. *'Sibirica'* (Siberian dogwood)

Cornus mas (Cornelian cherry)

Cotinus Coggygria (smoke bush)

Cotoneaster apiculatus (cranberry cotoneaster)

Cytisus species (broom)

Daphne Mezereum (February daphne)

Deutzia species (deutzia)

Enkianthus campanulatus (redvein enkianthus)

Fuchsia species (fuchsia, lady's eardrops)

Hamamelis virginiana (witch hazel)

Hibiscus syriacus (rose of Sharon, shrub althea)

Hydrangea macrophylla, also called *Hydrangea hortensis* (common bigleaf hydrangea, house hydrangea)

Hydrangea paniculata cv. *'Grandiflora'* (peegee hydrangea)

Paeonia suffruticosa (tree peony)

Philadelphus species (mock orange)

Potentilla fruticosa (bush cinquefoil)

Prunus glandulosa, double-flowered cultivars (dwarf flowering almond)

Rhododendron calendulaceum, also called *Azalea calendulacea* (flame azalea)

Rhododendron mucronulatum (Korean rhododendron)

Rhododendron Schlippenbachii, also called *Azalea Schlippenbachii* (royal azalea)

Rosa rugosa (rugosa rose)

Spiraea species (spirea, bridal wreath)

Tamarix ramosissima, also known as *Tamarix pentandra* (Odessa tamarisk)

Viburnum X carcephalum (fragrant snowball)

Viburnum plicatum, also called *Viburnum tomentosum sterile* (Japanese snowball)

Viburnum trilobum, also called *Viburnum americanum* (American cranberry bush)

Evergreen Shrubs

Abelia X grandiflora (glossy abelia)

Aucuba japonica (Japanese aucuba)

Chamaecyparis obtusa (Hinoki false cypress)

Chamaecyparis pisifera (Sawara false cypress)

Euonymus Fortunei (winter creeper)

Ilex X altaclarensis cv. 'Wilsonii' (Wilson holly)

Ilex Cassine (dahoon, dahoon holly)

Ilex cornuta (Chinese holly)

Ilex crenata (Japanese holly)

Ilex opaca (American holly)

Juniperus communis (common juniper)

Juniperus conferta (shore juniper)

Juniperus sabina (savin juniper)

Leucothoe Fontanesiana, also called *Leucothoe Catesbaei* (drooping leucothoe)

Mahonia Aquifolium (Oregon grape holly)

Nandina domestica (nandina, Chinese sacred bamboo)

Pieris floribunda (mountain andromeda)

Pinus aristata (bristlecone pine, hickory pine)

Pinus Mugo, also called *Pinus montana* (mugo pine, Swiss mountain pine)

Rhododendron carolinianum (Carolina rhododendron)

Rhododendron indicum cultivars (Indian azalea)

Rhododendron maximum (rosebay rhododendron, great laurel)

Skimmia japonica (Japanese skimmia)

Spartium junceum (Spanish broom)

Taxus baccata (English yew)

Deciduous Vines

Actinidia arguta (bower actinidia, tara vine)

Actinidia chinensis (Chinese actinidia)

Campsis X Tagliabuana (trumpet vine)

Celastrus scandens (American bittersweet)

Clematis hybrids (hybrid clematis)

Clematis montana (pink anemone clematis)

Hydrangea anomala subsp. *petiolaris,* also called *Hydrangea petiolaris,* or *Hydrangea scandens* (climbing hydrangea)

Lonicera Heckrottii (goldflame honeysuckle)

Lonicera japonica cv. 'Halliana' (Hall's honeysuckle)

Lonicera sempervirens (trumpet honeysuckle)

Parthenocissus quinquefolia, also called *Ampelopsis quinquefolia* (Virginia creeper, woodbine)

Parthenocissus tricuspidata, also called *Ampelopsis tricuspidata* (Boston ivy, Japanese creeper)

Polygonum aubertii (silver-fleece vine, silver-lace vine)

Pueraria lobata, also known as *Pueraria Thunbergiana* (kudzu)

Vitis coignetiae (glory vine)

Vitis species (grapevine species)

Wisteria floribunda (Japanese wisteria)

Wisteria sinensis, also called *Wisteria chinensis* (Chinese wisteria)

Evergreen Vines

Akebia quinata (five-leaf akebia)

Euonymus Fortunei (common winter creeper)

Hedera Helix (English ivy)

Lonicera sempervirens (trumpet honeysuckle)

Ground Covers

Aegopodium Podagraria (silver-edge bishop's weed, silver-edge goutweed)

Ajuga reptans cultivars (bugleweed, carpet bugle)

Arctostaphylos uva-ursi (bearberry, kinnikinnick)

Euonymus Fortunei 'Coloratas' (purple winter creeper)

Hedera Helix (English ivy)

Juniperus horizontalis cv. 'Wiltonii' (Wilton carpet juniper)

Juniperus horizontalis (creeping juniper)

Mahonia repens (creeping mahonia, dwarf holly grape)

Ophiopogon japonicus (mondo grass)

Pachysandra terminalis (Japanese pachysandra, Japanese spurge)

Paxistima Canbyi (Canby pachistima)

Rosmarinus officinalis cv. 'Prostratus' (rosemary)

Sedum species (stonecrop, live-forever)

Thymus praecox (mother-of-thyme)

Vinca minor (common periwinkle, trailing myrtle, creeping myrtle)

7

SOLVING
SPECIAL PROBLEMS
WITH PLANTS

PLANTS WERE FIRST VALUED for their production of food, fiber, and fuel, and only later for their beauty and medicinal powers. Now we realize the additional value of plants in improving our environment by building and holding soil, controlling water runoff, cleansing the air, and reducing the energy needed to maintain a comfortable home. Having first learned to manipulate plant materials for our sustenance and delight we now do so also to soothe and buffer those environmental conditions that degrade and even threaten our existence.

Air pollution specialists, acoustical engineers, soil conservation scientists, and sanitary and pollution control engineers have all studied plant systems to determine how plants may improve environmental quality. This chapter briefly describes further benefits that can be derived from careful landscape design. Most planting schemes can serve many purposes. The thoughtful landscape designer uses plants to solve several environmental problems and accepts the challenge of integrating energy and other environmental considerations in a single planting design.

PLANTS AND POLLUTANTS

Fair is foul and foul is fair:
Hover through fog and filthy air

Macbeth, Act 1, scene 1

Air pollution didn't happen overnight. It is an unfortunate by-product of civilization and humanity's desire for goods and services that require heavy industry and mass production.

Machines and factories sometimes taint the air with dirt, sand, fly ash, dust, smoke, and diesel and other fumes. The aesthetic pall of a blanket of particulate soot is obvious, but the insidious effects of colorless gases, including sulfur dioxide, hydrogen fluoride, ozone, oxides of nitrogen, peroxyacetyl nitrate (PAN), carbon dioxide, carbon monoxide, and pesticide aerosols, must also be recognized.

Some plants, especially conifers, wither when enshrouded and encrusted with pollutants. Patches of dead tissue, leaf drop, dwarfing, and stippling are all signs of vulnerability to pollution. Other plants, however, have a stronger resistant or recuperative nature. They continue to put forth a fresh garb of greenery in spite of overwhelming environmental odds. The ample delicate foliage of resistant species betrays little evidence of the fierce struggle that must constantly go on between vegetation and the airborne pollutants of town and country. In fact, some plant species not only withstand the siege of pollution over a lifetime of many decades, but they also purify the air of particulate dust, sulfur dioxide, and carbon dioxide.*

Some plants collect airborne particles, including dust and smoke, on their leaves, branches, stems, and leaf surfaces. The particles are then washed away by rain and fall to the ground. Plants that are particularly fuzzy or hairy, such as the small-leafed European linden (*Tilia cordata*),

*Charts on pages 183–212 in Appendix F indicate those plant species resistant to pollution.

are particularly adept at cleansing urban environments. But be cautioned that some fuzzy plant species will not endure unlimited pollution.

The value of vegetation for cleansing air of dust was documented in one German study that demonstrated that a greenbelt planted adjacent to a railroad station had only 300 dust particles per liter of air, although the neighboring terminal registered 5,000 dust particles per liter. Another study showed that air above a street without trees carried 10,000–12,000 dust particles per liter, while the air above a nearby tree-shaded street carried only 1,000–3,000 dust particles per liter.

The air purification system used by plants for filtering out particles aids the body in protecting the respiratory system against airborne dirt. Particulate dust can settle in and coat the lungs and air passages, increasing the likelihood of certain respiratory diseases.

Gaseous sulfur dioxide, which is a by-product of the combustion of most fuels and a key ingredient of urban smog, can be removed from the air by plants. The exact chemistry of this process is unknown. One Russian study suggested that a 500-meter-wide green area surrounding a factory reduced the area's sulfur dioxide concentration by 70 percent. Since most conifers are especially vulnerable to sulfur dioxide, they are not good species to plant in sulfur dioxide-polluted areas. Sulfur dioxide-resistant trees include Norway maple (*Acer platanoides*), the London plane (*Platanus X acerfolia*)

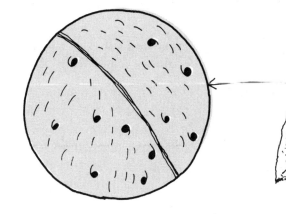

PUBESCENT LEAVES CATCH POLLUTANTS

and the small-leafed European linden.

The best known purifying action of plants is achieved through the photosynthetic process, which generates pure oxygen and sugar from the union of carbon dioxide and water. It is described by the following equation:

$$(6CO_2) + (6H_2O) \rightarrow (C_6H_{12}O_6) + (6O_2)$$

carbon dioxide	water	sugar	oxygen

Carbon dioxide is a by-product of respiration of all living animals. In the past fifty years the world level of this colorless gas has increased measurably. This means that plant systems are unable to purify air at a rate equal to the ability of man and animals to pollute it. Since the conversion of carbon dioxide into oxygen is vital to the survival of all animals, including man, a more desirable balance of plant and animal systems must be found. At least 150 square meters of leaf surface are thought to be needed to provide one person's annual oxygen needs. This means that every inhabitant of town centers ideally ought to have

thirty to forty square meters of greenery in trees, shrubs, and ground cover to produce sufficient oxygen. Needless to say, this requirement is not met in most urban areas. Fortunately, vegetation in rural areas partially compensates for this deficiency.

Plant species that are unable to tolerate excessive pollution are usually injured through their leaves. Such foliar injury is more common on evergreens than on deciduous species. This is because evergreens retain their leaves longer than deciduous plants and attempt to carry on the life processes during winter, when the concentrations of many airborne pollutants are at their highest. Such pollution causes conifers to lose their needles prematurely. This precocious balding means that trees can't maintain their normal levels of food production. Undernourished and weakened, they are vulnerable to attack by many insects, diseases, and other environmental stresses. Death often follows.

Air pollution often causes deciduous trees to lose their leaves, too. But because their leaves are regenerated every year, air pollution damage to these trees is not as severe.

To avoid pollution-related injury in your landscape, look out for nearby sources of pollution before beginning a planting program, then plant only vegetation known to tolerate local pollutants. Gardeners in rural areas are not exempt from this caution. Certain pollutants, such as ozone, travel great distances from their urban origin and others, such as pesticide aerosols and the road salt used to melt snow, are widespread in rural regions. Fortunately, there are relatively insensitive cultivars within many species, suggesting that a careful landscape design will not only avoid pollution-related plant injury but will also achieve a measure of pollution abatement.

PLANTING TO CONTROL GLARE AND REFLECTION

Modern society inhabits a shiny world. Smooth, polished, and highly reflective surfaces on glass, buildings, automobiles, and other objects accentuate and reflect natural sunshine and electric light. The resulting glare and reflection can cause considerable visual discomfort. The perception of glare occurs when the eye fails to accommodate successfully to a sharp streak of light in a relatively dim environment. Reflection is produced when light is bounced off a shiny surface such as water, glass, enameled steel, white pebbles, or snow.

Traditionally, fences, walls, and screens made of aluminum, wood, fiber glass, and canvas have been used to shade and soften glare and reflec-

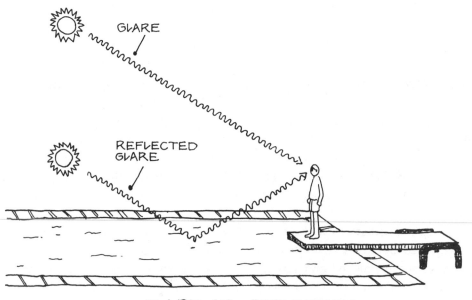

GLARE VS. REFLECTION

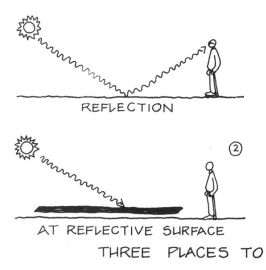

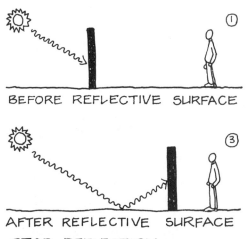

REFLECTION

BEFORE REFLECTIVE SURFACE

AT REFLECTIVE SURFACE

AFTER REFLECTIVE SURFACE

THREE PLACES TO STOP REFLECTION

tion. However, many of these materials collect and reradiate heat and are expensive, inflexible, or artificial in appearance. Recently, plants have become the favored materials for reducing glare and reflection, because they do not have these drawbacks. Careful selection of plants for appropriate size, shape, and foliage density can help to fine-tune the screening of light. In addition, vegetation has the special advantage of selectively filtering red and blue light, which are most objectionable to the human eye, and transmitting inoffensive green light. In winter, deciduous plants permit additional light to penetrate, providing dynamic natural control of changing light levels.

Plants are best at preventing glare when they screen sun to produce a gradual change in brightness, eliminating sharp changes in intensity. Trees shading an exit to a tunnel or vines covering a trellis can control glare in this way.

Reflected light can be controlled at any of three points: between the source of light and the reflective surface, at the reflective surface itself, or between the reflective surface and the viewer's eye. For example, if you wish to stop reflection by preventing light from hitting a reflective surface, plant trees and shrubs to shade the surface from the light source. Reflection can be obstructed at the reflective surface itself by placing ground covers, including plants and wood chips, over bare earth, sand, or pavement. Water lilies on a pond can prevent reflection off water. Finally, reflected light can be captured and controlled after it bounces off the reflective surface by planting a screen of hedges, shrubs, or trees between the reflective surface and the viewer.

ACOUSTICAL EFFECTS OF PLANTS

Plants by themselves are usually ineffective sound buffers because they

ATTENUATION BY DISTANCE   ATTENUATION BY BARRIER

TWO METHODS OF SOUND ATTENUATION

have too little mass to absorb and deaden sound waves. Indeed, their rustlings, movement, and tendency to reflect or resonate sound may add to the noise level. However, a complete landscape scheme that uses berms, ground covers, and plowed earth can absorb sound and reduce the level of noise.

Sound is formed by waves of energy, which can be weakened or muffled by two methods. The first is normal attenuation because of distance. The farther a sound wave travels, the more energy it loses and

the quieter it seems. The second method is excess attentuation resulting from the introduction of a barrier between the sound source and the receiver. When sound waves strike a barrier, part is reflected back toward the source, part is scattered away from the source, part is transmitted through the barrier, and finally the remaining sound is absorbed by the barrier itself. Desirable sound mufflers selectively deflect the sound in directions away from the receiver or use high mass to absorb and deaden the sound wave.

Most plants are poor sound ab-

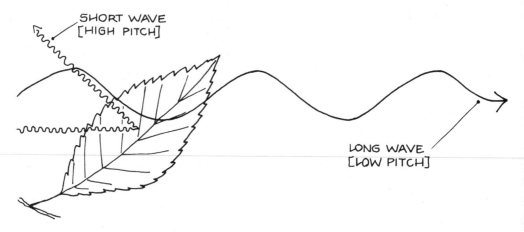

SHORT WAVE
[HIGH PITCH]

LONG WAVE
[LOW PITCH]

LOW PITCH [LONG SOUND WAVE] BYPASSING LEAF

sorbers because they have insufficient mass to absorb sound energy completely. Those few species that have been shown to effectively absorb and attenuate sound have especially thick, fleshy leaves or stems and include rubber plants (*Schefflera* species) and corn (*Zea mays*), which may reduce high-pitched noises such as whistles considerably—by as much as twenty decibels. Unfortunately, corn is rarely thought of as an appropriate landscape material.

Secondly, many irritating sound waves are long enough so they can simply travel around plant parts and evade whatever loose mass there is. For example, the needles of cedar (*Cedrus* species), hemlock (*Tsuga* species), or pine (*Pinus* species) are so ineffective at trapping sounds that a 100-foot-wide strip of these trees will reduce high-pitched noises by only a modest level of five decibels, because the needles are small in comparison to the length of the sound wave.

Finally, branches, twigs, fruits, and leaves can make their own sounds. This "white" noise may or may not be effective in masking unpleasant noise, depending on your location.

However, it must be noted in plants' favor that they can effectively scatter sound. The ground surface in forested or plowed areas is sufficiently roughened up to increase its absorption of sound. Thus, the sound which gets scattered to the ground by plants is then absorbed by the earth.

LANDSCAPED BERM DEADENS SOUND

Plant systems are at their best at controlling sound when used in a total landscape plan that incorporates berms, plowed earth, and ground covers, because earth forms have enough mass to absorb sound waves and deaden them. Within the earth, the energy of the sound wave is converted into a small amount of heat energy. Berms can deflect sound waves up and away from living areas, too. A berm that is built up as high as possible against an outside wall will dramatically reduce the noise reaching a home. If this strategy is inappropriate, build a berm some distance from the home and plow or rake the side facing the noise and plant it with ground cover. The ground cover will hold the soil in place and buffer select high-pitched sounds. Rough soil is better at absorbing sound, especially those low-pitched sounds that come from traffic. If you need a system to block noise but can't use a berm, build a cinder block or concrete wall between yourself and the noise and screen it with thick plantings. Remember that what stops sound most effectively is unbroken mass, and if plants are used, those with wide, continuous, dense, and heavy foliage make the best sound attenuators.

PLANTS THAT FEND OFF FLAMES

Those who live in the hot, arid regions of the American Southwest, where dry brush covers much of the native landscape, always face the threat of fire. This potential hazard is close at hand during the summer months when dry winds can whip a small fire into a devouring giant. As real as the threat of fire is, surprisingly few homes are armored against it. The lack of such defense is regrettable, especially since landscape design can offer a protective barrier.

A garden that resists fires is designed to follow four key guidelines: it is cleared of highly combustible dead brush; it uses water-retaining succulents and low-matted species that don't burn well; it avoids plants with flammable oils, including chamise (*Adenostoma fasiculatum*), rosemary (*Rosmarinus officinalis*), and eucalyptus trees; and it uses nonflammable ground covers, including raked earth, slate, and pebbles.

Eucalyptus species are common in arid regions but should be avoided where brush fires are a threat.

The resulting landscape is pleasant to look at and practical. By restricting plants to select native species, the landscape looks as natural as the surrounding hills, requires little water and energy-intensive maintenance, and helps to protect the house from brush fires. Dwarf coyote brush (*Baccharis pilularis*), salt bush (*Atriplex* species), yucca species, manzanita (*Arctostaphylos* species), and Saint Catherine's lace (*Eriogonum giganteum*) can form the backbone of such a garden. Most are low-growing plants, so there is little foliage to burn.

They're naturally well groomed so they don't accumulate too much deadwood or debris.

But the way plants are used in the landscape is as important as the selection of varieties. Restraint is essential. In the ideal arrangement, there is plenty of open space between plants, an uninhibited use of gray gravel and bare earth separates plants, and, in some places, ground-hugging ground covers isolate the more combustible species. This landscape design prevents a brush fire from traveling rapidly from plant to plant through the garden. Such a landscape will look odd if each plant is a different species, but creating a greenbelt of a very limited number of species and planting in great drifts give the garden a unified look. For the most part, the garden is green and gold, like the Arizona, New Mexico, and Southern California hillsides, the native home of many attractive succulent species.

PLANTING TO CONTROL EROSION

Plants and landscaping protect the soil from erosion, the wearing away and loss of the time-mellowed organic matter in the top seven or eight inches of earth. Nature needs about 500 years to create each inch of topsoil. If this blanket of topsoil is washed or blown away and the crusty, infertile subsoil exposed, the result is sparse or sickly vegetation. Soil nourishes all plant life, but in turn, vegetation protects soil from being scattered by wind and rain, the two key eroding forces.

Wind can carry away desirable topsoil as dirt and dust, depositing it elsewhere where it may be an undesirable nuisance, creating safety and health hazards by reducing visibility and entering the human respiratory system. Plant designs that serve as windbreaks control erosion by slowing wind velocity.* Tamarisk (*Tamarix* species), white mulberry (*Morus alba*), black locust (*Robinia Pseudoacacia*), and cottonwood (select *Populus* species) planted in parallel rows about six feet apart are hardy and effective wind-breaks. Other plant species with fibrous, shallow root systems also control wind erosion by holding surface soil in place. Ground covers including kudzu vine (*Pueraria lobata*), ivy (*Hedera Helix*), or ice plant (*Mesembryanthemum*) are especially good for this purpose.

Water is the most common soil-eroding agent. It erodes earth by the impact of raindrops on bare soil, displacing it, and carrying it off. As water runs off saturated soils, it carries loose particles with it, acting as a scouring agent and removing more precious top-soil. Plants can prevent and control this water-caused erosion in at least three ways. Leaves and branches interrupt rainfall, reducing the full velocity and force with which it hits the ground and carries away soil. Second, giant, underground nets of plant roots

*The ability of windbreaks to control air movements is described in Chapter 2.

clasp soil in place. Finally, leaves and other dead parts of plants on the soil surface add organic matter to the soil, loosening it and improving its ability to retain water successfully.

Modern engineering techniques have developed high-technology means for retaining topsoil. But well-planted grounds, covered with trees, bushes, grass, and other ground covers, offer a far more attractive safety belt for eroding soils.

ENERGY-EFFICIENT GREENHOUSE DESIGN

A solar greenhouse that fosters the growth of plants for your landscape could also help to heat your home this winter, even if you live in the cooler regions of the United States.

Greenhouses are among the most poorly understood and underutilized structures. The earliest designs, built with south-facing, insulated glass walls by the Dutch and English during the eighteenth and nineteenth centuries, were energy efficient. But because many poorly designed, ineffi-

PLANTS   PREVENT   WIND   EROSION

WATER ON BARE SOIL

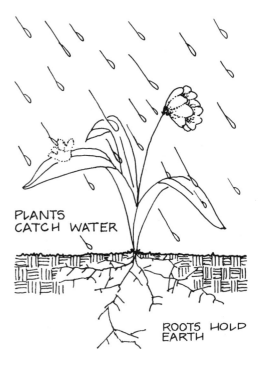

PLANTS CATCH WATER

ROOTS HOLD EARTH

PLANTS PREVENT WATER EROSION

cient conservatories were also built, by the turn of the twentieth century glass rooms had gained a reputation for wasting heat. Most of the existing greenhouses were constructed during the period of extravagant energy use.

However, several modern designers have built and tested solar greenhouses that rival and surpass the designs of the earliest greenhouse architects. Such structures often generate more heat than they consume and can heat part of the house they are attached to. They are not very complicated and need not be expensive, but they must be very carefully designed, sited, and constructed. Exciting results for such greenhouses were obtained in Burlington, Vermont, one of the coldest and cloudiest cities in the United States. Even in Frobisher Bay, an isolated village on southern Baffin Island in Canada, 1,600 miles due north of Boston, a properly designed and insulated greenhouse could be easily solar-heated from April first through October first. (There, the daily average of fifteen hours of clear summer sunshine compensates for a mean daily outdoor air temperature of only 7°F.)

The necessary elements of a solar greenhouse are orientation of the structure to the south, proper tilting of the glass walls so that the winter sun strikes at an angle of 90° (this angle allows in maximum winter sunlight but rejects overheating summer sun), and tight-fitting double- or triple-glazed window walls. For maximum efficiency, the east and west sidewalls

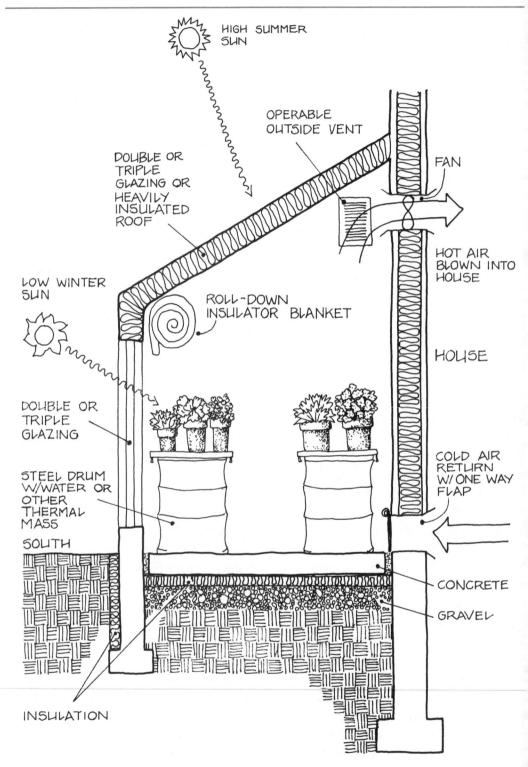

HIGH SUMMER SUN

OPERABLE OUTSIDE VENT

FAN

DOUBLE OR TRIPLE GLAZING OR HEAVILY INSULATED ROOF

HOT AIR BLOWN INTO HOUSE

LOW WINTER SUN

ROLL-DOWN INSULATOR BLANKET

HOUSE

DOUBLE OR TRIPLE GLAZING

COLD AIR RETURN W/ ONE WAY FLAP

STEEL DRUM W/WATER OR OTHER THERMAL MASS

SOUTH

CONCRETE

GRAVEL

INSULATION

ENERGY EFFICIENT GREENHOUSE

should be minimized, and a system developed for storing excess energy. Drums of water, masonry walls, or concrete floors laid on a thick, insulated bed of gravel are common thermal-storage systems. Special fluids and eutectic salts, which store radiant heat, change state at convenient temperatures (for example 81°F.) and may be embedded in building systems, are now sold in premanufactured containers. Of these, water is by far the most economical system for storing radiant heat. Growers may want to abandon the traditional planting tables in favor of water-filled oil drums covered with a metal grate. They can serve as both working tables and storage tanks for solar energy. A water-filled tank in the center of the greenhouse may also store heat and provide space for raising fish. These storage systems keep the air temperature in the greenhouse from getting too hot during daylight, while at night they release heat into the air to keep the temperature from dropping too much. The net result is that the greenhouse warms part of your house during the day but does not get too cold overnight.

As an alternative to these water-tank storage systems (or as a supplement to them, depending on how efficient you want to be) greenhouses can be fitted with devices to reduce overnight heat loss further. They include heavy curtains, movable insulation panels or blankets, or a polystyrene bead wall, air-blown balls of polystyrene plastic confined between two glass panes. Use of these various thermal curtains can increase the net heat gain by about 50 percent.

The configuration of the greenhouse significantly affects its performance. The most thermally efficient solar addition has a partially solid, well-insulated roof. This partial roof will obstruct the unwanted high summer sun but won't impede the rays from the low winter sun. Greenhouse builders who choose all-glass greenhouses sacrifice some efficiency. In summer, excess heat and sunshine on the end walls of the greenhouse should be eliminated by using aluminum and plastic shades that roll down from the roof, solar-blocking films that stick to glass, or the traditional, white greenhouse paint.

The rewards for careful greenhouse construction are related to the number of design details added to it. A simple, single-glazed greenhouse attached to the home will result in a net energy deficit for the dwelling. Heat loss can be avoided only if the greenhouse is sealed off from the house during the winter. This type of unheated glass house is vulnerable to extreme fluctuations in daily temperature, limiting the number of plant species that may be grown inside. A double-glazed greenhouse operates at about a break-even point, depending on local climate; it neither contributes energy to the home nor siphons it off. However, a double-glazed structure with an insulated roof and an internal thermal storage system will heat itself and offer a net energy gain to the structure as well, thus reducing winter heating bills.

PSYCHOLOGICAL BENEFITS OF LANDSCAPING

Long before scientists measured the ability of plants to control pollution, erosion, reflection, and noise, they recognized that plants could alter the perception of environmental eyesores. In certain situations, plants do not physically ameliorate an environmental problem but, because they reduce awareness of a nuisance, they offer a real, positive psychological effect.

For example, we are often surrounded with areas, activities, and objects we would rather not see. We screen or hide them to make the total environment more acceptable. Plants make effective screens, even though they grow and change and are less predictable than fences, walls, or architecture. They have the benefit of a natural appearance and a rich diversity of form, texture, and color.

Typical areas in our contemporary environment that may be screened by plants include highways, junkyards, service stations, construction sites, storage areas, parking lots, industrial and power facilities, athletic fields and arenas, roadways, driveways, and outdoor air-conditioners. Landscape design, including plants and earth forms, can do an efficient job of screening ugliness.

In   an   increasingly   congested

PLANTS SCREENING TRASH

PLANTS SCREENING JUNKYARD

PLANT DESIGN ALLOWS PRIVACY

world, plants can also convey an improved sense of seclusion. Privacy may be enhanced by plants in such settings as patios, terraces in high rise buildings, and public gathering areas. Plantings can be used to provide barriers at any scale. An individual can be offered an illusion of privacy by loose plantings of hibiscus, forsythia, or honeysuckle (*Lonicera* species). At the other end of the scale, an entire building site may be assured of absolute privacy by the implementation of a complex landscape design using earthforms, ponds and pools, and dense stands of spruce trees (*Picea* species) with clumps of birch (*Betula papyrifera* or *Betula populifolia*) in front. The amount of privacy needed must be

determined before selecting an appropriate landscape design.

Such plantings can also give an illusion of security, which may or may not be an advantage, depending on your neighborhood.

As indicated earlier, most plants are ineffective absorbers of sound, but they do produce their own "white noise," which may mask unpleasant sounds. Winds moving through pine needles and the rustle of leaves, either on the trees or on the ground, all produce pleasant sounds which can reduce the listener's awareness of offensive noises. Some trees, such as cottonwood (*Populus deltoides),* have leaf and petiole structures that rustle in the slightest breeze. In addition, landscaped grounds attract mammals and birds that contribute diversionary noises. In almost all cases, these sounds of nature, even when quite loud, are preferable to the sounds of industry. Thus, although plants are ineffective sound barriers themselves, they do offer positive psychological masks for unpleasant sounds.

Another aspect of landscaping that rarely receives sufficient credit is the psychological benefit derived from actually creating and maintaining attractive grounds. Gardening is being rediscovered as an important therapeutic tool because of its relaxed pace and its ability to help people work out contained frustrations.

Annually, at least one of every two households plans a garden and anticipates invigorating exercise, relaxation in an attractive and tranquil setting, and a harvest of produce and flowers. But for many, the greatest rewards of working with the soil are the release of tensions and the sense of satisfaction and accomplishment that come with seeing almost immediate results to one's gardening efforts. Even the laborious chores of loosening soil, building retaining walls, clearing brush, or pulling recalcitrant weeds can serve the desirable goal of offering a productive channel for venting contained hostilities.

Those who work with the soil learn of the vagaries of nature, but also of the great resiliency in life. Gardeners learn, too, that there is enormous potential for discovering novel solutions to challenging problems. These are among the more important psychological benefits of establishing a landscape program.

8

LOOKING AHEAD

Attacking the Energy Problem

IN THE COURSE OF reading this book you have probably asked yourself, "If the use of landscape design is such an effective means of conserving energy, why hasn't it received more widespread public recognition?"

The answer is simple. Landscape design is a passive, energy-saving technique and relies on quality design in simple materials, not on complex technological fabrications. It saves energy by *reducing demand* for energy at the point of use, the home or office. In contrast, the most visible and favored strategy for resolving the energy crisis encourages the development of systems that *increases production* such as nuclear power plants. Because passive conservation techniques do not fall within the preferred strategy for elim-

inating the energy shortage, they receive little attention and even less financial support.

By all estimates, it is cheaper to reduce the need for existing sources of energy by applying passive conservation techniques, including landscape design, insulation, weather stripping, caulking, and thermal window shades, than to create new energy sources. This rule becomes more evident as the true costs are revealed for developing new energy sources, such as nuclear power and synthetic fuels.

The results of these two investment strategies, high technology to develop new energy sources and simpler passive systems to reduce demand for existing energy sources, are contrasted in the following example.

To date, the government has already spent more than $200 billion subsidizing the nuclear and fossil fuel industries and has made a commitment to spend at least $80 billion more developing synthetic fuels. Such investments have no guaranteed results and to date have not produced the hoped-for energy bonanza.

If, instead, just the $80 billion being invested in synthetic fuels was distributed to each of the approximately 50 million American families, it could buy about $1,600 worth of insulation or purchase a modest solar hot-water heater. Retrofitting the average single-family home in the Northeast with this insulation would guarantee savings of five to ten barrels of oil per house per year. The same $1,600, if invested in a solar hot-water heater used to heat domestic water for a home in the South, would guarantee savings of about four barrels of oil per house per year. That's a savings of at least 200 million barrels of oil per year!

But the government is not investing large sums in the development of small-scale passive solar collectors. Instead, it is investing in multi-million-dollar arrays of reflective dishes that direct sunshine to giant "power towers" in the desert. These towers heat water into steam that runs a turbine and produces electricity that is distributed via an expensive system of trunk lines (where there is a marked energy loss), is then sold by private utilities to individual households, and finally runs through a coil and heats water (which is what the home solar hot-water heater does in the first place).

This strategy of investing huge sums in projects to develop new sources of energy instead of making impressive investments in passive energy-saving techniques has resulted in a lopsided national energy program that favors high technology gadgetry in lieu of lower-cost passive systems such as energy-efficient landscape design. Increased investment in the development of passive systems that conserve energy at the point of use—the home and business—will not produce new fuels for transportation and industry. But it will release energy now consumed by business and residential heating and cooling systems, which may be redirected to these other needs.

Positive Steps

Despite its less-than-ideal research and development strategy, other aspects of the government's energy program have produced commendable results. The establishment of federal Building and Energy Performance Standards (BEPS), which state the maximum amount of energy that may be used to maintain heating, lighting and cooling in buildings, could go a long way toward conserving energy. These building codes are in the process of being implemented and are descendants of the earlier pioneer codes that were created in the 1970s by states and municipalities trying to enforce greater conservation in their domains. However, the new federal codes have three important advantages over earlier ones.

First, the BEPS codes are performance codes rather than prescriptive ones. This means that they set standards for energy use for every new structure but don't state what combination of energy-saving techniques must be used to meet the standards. The techniques used to build the structure are left to the designer. In contrast, the old prescriptive codes set specific construction guidelines, including permissible percentage of wall space devoted to glass and minimum insulation values for walls and ceilings, but did not state what the ultimate energy-saving goal should be. The establishment of performance codes presents the opportunity for energy-efficient landscape design to demonstrate its energy-saving potential.

Secondly, the new BEPS codes will be more strictly enforced than earlier regional building energy codes. Those states that now have energy codes have no uniform method of enforcement and usually rely on local enforcement. Local governments, in turn, must depend on the astuteness and honesty of their building commissioners, who have few penalties for miscreants. If and when the new BEPS codes are finally established, all new structures financed with federal funds must meet the code. This is a particularly strong point for enforcement, since the construction of many new homes involves federally financed Veterans Administration (VA), Housing and Urban Development (HUD), and/or Federal Housing Administration (FHA) loans.

Finally, the BEPS codes are far stricter than earlier energy codes. They define the *total* maximum energy budget, in Btus per square feet, that can be used to run a building. The total budgets are adjusted to account for the different climatic regions throughout the United States. These codes were developed after the federal government asked 168 architects across the country to redesign selected projects for greater energy efficiency. Of these redesigns, the top 50 percent were selected as models of the state-of-the-art in energy conservation. The BEPS guidelines were established from these redesigns and will challenge designers to use all potential energy-saving strategies to meet the new stringent goals for conservation. Passive design techniques such as careful landscape planning and siting of buildings and windows should receive increased attention from architects as a result of the implementation of BEPS guidelines. A BEPS type of code will have only a small overall effect in its early years, simply because there will be a lot of energy wasters still around, but its long-term (fifty years and more) effect will be tremendous.

Another federal program that is

helping to resolve the energy crisis is the tax credits for residential energy conservation. The tax credits encourage individuals to buy expensive equipment that helps to reduce home energy consumption. As passed by Congress in 1978, the program provides tax credits of 15 percent of the cost, up to $300, of installing insulation, caulking, and other select conservation materials. For installing gadgetry such as geothermal or wind-driven power generators and solar heating systems that produce renewable energy, the tax credits began at 30 percent of the first $2,000 invested and 20 percent of the next $8,000, up to a total tax credit of $2,200.

The response to these incentives has been very good. The Internal Revenue Service computed that in the first twenty-one months of the program taxpayers reported investing $139 million in conservation programs. In 1980 the tax credits for investments in renewable energy sources were increased from 22 to 40 percent of the first $10,000 invested. However, credits for use of passive conservation materials were not increased, on the grounds that such an increase would be too expensive in lost tax dollars and that homeowners already had sufficient incentive. This is another example of the government supporting high-technology gadgetry instead of cheaper, more efficient passive design. The current credits, although admirable, are still too limited in scope and stifle innovative design solutions to the energy crisis. For example, pas-

sive solar houses, which may use south-facing glass, insulation, heat-storing materials, and energy-efficient landscape design, are not eligible for existing tax credits. The credits should be based on how well a house performs, not on what kind of mechanical equipment it uses. To continue to provide sufficient incentive for homeowners to install insulation, clock thermostats, and other energy-efficient measures, the existing 15 percent credit for materials should be increased, perhaps to 50 percent of the improvement costs. Energy conservation in homes should be as highly subsidized as other forms of energy production.

The "solar bank act" may help to fulfill this goal by providing immediate financing and subsidies of as much as $750 million through low-interest loans for renewable energy-producing equipment, and up to $3.35 billion in government-supported loans for conservation materials. Unlike the tax credits, which are available to all taxpaying homeowners, these loans are made on the basis of income and are available to tenants, farmers, and commercial and non-profit organizations.

Another branch of government that has offered generous energy aid to the average citizen is the U.S. Department of Agriculture and its affiliated land grant universities and local Extension offices. They have produced a variety of easy-to-read publications that foster awareness of the energy problem and offer suggestions for conservation. County Extension agents have long been known for giving horticultural advice; now many offer energy advice as well.

The government has also established the National Solar Heating and Cooling Information Center (P.O. Box 1607, Rockville, Md 20850) to help citizens learn to use conservation techniques.

Our emphasis on government's contributions to the resolution of the energy shortage is not meant to imply that only the government has the resources to solve the problem. But government establishes the national policies that set the incentives for business, universities, or federal agencies.

Promising Research

The full value of energy-efficient landscape design (and other passive conservation techniques) will be realized only after it is explored as vigorously as "big energy" production systems. However, lack of sufficient support has not caused the field to languish completely. Modest research efforts made by enthusiastic researchers in the United States and elsewhere are helping to transform energy-efficient landscape design from an imprecise art to a more exact science.

Many disciplines are contributing to the refinement of the science of energy-efficient landscape design including plant physiology, agronomy, architecture, engineering, and land-

scape architecture. An unforeseen discipline that has given impetus to the field is computer graphics. It is a mathematically based technique that translates complex physical phenomena such as environmental and engineering data into pictures. Computer graphics permits designers and their clients to communicate with a computer using pictures. Using this technique, an architect traces a preliminary design of a building on a computer's drawing board, an electronic device that detects the position of the stylus, or drawing tool. The programmed computer automatically analyzes the drawn floor plan and translates it into mathematical statements comprehensible to the computer.

Once the structure's specifications are translated into the computerized netherworld of equations and coordinates, the architect can tell the computer to display the building from any angle, inside or out, or to position it in a setting that has been previously

described to the computer. More important is the ability of a sophisticated computer program to measure the energy needed to maintain a comfortable environment for residents.

However, when this system was first tested in the mid-1970s, it was found that the computer's assessment of the energy needed to heat and cool a building was inaccurate by as much as 30 percent. An investigation revealed that the early computer simulations of a building's energy needs for heating and cooling failed to consider two important sets of environmental considerations: the activities of the people in the building—exercising, working, cooking, or sleeping—and the surrounding landscape.

The research goal of one of the authors (Schiler) is to determine how landscape affects a building's energy needs.

Because trees that block sun have the single largest impact on a structure's energy requirements, these plants were studied first. This meant taking photos of trees, scanning the photos to determine the trees' density and ability to block sun, and quantify-

ing the results for input to a computer. Trees were studied in full foliage and bare. It was found that the density of trees is extremely consistent within a given species, but varies greatly from species to species. For example, a Norway maple *(Acer platanoides)* in full foliage intercepts 90 percent of the sun's light, but a honey locust *(Gleditsia triacanthos)* screens only 50 percent. The results of this research, which measures and compares the sun-blocking ability of thirty plant species, is presented on pages 181–182 in Appendix E. These studies are the sources of some of the estimates on energy savings cited in earlier chapters.

The second phase of this research will refine the initial computer program by adding data on how plants affect airflow. Information is now available on how straight lines of trees affect wind but little data is available on how other groupings of trees or randomly placed specimens affect airflow. Another goal for scientific investigation is to quantify the ability of plant species with small foliage such as vines and ground covers to block sun. When these three phases of the study are completed it will be possible to use computer graphics techniques to measure exactly the impact of a *proposed* landscape design on a home's energy requirements. Because the cost of computer equipment is falling rapidly, many of the larger architectural and landscape architecture firms could have access to these techniques within ten years.

It must be stressed that computers are used to aid the design process and not to substitute for aesthetic creativity. Their strength is that they quantify the impact of a proposed design on a building's energy needs, remove the tedium of numerical calculations, and in fact free the designer to spend more time creatively.

Trends

The current energy shortage stresses that the concerns of the architect and the landscape designer must be broader than aesthetics. They must use and refine the scientific principles of passive design to reduce the consumption of energy by residential and business structures, which now amounts to about 30 percent of the nation's total annual energy use. Unfortunately, the architectural professions have not consistently supported this cause as well as they could. Most awards and publicity in the profession go to people who design stylish, sculptural homes, offices, and gardens, not to people who create energy-efficient designs.

Good design and applied science are not mutually exclusive. Their synthesis is essential if we will respond effectively to the challenge to use less energy in the home and the workplace. Indeed, the development of energy-efficient landscape design into a precise, quantifiable technique should be one more exciting result of the integration of art and science.

APPENDICES

THE ZONES OF PLANT HARDINESS

A

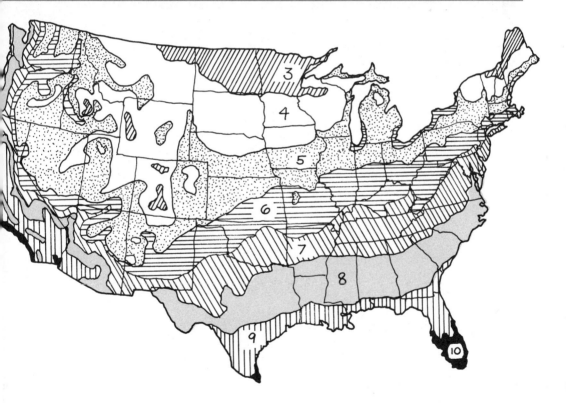

APPROXIMATE RANGE OF AVERAGE ANNUAL MINIMUM
TEMPERATURES FOR EACH ZONE

ZONE 3	-40°F TO -30°F		ZONE 7	0°F TO 10°F
ZONE 4	-30°F TO -20°F		ZONE 8	10°F TO 20°F
ZONE 5	-20°F TO -10°F		ZONE 9	20°F TO 30°F
ZONE 6	-10°F TO 0°F		ZONE 10	30°F TO 40°F

B

LATITUDES OF NORTH AMERICA

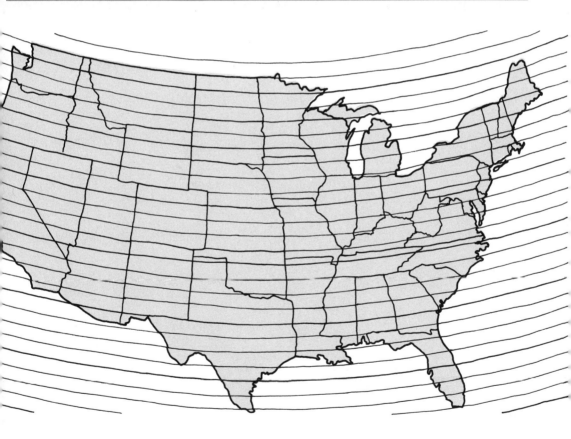

THE LATITUDES OF NORTH AMERICA

TABLE OF SOLAR ANGLES FOR U.S.

26.0 DEGREES NORTH LATITUDE

Winter solstice, December 22			**Spring and Fall Equinox, March 21, Sept 24**			**Summer solstice, June 22**		
Time	∝ **Altitude Angle**	β **Bearing Angle**	**Time**	∝ **Altitude Angle**	β **Bearing Angle**	**Time**	∝ **Altitude Angle**	β **Bearing Angle**
7:00 a.m.	2.23	117.51	7:00	13.26	97.07	6:00 a.m.	10.04	68.70
8:00 a.m.	13.76	125.11	8:00 a.m.	26.50	104.59	7:00 a.m.	22.82	74.03
9:00 a.m.	24.12	134.70	9:00 a.m.	39.23	114.10	8:00 a.m.	35.92	78.85
10:00 a.m.	32.66	146.98	10:00 a.m.	50.83	127.66	9:00 a.m.	49.24	83.55
11:00 a.m.	38.46	162.34	11:00 a.m.	59.88	148.94	10:00 a.m.	62.69	88.83
12:00 noon	40.55	180.00	12:00 noon	63.59	180.00	11:00 a.m.	76.14	97.39
1:00 p.m.	38.46	197.65	1:00 p.m.	59.88	211.05	12:00 noon	87.44	180.00
2:00 p.m.	32.66	213.01	2:00 p.m.	50.83	232.33	1:00 p.m.	76.14	262.60
3:00 p.m.	24.12	225.30	3:00 p.m.	39.23	245.90	2:00 p.m.	62.69	271.16
4:00 p.m.	13.76	234.88	4:00 p.m.	26.50	255.40	3:00 p.m.	49.24	276.44
5:00 p.m.	2.23	242.48	5:00 p.m.	13.26	262.93	4:00 p.m.	35.92	281.14
						5:00 p.m.	22.82	285.96
						6:00 p.m.	10.04	291.29

28.0 DEGREES NORTH LATITUDE

	Winter solstice, December 22			Spring and Fall Equinox, March 21, Sept. 24			Summer solstice, June 22	
	α Altitude	β Bearing		α Altitude	β Bearing		α Altitude	β Bearing
Time	Angle	Angle	Time	Angle	Angle	Time	Angle	Angle
7:00 a.m.	1.31	117.57	7:00 a.m.	13.01	97.53	6:00 a.m.	10.76	69.04
8:00 a.m.	12.60	125.49	8:00 a.m.	25.98	105.54	7:00 a.m.	23.35	74.85
9:00 a.m.	22.70	135.31	9:00 a.m.	38.39	115.56	8:00 a.m.	36.28	80.28
10:00 a.m.	30.98	147.65	10:00 a.m.	49.58	129.54	9:00 a.m.	49.42	85.87
11:00 a.m.	36.56	162.80	11:00 a.m.	58.16	150.62	10:00 a.m.	62.66	92.70
12:00 noon	38.55	180.00	12:00 noon	61.59	180.00	11:00 a.m.	75.75	105.23
1:00 p.m.	36.56	197.19	1:00 p.m.	58.16	209.38	12:00 noon	85.44	180.00
2:00 p.m.	30.98	212.34	2:00 p.m.	49.58	230.45	1:00 p.m.	75.75	254.76
3:00 p.m.	22.70	224.68	3:00 p.m.	38.39	244.43	2:00 p.m.	62.66	267.29
4:00 p.m.	12.60	234.50	4:00 p.m.	25.98	254.45	3:00 p.m.	49.42	274.12
5:00 p.m.	1.31	242.42	5:00 p.m.	13.01	262.46	4:00 p.m.	36.28	279.71
						5:00 p.m.	23.35	285.14
						6:00 p.m.	10.76	290.95

30.0 DEGREES NORTH LATITUDE

Winter solstice, December 22			Spring and Fall Equinox, March 21, Sept. 24			Summer solstice, June 22		
7:00 a.m.	0.38	117.60	7:00 a.m.	12.74	97.98	6:00 a.m.	11.47	69.41
8:00 a.m.	11.44	125.84	8:00 a.m.	25.43	106.47	7:00 a.m.	23.86	75.70
9:00 a.m.	21.27	135.87	9:00 a.m.	37.50	116.95	8:00 a.m.	36.59	81.74
10:00 a.m.	29.28	148.26	10:00 a.m.	48.28	131.29	9:00 a.m.	49.53	88.21
11:00 a.m.	34.64	163.22	11:00 a.m.	56.40	152.11	10:00 a.m.	62.50	96.54
12:00 noon	36.55	180.00	12:00 noon	59.59	180.00	11:00 a.m.	75.01	112.52
1:00 p.m.	34.64	196.77	1:00 p.m.	56.40	207.88	12:00 noon	83.44	180.00
2:00 p.m.	29.28	211.73	2:00 p.m.	48.28	228.70	1:00 p.m.	75.10	247.47
3:00 p.m.	21.27	224.12	3:00 p.m.	37.50	243.04	2:00 p.m.	62.50	263.45
4:00 p.m.	11.44	234.15	4:00 p.m.	25.43	253.52	3:00 p.m.	49.53	271.78
5:00 p.m.	0.38	242.40	5:00 p.m.	12.74	262.01	4:00 p.m.	36.59	278.25
						5:00 p.m.	23.86	284.30
						6:00 p.m.	11.47	290.58

32.0 DEGREES NORTH LATITUDE

Winter solstice, December 22			Spring and Fall Equinox, March 21, Sept. 24			Summer solstice, June 22		
8:00 a.m.	10.26	126.15	7:00 a.m.	12.46	98.42	5:00 a.m.	0.54	62.40
9:00 a.m.	19.83	136.39	8:00 a.m.	24.85	107.37	6:00 a.m.	12.17	69.80
10:00 a.m.	27.57	148.83	9:00 a.m.	36.57	118.29	7:00 a.m.	24.34	76.56
11:00 a.m.	32.73	163.60	10:00 a.m.	46.94	132.91	8:00 a.m.	36.86	83.22
12:00 noon	34.55	180.00	11:00 a.m.	54.62	153.44	9:00 a.m.	49.55	90.55
1:00 p.m.	32.73	196.39	12:00 noon	57.59	180.00	10:00 a.m.	62.20	100.32
2:00 p.m.	27.57	211.16	1:00 p.m.	54.62	206.55	11:00 a.m.	74.23	119.09
3:00 p.m.	19.83	223.60	2:00 p.m.	46.94	227.08	12:00 noon	81.44	180.00
4:00 p.m.	10.26	233.84	3:00 p.m.	36.57	241.70	1:00 p.m.	74.23	240.90
			4:00 p.m.	24.85	252.62	2:00 p.m.	62.20	259.67
			5:00 p.m.	12.46	261.57	3:00 p.m.	49.55	269.44
						4:00 p.m.	36.86	276.77
						5:00 p.m.	24.34	283.43
						6:00 p.m.	12.17	290.19
						7:00 p.m.	0.54	297.60

34.0 DEGREES NORTH LATITUDE

Winter solstice, December 22			Spring and Fall Equinox, March 21, Sept. 24			Summer soltice, June 22		
	α	β		α	β		α	β
Time	Altitude Angle	Bearing Angle	Time	Altitude Angle	Bearing Angle	Time	Altitude Angle	Bearing Angle
8:00 a.m.	9.08	126.42	7:00 a.m.	12.15	98.86	5:00 a.m.	1.47	62.43
9:00 a.m.	18.38	136.87	8:00 a.m.	24.24	108.24	6:00 a.m.	12.85	70.22
10:00 a.m.	25.86	149.35	9:00 a.m.	35.61	119.57	7:00 a.m.	24.79	77.46
11:00 a.m.	30.81	163.95	10:00 a.m.	45.56	134.42	8:00 a.m.	37.07	84.72
12:00 noon	32.55	180.00	11:00 a.m.	52.82	154.63	9:00 a.m.	49.49	92.90
1:00 p.m.	30.81	196.05	12:00 noon	55.59	180.00	10:00 a.m.	61.78	104.00
2:00 p.m.	25.86	210.64	1:00 p.m.	52.82	205.36	11:00 a.m.	73.17	124.90
3:00 p.m.	18.38	223.12	2:00 p.m.	45.56	225.57	12:00 noon	79.44	180.00
4:00 p.m.	9.08	233.57	3:00 p.m.	35.61	240.42	1:00 p.m.	73.17	235.10
			4:00 p.m.	24.24	251.75	2:00 p.m.	61.78	255.99
			5:00 p.m.	12.15	261.14	3:00 p.m.	49.49	267.09
						4:00 p.m.	37.07	275.27
						5:00 p.m.	24.79	282.54
						6:00 p.m.	12.85	289.77
						7:00 p.m.	1.47	297.56

36.0 DEGREES NORTH LATITUDE

Winter solstice, December 22			Spring and Fall Equinox, March 21, Sept. 24			Summer solstice, June 22		
8:00 a.m.	7.88	126.66	7:00 a.m.	11.84	99.28	5:00 a.m.	2.39	62.49
9:00 a.m.	16.91	137.30	8:00 a.m.	23.60	109.08	6:00 a.m.	13.52	70.66
10:00 a.m.	24.13	149.82	9:00 a.m.	34.60	120.78	7:00 a.m.	25.21	78.37
11:00 a.m.	28.88	164.26	10:00 a.m.	44.14	135.83	8:00 a.m.	37.22	86.23
12:00 noon	30.55	180.00	11:00 a.m.	51.01	155.70	9:00 a.m.	49.35	95.23
1:00 p.m.	28.88	195.73	12:00 noon	53.59	180.00	10:00 a.m.	61.24	107.55
2:00 p.m.	24.13	210.17	1:00 p.m.	51.01	204.29	11:00 a.m.	71.95	129.95
3:00 p.m.	16.91	222.69	2:00 p.m.	44.14	224.16	12:00 noon	77.44	180.00
4:00 p.m.	7.88	233.33	3:00 p.m.	34.60	239.21	1:00 p.m.	71.95	230.04
			4:00 p.m.	23.60	250.91	2:00 p.m.	61.24	252.44
			5:00 p.m.	11.84	260.72	3:00 p.m.	49.35	264.77
						4:00 p.m.	37.22	273.76
						5:00 p.m.	25.21	281.62
						6:00 p.m.	13.52	189.33
						7:00 p.m.	2.39	297.50

38.0 DEGREES NORTH LATITUDE

Winter Solstice, December 22			Spring and Fall Equinox, March 21, Sept. 24			Summer Solstice, June 22		
8:00 a.m.	6.69	126.87	7:00 a.m.	11.51	99.68	5:00 a.m.	3.31	62.57
9:00 a.m.	15.44	137.69	8:00 a.m.	22.93	109.89	6:00 a.m.	14.18	71.13
10:00 a.m.	22.40	150.25	9:00 a.m.	33.56	121.94	7:00 a.m.	25.60	79.30
11:00 a.m.	26.96	164.55	10:00 a.m.	42.69	137.13	8:00 a.m.	37.33	87.75
12:00 noon	28.55	180.00	11:00 a.m.	49.18	156.67	9:00 a.m.	49.12	97.53
1:00 p.m.	26.96	195.45	12:00 noon	51.59	180.00	10:00 a.m.	60.58	110.94
2:00 p.m.	22.40	209.74	1:00 p.m.	49.18	203.32	11:00 a.m.	70.61	134.33
3:00 p.m.	15.44	222.30	2:00 p.m.	42.69	222.86	12:00 noon	75.44	180.00
4:00 p.m.	6.69	233.12	3:00 p.m.	33.56	238.05	1:00 p.m.	70.61	225.66
			4:00 p.m.	22.93	250.10	2:00 p.m.	60.58	249.05
			5:00 p.m.	11.51	260.31	3:00 p.m.	49.12	262.46
						4:00 p.m.	37.33	272.24
						5:00 p.m.	25.60	280.69
						6:00 p.m.	14.18	288.87
						7:00 p.m.	3.31	297.42

40.0 DEGREES NORTH LATITUDE

Winter Solstice, December 22			Spring and Fall Equinox, March 21, Sept. 24			Summer Solstice, June 22		
	∝	β		∝	β		∝	β
Time	Altitude Angle	Bearing Angle	Time	Altitude Angle	Bearing Angle	Time	Altitude Angle	Bearing Angle
8:00 a.m.	5.48	127.04	7:00 a.m.	11.17	100.08	5:00 a.m.	4.23	62.69
9:00 a.m.	13.95	138.05	8:00 a.m.	22.24	110.67	6:00 a.m.	14.82	71.62
10:00 a.m.	20.66	150.64	9:00 a.m.	32.48	123.04	7:00 a.m.	25.95	80.25
11:00 a.m.	25.03	164.80	10:00 a.m.	41.21	138.34	8:00 a.m.	37.38	89.28
12:00 noon	26.55	180.00	11:00 a.m.	47.34	157.54	9:00 a.m.	48.82	99.81
1:00 p.m.	25.03	195.19	12:00 noon	49.59	180.00	10:00 a.m.	59.81	114.17
2:00 p.m.	20.66	209.35	1:00 p.m.	47.34	202.45	11:00 a.m.	69.16	138.11
3:00 p.m.	13.95	221.94	2:00 p.m.	41.21	221.65	12:00 noon	73.44	180.00
4:00 p.m.	5.48	232.95	3:00 p.m.	32.48	236.95	1:00 p.m.	69.16	221.88
			4:00 p.m.	22.24	249.32	2:00 p.m.	59.81	245.82
			5:00 p.m.	11.17	259.91	3:00 p.m.	48.82	260.19
						4:00 p.m.	37.38	270.71
						5:00 p.m.	25.95	279.74
						6:00 p.m.	14.82	288.37
						7:00 p.m.	4.23	297.30

42.0 DEGREES NORTH LATITUDE

Winter solstice, December 22			Spring and Fall Equinox, March 21, Sept. 24			Summer solstice, June 22		
8:00 a.m.	4.28	127.17	7:00 a.m.	10.81	100.46	5:00 a.m.	5.15	62.84
9:00 a.m.	12.46	138.36	8:00 a.m.	21.52	111.42	6:00 a.m.	15.44	72.13
10:00 a.m.	18.91	150.99	9:00 a.m.	31.38	124.08	7:00 a.m.	26.27	81.22
11:00 a.m.	23.10	165.04	10:00 a.m.	39.70	139.46	8:00 a.m.	37.38	90.81
12:00 noon	24.55	180.00	11:00 a.m.	45.48	158.33	9:00 a.m.	48.44	102.04
1:00 p.m.	23.10	194.96	12:00 noon	47.59	180.00	10:00 a.m.	58.94	117.21
2:00 p.m.	18.91	209.00	1:00 p.m.	45.48	201.66	11:00 a.m.	67.63	141.38
3:00 p.m.	12.46	221.63	2:00 p.m.	39.70	220.53	12:00 noon	71.44	180.00
4:00 p.m.	4.28	232.82	3:00 p.m.	31.38	235.92	1:00 p.m.	67.63	218.61
			4:00 p.m.	21.52	248.57	2:00 p.m.	58.94	242.78
			5:00 p.m.	10.81	259.53	3:00 p.m.	48.44	257.96
						4:00 p.m.	37.38	269.19
						5:00 p.m.	26.27	278.77
						6:00 p.m.	15.44	287.86
						7:00 p.m.	5.15	297.15

44.0 DEGREES NORTH LATITUDE

Winter solstice, December 22			Spring and Fall Equinox, March 21, Sept. 24			Summer solstice, June 22		
8:00 a.m.	3.07	127.28	7:00 a.m.	10.44	100.83	5:00 a.m.	6.06	63.01
9:00 a.m.	10.96	138.63	8:00 a.m.	20.77	112.14	6:00 a.m.	16.04	72.67
10:00 a.m.	17.16	151.30	9:00 a.m.	30.24	125.06	7:00 a.m.	25.56	82.20
11:00 a.m.	21.16	165.24	10:00 a.m.	38.17	140.50	8:00 a.m.	37.32	92.33
12:00 noon	22.55	180.00	11:00 a.m.	43.62	159.05	9:00 a.m.	47.99	104.22
1:00 p.m.	21.16	194.75	12:00 noon	45.59	180.00	10:00 a.m.	57.98	120.07
2:00 p.m.	17.16	208.69	1:00 p.m.	43.62	200.94	11:00 a.m.	66.04	144.21
3:00 p.m.	10.96	221.36	2:00 p.m.	38.17	219.49	12:00 noon	69.44	180.00
4:00 p.m.	3.07	232.71	3:00 p.m.	30.24	234.93	1:00 p.m.	66.04	215.79
			4:00 p.m.	20.77	247.85	2:00 p.m.	57.98	239.92
			5:00 p.m.	10.44	259.16	3:00 p.m.	47.99	255.77
						4:00 p.m.	37.32	267.66
						5:00 p.m.	26.56	277.79
						6:00 p.m.	16.04	287.32
						7:00 p.m.	6.06	296.98

46.0 DEGREES NORTH LATITUDE

Winter solstice, December 22

Time	α Altitude Angle	β Bearing Angle
8:00 a.m.	1.86	127.35
9:00 a.m.	9.46	138.87
10:00 a.m.	15.41	151.58
11:00 a.m.	19.23	165.43
12:00 noon	20.55	180.00
1:00 p.m.	19.23	194.56
2:00 p.m.	15.41	208.41
3:00 p.m.	9.46	221.12
4:00 p.m.	1.86	232.65

Spring and Fall Equinox, March 21, Sept. 24

Time	α Altitude Angle	β Bearing Angle
7:00 a.m.	10.06	101.19
8:00 a.m.	20.01	112.82
9:00 a.m.	29.08	125.99
10:00 a.m.	36.62	141.46
11:00 a.m.	41.75	159.70
12:00 noon	43.59	180.00
1:00 p.m.	41.75	200.29
2:00 p.m.	36.62	218.53
3:00 p.m.	29.08	234.01
4:00 p.m.	20.01	247.17
5:00 p.m.	10.06	258.81

Summer solstice, June 22

Time	α Altitude Angle	β Bearing Angle
5:00 a.m.	6.96	63.22
6:00 a.m.	16.63	73.23
7:00 a.m.	26.82	83.20
8:00 a.m.	37.22	93.85
9:00 a.m.	47.46	106.34
10:00 a.m.	56.94	122.75
11:00 a.m.	64.39	146.66
12:00 noon	67.44	180.00
1:00 p.m.	64.39	213.33
2:00 p.m.	56.94	237.24
3:00 p.m.	47.46	253.65
4:00 p.m.	37.22	266.14
5:00 p.m.	26.82	276.79
6:00 p.m.	16.63	286.76
7:00 p.m.	6.96	296.77

48.0 DEGREES NORTH LATITUDE

Winter solstice, December 22

Time	α Altitude Angle	β Bearing Angle
8:00 a.m.	0.64	127.38
9:00 a.m.	7.95	139.07
10:00 a.m.	13.64	151.83
11:00 a.m.	17.29	165.60
12:00 noon	18.55	180.00
1:00 p.m.	17.29	194.40
2:00 p.m.	13.64	208.16
3:00 p.m.	7.95	220.92
4:00 p.m.	0.64	232.61

Spring and Fall Equinox, March 21, Sept. 24

Time	α Altitude Angle	β Bearing Angle
7:00 a.m.	9.66	101.53
8:00 a.m.	19.22	113.48
9:00 a.m.	27.89	126.86
10:00 a.m.	35.04	142.35
11:00 a.m.	39.87	160.29
12:00 noon	41.59	180.00
1:00 p.m.	39.87	199.70
2:00 p.m.	35.04	217.64
3:00 p.m.	27.89	233.13
4:00 p.m.	19.22	246.51
5:00 p.m.	9.66	258.46

Summer solstice, June 22

Time	α Altitude Angle	β Bearing Angle
5:00 a.m.	7.86	63.45
6:00 a.m.	17.20	73.81
7:00 a.m.	27.03	84.21
8:00 a.m.	37.06	95.36
9:00 a.m.	46.86	108.40
10:00 a.m.	55.82	125.25
11:00 a.m.	62.70	148.81
12:00 noon	65.44	180.00
1:00 p.m.	62.70	211.18
2:00 p.m.	55.82	234.75
3:00 p.m.	46.86	251.59
4:00 p.m.	37.06	264.63
5:00 p.m.	27.03	275.78
6:00 p.m.	17.20	286.18
7:00 p.m.	7.86	296.54

50.0 DEGREES NORTH LATITUDE

Winter solstice, December 22

Time	α Altitude Angle	β Bearing Angle
9:00 a.m.	6.44	139.24
10:00 a.m.	11.88	152.04
11:00 a.m.	15.35	165.74
12:00 noon	16.55	180.00
1:00 p.m.	15.35	194.25
2:00 p.m.	11.88	207.95
3:00 p.m.	6.44	220.75

Spring and Fall Equinox, March 21, Sept. 24

Time	α Altitude Angle	β Bearing Angle
7:00 a.m.	9.26	101.85
8:00 a.m.	18.42	114.10
9:00 a.m.	26.68	127.68
10:00 a.m.	33.45	143.18
11:00 a.m.	37.98	160.83
12:00 noon	39.59	180.00
1:00 p.m.	37.98	199.17
2:00 p.m.	33.45	216.81
3:00 p.m.	26.68	232.31
4:00 p.m.	18.42	245.89
5:00 p.m.	9.26	258.14

Summer solstice, June 22

Time	α Altitude Angle	β Bearing Angle
4:00 a.m.	0.57	52.61
5:00 a.m.	8.75	63.71
6:00 a.m.	17.74	74.42
7:00 a.m.	27.22	85.23
8:00 a.m.	36.84	96.86
9:00 a.m.	46.20	110.39
10:00 a.m.	54.63	127.56
11:00 a.m.	60.97	150.69
12:00 noon	63.44	180.00
1:00 p.m.	60.97	209.30
2:00 p.m.	54.63	232.43
3:00 p.m.	46.20	249.60
4:00 p.m.	36.84	263.13
5:00 p.m.	27.22	274.76
6:00 p.m.	17.74	285.57
7:00 p.m.	8.75	296.28
8:00 p.m.	0.57	307.38

D

TABLE OF TANGENTS

Angle	Tangent	Angle	Tangent	Angle	Tangent
1.00	0.017	31.00	0.601	61.00	1.804
2.00	0.035	32.00	0.625	62.00	1.881
3.00	0.052	33.00	0.649	63.00	1.963
4.00	0.070	34.00	0.675	64.00	2.050
5.00	0.087	35.00	0.700	65.00	2.145
6.00	0.105	36.00	0.727	66.00	2.246
7.00	0.123	37.00	0.754	67.00	2.356
8.00	0.141	38.00	0.781	68.00	2.475
9.00	0.158	39.00	0.810	69.00	2.605
10.00	0.176	40.00	0.839	70.00	2.747
11.00	0.194	41.00	0.869	71.00	2.904
12.00	0.213	42.00	0.900	72.00	3.078
13.00	0.231	43.00	0.933	73.00	3.271
14.00	0.249	44.00	0.966	74.00	3.487
15.00	0.268	45.00	1.000	75.00	3.732
16.00	0.287	46.00	1.036	76.00	4.011
17.00	0.306	47.00	1.072	77.00	4.331
18.00	0.325	48.00	1.111	78.00	4.705
19.00	0.344	49.00	1.150	79.00	5.145
20.00	0.364	50.00	1.192	80.00	5.671
21.00	0.384	51.00	1.235	81.00	6.314
22.00	0.404	52.00	1.280	82.00	7.115
23.00	0.424	53.00	1.327	83.00	8.144
24.00	0.445	54.00	1.376	84.00	9.514
25.00	0.466	55.00	1.428	85.00	11.430
26.00	0.488	56.00	1.483	86.00	14.300
27.00	0.510	57.00	1.540	87.00	19.081
28.00	0.532	58.00	1.600	88.00	28.635
29.00	0.554	59.00	1.664	89.00	57.286
30.00	0.577	60.00	1.732	90.00	∞

Angle	Tangent	Angle	Tangent	Angle	Tangent
91.00	− 57.286	141.00	− 0.810	191.00	0.194
92.00	− 28.635	142.00	− 0.781	192.00	0.213
93.00	− 19.082	143.00	− 0.754	193.00	0.231
94.00	− 14.301	144.00	− 0.727	194.00	0.249
95.00	− 11.430	145.00	− 0.700	195.00	0.268
96.00	− 9.514	146.00	− 0.675	196.00	0.287
97.00	− 8.144	147.00	− 0.649	197.00	0.306
98.00	− 7.115	148.00	− 0.625	198.00	0.325
99.00	− 6.314	149.00	− 0.601	199.00	0.344
100.00	− 5.671	150.00	− 0.577	200.00	0.364
101.00	− 5.145	151.00	− 0.554	201.00	0.384
102.00	− 4.705	152.00	− 0.532	202.00	0.404
103.00	− 4.332	153.00	− 0.510	203.00	0.424
104.00	− 4.011	154.00	− 0.488	204.00	0.445
105.00	− 3.732	155.00	− 0.466	205.00	0.466
106.00	− 3.487	156.00	− 0.445	206.00	0.488
107.00	− 3.271	157.00	− 0.424	207.00	0.510
108.00	− 3.078	158.00	− 0.404	208.00	0.532
109.00	− 2.904	159.00	− 0.384	209.00	0.554
110.00	− 2.747	160.00	− 0.364	210.00	0.577
111.00	− 2.605	161.00	− 0.344	211.00	0.601
112.00	− 2.475	162.00	− 0.325	212.00	0.625
113.00	− 2.356	163.00	− 0.306	213.00	0.649
114.00	− 2.246	164.00	− 0.287	214.00	0.675
115.00	− 2.145	165.00	− 0.268	215.00	0.700
116.00	− 2.050	166.00	− 0.249	216.00	0.727
117.00	− 1.963	167.00	− 0.231	218.00	0.781
118.00	− 1.881	168.00	− 0.213	219.00	0.810
119.00	− 1.804	169.00	− 0.194	220.00	0.839
120.00	− 1.732	170.00	− 0.176	221.00	0.869
121.00	− 1.664	171.00	− 0.158	222.00	0.900
122.00	− 1.600	172.00	− 0.141	223.00	0.933
123.00	− 1.540	173.00	− 0.123	224.00	0.966
124.00	− 1.483	174.00	− 0.105	225.00	1.000
125.00	− 1.428	175.00	− 0.087	266.00	1.036
126.00	− 1.376	176.00	− 0.070	227.00	1.072
127.00	− 1.327	177.00	− 0.052	228.00	1.111
128.00	− 1.280	178.00	− 0.035	229.00	1.150
129.00	− 1.235	179.00	− 0.017	230.00	1.192
130.00	− 1.192	180.00	− 0.000	231.00	1.235
131.00	− 1.150	181.00	0.017	232.00	1.280
132.00	− 1.111	182.00	0.035	233.00	1.327
133.00	− 1.072	183.00	0.052	234.00	1.376
134.00	− 1.036	184.00	0.070	235.00	1.428
135.00	− 1.000	185.00	0.087	236.00	1.483
136.00	− 0.966	186.00	0.105	237.00	1.540
137.00	− 0.933	187.00	0.123	238.00	1.600
138.00	− 0.900	188.00	0.141	239.00	1.664
139.00	− 0.869	189.00	0.158	240.00	1.732
140.00	− 0.839	190.00	0.176	241.00	1.804

Angle	Tangent	Angle	Tangent	Angle	Tangent
242.00	1.881	282.00	− 4.705	322.00	− 0.781
243.00	1.963	283.00	− 4.332	323.00	− 0.754
244.00	2.050	284.00	− 4.011	324.00	− 0.727
245.00	2.144	285.00	− 3.732	325.00	− 0.700
246.00	2.246	286.00	− 3.487	326.00	− 0.675
247.00	2.356	287.00	− 3.271	327.00	− 0.649
248.00	2.475	288.00	− 3.078	328.00	− 0.625
249.00	2.605	289.00	− 2.904	329.00	− 0.601
250.00	2.747	290.00	− 2.748	330.00	− 0.577
251.00	2.904	291.00	− 2.605	331.00	− 0.554
252.00	3.078	292.00	− 2.475	332.00	− 0.532
253.00	3.271	293.00	− 2.356	333.00	− 0.510
254.00	3.487	294.00	− 2.246	334.00	− 0.488
255.00	3.732	295.00	− 2.145	335.00	− 0.466
256.00	4.011	296.00	− 2.050	336.00	− 0.445
257.00	4.331	297.00	− 1.963	337.00	− 0.424
258.00	4.705	298.00	− 1.881	338.00	− 0.404
259.00	5.144	299.00	− 1.804	339.00	− 0.384
260.00	5.671	300.00	− 1.732	340.00	− 0.364
261.00	6.314	301.00	− 1.664	341.00	− 0.344
262.00	7.115	302.00	− 1.600	342.00	− 0.325
263.00	8.144	303.00	− 1.540	343.00	− 0.306
264.00	9.514	304.00	− 1.483	344.00	− 0.287
265.00	11.430	305.00	− 1.428	345.00	− 0.268
266.00	14.300	306.00	− 1.376	346.00	− 0.249
267.00	19.080	307.00	− 1.327	347.00	− 0.231
268.00	28.635	308.00	− 1.280	348.00	− 0.213
269.00	57.286	309.00	− 1.235	349.00	− 0.194
270.00	788935.938	310.00	− 1.192	350.00	− 0.176
271.00	− 57.286	311.00	− 1.150	351.00	− 0.158
272.00	− 28.635	312.00	− 1.111	352.00	− 0.141
273.00	− 19.082	313.00	− 1.072	353.00	− 0.123
274.00	− 14.301	314.00	− 1.036	354.00	− 0.105
275.00	− 11.431	315.00	− 1.000	355.00	− 0.087
276.00	− 9.515	316.00	− 0.966	356.00	− 0.070
277.00	8.145	317.00	0.933	357.00	0.052
278.00	− 7.116	318.00	− 0.900	358.00	− 0.035
279.00	− 6.314	319.00	− 0.869	359.00	− 0.017
280.00	− 5.671	320.00	− 0.839	360.00	− 0.000
281.00	− 5.145	321.00	− 0.810		

TABLE OF
TREE DENSITIES

This chart describes the sun-blocking ability of various trees, which is expressed in the last two columns as percentages of visible radiation blocked by a species in full foliage.

Scientific Name	Common Name	Density	Range
Acer ginnala	Amur Maple	91	90-92
Acer platanoides	Norway Maple	90	85-94
Acer rubrum	Red Maple	83	78-92
Acer saccharinum	Silver Maple	79	72-86
Acer saccharum	Sugar Maple	84	73-97
Aesculus hippocastum	Common Horse Chestnut	85	73-91
Alnus glutinosa	European Alder	83	81-85
Amelanchier canadensis	Serviceberry	77	75-80
Betula pendula	European White Birch	81	76-86
Carya glabra	Pignut Hickory	86	82-90
Carya ovata	Shagbark Hickory	77	72-85
Catalpa speciosa	Western Catalpa	76	70-82
Cercidiphyllum japonicum	Katsura Tree	78	71-82
Corylus Colurna	Turkish Hazelnut	80	70-90
Fagus sylvatica	European Beech	88	85-93
Fraxinus pennsylvanica	Green Ash, Red Ash	80	71-90
Ginkgo biloba	Ginkgo, Maidenhair	78	75-82
Gleditsia triacanthos	Honey Locust	62	49-75
Juglans cinerea	Butternut	75	69-80
Larix decidua	European Larch	73	58-88

Scientific Name	Common Name	Density	Range
Picea pungens	Colorado Spruce	80	72-87
Pinus Strobus	White Pine	72	70-75
Populus deltoides	Cottonwood	85	80-90
Populus nigra	Lombardy Poplar	86	81-91
Populus tremuloides	Quaking Aspen	69	67-71
Pyrus communis	Common Pear	80	77-87
Quercus alba	White Oak	75	62-87
Quercus robur	English Oak	81	77-87
Quercus rubra	Northern Red Oak	81	77-88
Salix alba	White Willow, Golden Willow	84	71-93
Sophora japonica	Japanese Pagoda Tree	78	75-82
Tilia americana	Basswood	88	86-94
Tilia cordata	Small-leaved European Linden	83	73-88
Tilia tomentosa	Silver Linden	90	88-92
Zelkova serrata	Japanese Zelkova	76	70-81

Technical Note:

The above table shows the comparative densities of some trees commonly found in North America. These are visual densities or overall occlusion, and do not represent density of specific spectra, since foliage varies in its transmission depending on light wavelength. Values may be prorated to determine exact radiant heat gain based on percentage stem material vs. percentage leaf material. For further information, contact Prof. Schiler, Department of Architecture, Cornell University.

Special thanks are due to Cornell University, Program of Computer Graphics, Department of Architecture, and Graduate School, and to Curt Westergaard, graduate student in Landscape Architecture.

LISTS OF PLANTS ACCORDING TO SIZE AND FORM

TALL DECIDUOUS TREES (OVER THIRTY-FIVE FEET)

Name	Hardiness Zones	Growth Rate	Comments
Acer macrophyllum (big-leafed maple, California maple)	3, 4, 5, 6, 7	Variable	Globe-shaped. Chloride-tolerant. Yellow and orange fall foliage.
Acer platanoides (Norway maple)	3, 4, 5, 6, 7, 8, 9	Medium	Columnar- or globe-shaped. Grows in cities. Low maintenance. Yellow fall foliage.
Acer rubrum (red maple, scarlet maple, swamp maple)	3, 4, 5, 6, 7, 8	Fast	Globe-shaped. Sensitive to salt, nitrous oxide. Tolerant of sulfur dioxide, ozone. Red or yellow fall foliage.
Acer saccharinum (silver maple, soft maple)	3, 4, 5, 6, 7, 8	Fast	Pendulous branches. Red and yellow fall foliage. Source of commercial wood.
Acer saccharum (sugar maple, rock maple)	3, 4, 5, 6, 7, 8	Fast	Columnar- or globe-shaped. Sensitive to salt, nitrous oxide. Tolerant of sulfur dioxide, ozone. Must remove dead wood. Good fall color.
Aesculus X carnea cv. 'Briottii' (ruby horse chestnut)	4, 5, 6	Slow	Oval-shaped. Salt-tolerant. Must remove dead fruit and flowers. Susceptible to mildew. Red blossoms, horse chestnuts.

Betula papyrifera (canoe birch, paper birch, white birch)	2, 3, 4	Medium	Columnar-shaped. Needs dark night (i.e., won't tolerate electric night lights). Tolerant of salt, chloride. Sensitive to sulfur dioxide, 2-4-D. Must be sprayed. Resistant to birch borer. White bark.
Betula pendula (European white birch)	3, 4, 5, 6, 7, 8, 9, 10	Fast	Weeping. Prefers medium shade. Tolerant of salt, ozone, chloride. Sensitive to sulfur dioxide, 2-4-D. Subject to borers.
Bursera simaruba (gumbo-limbo, West Indian birch)	9, 10	Medium	Red, peeling bark. Good shade tree.
Carya ovata (shagbark hickory)	to zone 5	Slow	Oval-shaped. Hard wood. Salt-tolerant. Yellow fall foliage.
Castanea mollissima (Chinese chestnut)	to zone 5	Medium	Low, oval-shaped. Medium shade. Resistant to chestnut blight. Yellow flowers.
Cercidiphyllum japonicum (katsura tree)	5, 6, 7, 8, 9	Fast	Oval-shaped. Disease-free. Distinctive foliage.
Cladrastis lutea (American yellowwood)	4, 5, 6, 7, 8, 9	Medium	Globe-shaped. Sensitive to 2-4-D. Needs spray against oyster scale. Weak wood. White blossoms.
Cornus Nuttallii (Pacific dogwood, mountain dogwood)	6, 7, 8, 9	Medium	Globe-shaped, horizontal branching. Sensitive to 2-4-D. Bright red fruit, flowers.
Fagus sylvatica (European beech)	4, 5, 6, 7, 8	Slow	Globe-shaped. Needs full sun. Sensitive to fluoride. Susceptible to beech bark disease. Bronze fall foliage.
Fraxinus pennsylvanica (green ash)	3, 4, 5, 6, 7, 8, 9	Fast	Oval-shaped. Tolerant of sulfur dioxide, 2-4-D. Sensitive to fluoride, ozone. Weak wood. Yellow fall color.
Fraxinus velutina var. *glabra* (Modesto ash, Arizona ash)	5, 6, 7	Fast	Tolerant of fluorine, 2-4-D.
Ginkgo biloba (ginkgo, maidenhair tree)	5, 6, 7, 8, 9, 10	Slow	Columnar. Thrives in city. Tolerant of sulfur dioxide. Sensitive to nitrous oxide, ozone. No diseases. Yellow fall foliage. Female produces obnoxious, smelly fruit.
Gleditsia triacanthos var. *inermis* (thornless honey locust)	5, 6, 7, 8, 9	Fast	Low, globe-shaped. Grows in cities. Sensitive to ozone. Must remove pods, needs some spraying. Strong wood. Pest-resistant. Yellow fall foliage.

Jacaranda mimosifolia (green ebony)	10	Medium	Globe-shaped. Sensitive to salt. Blue, showy flowers. Fernlike leaves.
Koelreuteria paniculata (golden-rain tree, varnish tree)	5, 6, 7, 8, 9, 10	Medium	Globe- or columnar-shaped. Needs full sun. Grows in cities. Tolerant of salt. Low maintenance. Pest-free. Yellow flowers, fruit.
Larix decidua (European larch)	to zone 3	Fast	Pyramidal-shaped. Sensitive to nitrous oxide, chloride, ozone. Tolerant of PAN,* sulfur dioxide. Susceptible to insects. Yellow fall foliage.
Liquidambar Styraciflua (sweet gum)	5, 6, 7, 8, 9, 10	Medium	Pyramidal-shaped. Sensitive to ozone, chloride. Tolerant of 2-4-D. Needs no special maintenance. Pest-resistant. Good fall color.
Liriodendron Tulipifera (tulip tree)	4, 5, 6, 7, 8, 9	Fast	Oval-shaped. Needs sun. Sensitive to ozone, PAN, smog. Tolerant of sulfur dioxide. Weak wood. Resistant to gypsy moth. Yellow flowers, yellow fall foliage.
Magnolia heptapeta (Yulan magnolia)	4, 5, 6, 7, 8	Medium	Pyramidal-shaped. Prefers medium shade. White fragrant flowers.
Morus alba (white mulberry)	to zone 4	Medium	Globe-shaped. Sensitive to salt, ozone.
Nyssa sylvatica (black tupelo, black gum, sour gum, pepperidge)	5, 6, 7, 8, 9	Slow	Pyramidal-shaped. Tolerant of sulfur dioxide. Sensitive to chloride. Low maintenance. No pests. Good fall foliage.
Paulownia tomentosa (princess tree, royal paulownia, karri tree)	7, 8, 9, 10	Medium	Globe-shaped. Medium shade. Sensitive to fluoride. Lavender flowers.
Pistacia chinensis (Chinese pistachio)	6, 7, 8, 9, 10	Slow	Flowers, red fall foliage.
Platanus X acerifolia (London plane tree)	5, 6, 7, 8, 9	Fast	Globe-shaped. Needs sun. Grows in cities. Sensitive to 2-4-D. Tolerant of fluorine. Low maintenance. Resistance to anthracnose. Fruit.
Platanus occidentalis (eastern sycamore)	4, 5, 6, 7, 8, 9	Fast	Globe-shaped. Tolerant of salt, sulfur dioxide. Sensitive to ozone. Spray twice annually. Susceptible to anthracnose.
Platanus racemosa (California plane tree)	10	Fast	Globe-shaped. Sensitive to ozone. Tolerant of fluoride. Spray twice annually. Susceptible to anthracnose.

PAN refers to peroxyacetyl nitrate.

Populus alba cv. 'Pyramidalis,' also known as *Populus bolleana* (Bolleana poplar)	to zone 4	Fast	Columnar-shaped. Roots likely to stop drains or cause heaving of sidewalks.
Pyrus Calleryana (Callery pear)	6, 7, 8, 9, 10	Medium	Oval-shaped. Pollution-resistant. Good street tree. Resistant to fire blight. Good fall color.
Quercus alba (white oak)	4, 5, 6, 7, 8, 9, 10	Slow	Globe-shaped with horizontal branches. Tolerant of ozone. Sensitive to salt. Low maintenance. Susceptible to scale.
Quercus coccinea (scarlet oak)	4, 5, 6, 7, 8	Slow	Globe-shaped. Needs full sun. Grows in cities. Good fall color.
Quercus macrocarpa (mossy-cup oak, bur oak)	4, 5, 6, 7, 8, 9	Slow	Globe-shaped. Sensitive to salt.
Quercus nigra (water oak)	6, 7, 8, 9, 10	Slow	Globe-shaped.
Quercus palustris (pin oak, Spanish oak)	5, 6, 7, 8, 9, 10	Slow	Pyramidal-shaped. Needs full sun. Sensitive to salt, ozone. Susceptible to horned oak gall. Red fall foliage.
Quercus phellos (willow oak)	6, 7, 8, 9	Medium	Pyramidal-shaped. Grows in cities. Low maintenance. No pests. Yellow fall foliage.
Quercus rubra (northern oak)	5, 6, 7, 8	Slow	Globe-shaped. Grows in cities. Susceptible to oak wilt. Good fall color.
Quercus virginiana (live oak, southern live oak)	7, 8, 9, 10	Medium	Upright. Needs full sun. Tolerates salt spray. Sensitive to ozone. Low maintenance.
Robinia Pseudoacacia (black locust, false acacia, yellow locust)	to zone 3	Fast	Columnar-shaped. Tolerant of sulfur dioxide, salt, fluoride. Sensitive to ozone, nitrous oxide. Needs treatment for borers. Weak wood. White flowers.
Salix alba (golden weeping willow)	to zone 2	Fast	Weeping. Tolerant of salt. Sensitive to sulfur dioxide, ozone. Weak wood. Yellow fall color.
Sophora japonica (Japanese pagoda tree, Chinese scholar tree)	5, 6, 7, 8, 9, 10	Medium	Globe-shaped. Grows in cities. Resistant to salt. Needs pruning to maintain shape. Susceptible to twig blight. Flowers.
Sorbus Aucuparia (European mountain ash, rowan tree)	3, 4, 5, 6, 7, 8	Slow	High, globe-shaped. Tolerant of fluoride, ozone. Sensitive to sulfur dioxide. Susceptible to borers, fire blight. White flowers, orange-red fruit.

Stewartia Pseudocamellia (Japanese stewartia)	8, 9, 10	Fast	Oval-shaped. Needs sun to medium shade.
Taxodium distichum (swamp cypress)	5, 6, 7, 8, 9, 10	Medium	Columnar-shaped. Needs sun. Reddish brown fall foliage.
Tilia americana (American linden, basswood)	3, 4, 5, 6, 7, 8	Medium	Pyramidal. Sensitive to salt, ozone, nitrous oxide. Tolerant of fluoride. Susceptible to Japanese beetle. Fragrant blooms.
Tilia cordata (little leaf linden)	4, 5, 6, 7, 8	Medium	Pyramidal-shaped. Grows in cities. Tolerant of fluoride. Must be sprayed and pruned. Susceptible to Japanese beetle. Fragrant blooms.
Tilia tomentosa (silver linden)	4, 5, 6, 7, 8	Medium	Pyramidal-shaped. Fragrant blooms.
Ulmus parvifolia (Chinese elm)	6, 7, 8	Fast	Globe-shaped. Tolerates salt. Sensitive to ozone, sulfur dioxide, 2-4-D. Less susceptible to Dutch elm disease.
Ulmus procera (English elm)	to zone 6	Fast	Propagated by suckers. Popular tree in Northeast.
Zelkova serrata (Japanese zelkova)	5, 6, 7, 8, 9, 10	Medium	Globe-shaped. Grows in cities. Susceptible to Dutch elm disease, beetles. Yellow fall foliage.

SHORT DECIDUOUS TREES
(UNDER THIRTY-FIVE FEET)

Name	Hardiness Zones	Growth Rate	Comments
Acer Ginnala (Amur maple)	3, 4, 5, 6, 7, 8	Slow	Globe-shaped. Sensitive to salt. Good fall color.
Acer palmatum (Japanese maple)	6, 7, 8, 9	Slow	Low, globe-shaped. Prefers medium shade. Sensitive to nitrous oxide, salt. No special maintenance required. Red foliage on some cultivars.
Albizia Julibrissin (silk tree, mimosa tree)	7, 8, 9, 10	Fast	Horizontal branching. Needs sun. Grows in cities. Sensitive to salt.
Amelanchier canadensis (downy serviceberry)	5, 6, 7, 8	Medium	Globe-shaped. Grows in shade. Salt sensitive. White blossoms, red fall foliage.
Amelanchier X grandiflora (apple serviceberry)	3, 4, 5, 6, 7, 8	Medium	Globe-shaped. Grows in shade. Sensitive to salt. Red flowers.

Amelanchier canadensis (shadblow, serviceberry)	to zone 4	Medium	Showy, early spring bloom. Edible fruit.
Bauhinia variegata (Buddhist bauhinia, mountain ebony, orchid tree)	9, 10	Medium	Globe-shaped. Needs full sun. White flowers.
Cercidium floridum (palo verde)	7, 8, 9, 10	Medium	Globe-shaped. Yellow flowers.
Cercis canadensis (eastern redbud)	5, 6, 7, 8, 9	Medium	Globe-shaped. Grows in shade. Sensitive to 2-4-D. Pink flowers. Colored fall foliage.
Chilopsis linearis (desert willow)	8, 9, 10	Medium	Prefers full sun. May need watering. White-to-pink fragrant flowers.
Chionanthus virginicus (fringe tree)	5, 6, 7, 8, 9	Medium	Globe-shaped. Prefers full sun. White flowers, yellow fall color.
Cornus florida (flowering dogwood)	5, 6, 7, 8	Medium	Globe-shaped, horizontal branching. Grows in shade. Tolerant of sulfur dioxide. Sensitive to 2-4-D. Susceptible to dogwood borer. Flowers, bright-red fruit.
Cornus Kousa (Chinese dogwood)	5, 6, 7, 8, 9	Medium	Globe-shaped. Sensitive to 2-4-D. Flowers, fruit, distinctive foliage.
Crataegus laevigata, also known as *Crataegus Oxycantha* (English hawthorn)	5, 6, 7, 8	Slow	Low, globe-shaped. Sensitive to salt. Flowers, distinctive foliage.
Crataegus mollis (downy hawthorn)	4, 5	Medium	Low, globe-shaped. Sensitive to salt. White flowers, red fruit, useful for jellies.
Crataegus Phaenopyrum (Washington hawthorn)	5, 6, 7, 8	Medium	Low, globe-shaped. Grows in cities. Sensitive to salt. Weak wood. Susceptible to borers, scale. White flowers, red fruit.
Delonix regia (poinciana regia poinciana tree, royal flame)	10	Medium	Weeping, scarlet, showy flowers.
Elaeagnus angustifolia (Russian olive, oleaster, silver berry)	3, 4, 5, 6, 7, 8, 9	Fast	Irregular-shape. Prefers full sun. Tolerant of fluoride, chloride. Grows in cities. Pest-free. Distinctive foliage.
Halesia carolina (Carolina silverbell, wild olive, shittim wood, opposum wood)	5, 6, 7, 8, 9, 10	Medium	Globe-shaped. Flowers, attractive fruit

Koelreuteria elegans (Chinese flame tree, flame-gold)	9, 10	Medium	Globe-shaped. Needs sun. Flowers, orange seed pods.
Laburnum X Watereri, also known as *Laburnum X Vossii* (golden chain tree)	5, 6, 7, 8, 9	Fast	Globe-shaped. Medium shade. Yellow flowers.
Lagerstroemia indica (crape myrtle)	7, 8, 9	Medium to fast	Globe-shaped. Needs full sun. Needs watering. Susceptible to mildew. Flowers.
Magnolia X Loebneri cv. 'Merrill' (Merrill magnolia)	4, 5, 6, 7, 8	Medium	Pyramidal-shaped. Prefers medium shade. White flowers.
Magnolia X Soulangiana (saucer magnolia)	5, 6, 7, 8, 9, 10	Medium	Globe-shaped. Prefers full shade. Grows in cities. Requires selective pruning. Susceptible to magnolia scale. Attractive flowers.
Magnolia stellata (star magnolia)	5, 6, 7, 8, 9, 10	Medium	Globe-shaped. Prefers medium shade. Grows in cities. Requires selective pruning. Susceptible to borers, scale. Fragrant flowers.
Malus X atrosanguinea (Carmine crab apple)	4, 5, 6, 7, 8	Medium	Globe-shaped. Semisensitive to salt. Flowers, fruit.
Malus baccata (Siberian crab apple)	2, 3, 4, 5, 6, 7	Medium	Globe-shaped. Semisensitive to salt. Flowers, fruit.
Malus floribunda (showy crab apple)	5, 6, 7, 8	Medium	Low, globe-shaped. Semisensitive to salt. Susceptible to borers, scale. Flowers, fruit.
Malus ioensis (Prairie crab apple, wild crab apple)	2, 3, 4, 5, 6, 7, 8	Medium	Globe-shaped. Semisensitive to salt. Susceptible to borers, scale. Flowers, fruit.
Malus X purpurea (purple crab apple)	4, 5, 6, 7, 8	Medium	Globe-shaped. Semisensitive to salt. Susceptible to borers, scale. Flowers, fruit.
Morus alba (white mulberry)	to zone 4	Medium	Globe-shaped. Sensitive to salt.
Oxydendrum arboreum (sorrel tree, sourwood)	5, 6, 7, 8, 9	Slow	Globe-shaped. Takes sun or shade. Grows in cities. Tolerant of sulfur dioxide. Low maintenance. Flowers, distinctive foliage.
Parkinsonia aculeata (Jerusalem thorn)	10	Medium	Yellow color. Yellow flowers.
Phellodendron amurense (Amur cork tree)	4, 5, 6, 7	Fast	Globe-shaped. Grows in cities. Insect-free. Yellow fall foliage.

Prosopis glandulosa (honey mesquite)	7, 8, 9	Medium	Weeping. Susceptible to boring mollusk. Flowers.
Prunus X *blireiana* (blireiana plum, purple leaf plum)	5, 6, 7, 8, 9	Fast	Low, globe-shaped. White flowers, purple leaves.
Prunus cerasifera (cherry plum)	4, 5, 6	Fast	Low, globe-shaped. Tolerant of fluoride. Light-pink flowers, fruit.
Prunus dulcis (almond tree)	7, 8, 9	Fast	Low, globe-shaped. Sensitive to salt. White flowers. Many cultivars grown commercially in California.
Prunus serrulata (Oriental cherry)	6, 7, 8	Fast	Low, globe-shaped. Tolerant of fluoride. Flowers.
Prunus subhirtella (Higan cherry)	6, 7, 8, 9	Fast	Low, globe-shaped. Semisensitive to fluorine. Sensitive to smog. Flowers.
Prunus virginiana (chokecherry)	2, 3, 4, 5, 6, 7, 8	Fast	Low, globe-shaped. Tolerant of salt.
Prunus yedoensis (Yoshino cherry, Japanese flowering cherry)	6, 7, 8, 9	Fast	Low, globe-shaped. Semisensitive to fluoride. Flowers.
Pyrus communis (pear tree)	to zone 5	Medium	Oval-shaped. Sensitive to sulfur dioxide, nitrous oxide. Needs spraying. Subject to scale and fire blight. White flowers.
Salix babylonica (Babylon weepng willow)	to zone 5	Fast	Weeping. Full sun. Tolerant of salt. Sensitive to sulfur dioxide, ozone. Weak wood. Needs pruning. Yellow fall foliage.
Sapium sebiferum (Chinese tallow tree)	to zone 4	Medium	Good street tree.
Sorbus americana (American mountain ash, dogberry, missey-moosey)	to zone 2	Medium to slow	Shrubby. Hardy. Thrives in dry soils.
Sorbus decora (showy mountain ash)	2, 3, 4, 5, 6	Fast	Globe-shaped. Tolerant of salt.
Syringa reticulata var. *japonica* (Japanese tree lilac)	4, 5, 6, 7, 8	Medium	Globe-shaped. Prefers full sun. Tolerant of salt. Fruit, flowers.
Ulmus pumila (dwarf elm, Siberian elm)	3, 4, 5, 6, 7, 8	Fast	Globe-shaped. Sensitive to ozone, sulfur dioxide, 2-4-D. Tolerates salt. Weak wood. Less susceptible to Dutc elm disease.

EVERGREEN TREES OVER THIRTY-FIVE FEET

Name	Hardiness Zones	Growth Rate	Comments
Abies balsamea (balsam fir)	to zone 3	Medium	Does not thrive where growing season is hot or where air is polluted.
Abies concolor (white fir, concolor fir)	4, 5, 6, 7, 8, 9	Fast	Pyramidal-shaped. Semisensitive to ozone, sulfur dioxide. Grows in cities.
Araucaria heterophylla (Norfolk Island pine)	10	Medium	Pyramidal-shaped.
Calocedrus decurrens, also known as *Libocedrus decurrens* (California incense cedar)	6, 7, 8, 9, 10	Slow	Semisensitive to ozone.
Casuarina equisetifolia (horsetail tree, South Sea ironwood)	9, 10	Fast	Pyramidal-shaped. Resistant to salt.
Cedrus atlantica v. 'Glauca' (blue atlas cedar)	to zone 4	Medium	Pyramidal-shaped. Low maintenance. Stark effect.
Cedrus Deodara (deodar cedar)	7, 8	Slow to Medium	Pyramidal-shaped. Low maintenance.
Ceratonia Siliqua (carob tree)	10	Slow	Globe-shaped. Low maintenance. Disease-free.
Chamaecyparis Lawsoniana (Lawson cypress, Port Orford cedar)	6, 7	Fast	Pyramidal-shaped. Prefers full sun. Sensitive to salt. Prized for many ornamental forms.
Cryptomeria japonica (Japanese cedar)	7, 8	Fast	Pyramidal-shaped. Thrives in fertile, moist soil and clean air.
Cupressus arizonica (Arizona cypress)	6, 7, 8, 9	Medium to Slow	Pyramidal-shaped.
Cupressus sempervirens (Italian cypress)	8, 9	Medium to Slow	Pyramidal-shaped.
Eucalyptus polyanthemos (red box gum, silver dollar tree, Australian beech)	9, 10	Fast	Globe-shaped.
Eucalyptus rudis (desert gum)	9, 10	Fast	Globe-shaped.

Ficus benjamina (weeping fig, Java fig, weeping Chinese banyan, Benjamin fig, small-leafed rubber plant)	8, 9, 10	Medium	Weeping. Prefers full sun. Pest-resistant. Fruit.
Grevillea robusta (silk oak)	10	Fast	Columnar-shaped. Thrives in full sun or full shade. Decorative street tree. Weak wood. Pest-resistant. Orange flowers.
Magnolia grandiflora (Southern magnolia, bull bay)	7, 8, 9, 10	Medium	Pyramidal-shaped. Prefers full sun. Grows in cities. Low maintenance. Flowers, fruit, distinctive foliage.
Picea Abies cultivars, also known as *Picea excelsa* (Norway spruce)	3, 4, 5, 6	Fast	Pyramidal-shaped. Prefers medium shade. Sensitive to salt. Susceptible to spruce gall aphids, mites. Cones.
Picea glauca cv. 'Densata' (Black Hills spruce, white spruce)	3, 4, 5	Slow	Pyramidal with drooping branchlets. Tolerant of PAN, sulfur dioxide, salt. Susceptible to red spider mites, aphids.
Picea pungens (Colorado blue spruce)	3, 4, 5, 6	Medium	Pyramidal-shaped. Tolerant of ozone, PAN. Sensitive to nitrous oxide. Susceptible to mites, aphids, canker.
Pinus banksiana (jackpine, gray pine, scrub pine)	2, 3, 4, 5, 6, 7, 8	Medium	Prefers full sun. Irregular-shaped. Sensitive to ozone. Tolerant of sulfur.
Pinus canariensis (Canary Island pine)	8, 9, 10	Fast	Pyramidal-shaped.
Pinus caribaea (slash pine, swamp pine, Cuban pine)	9, 10	Fast	Pyramidal-shaped.
Pinus nigra subsp. *Laricio* (black pine, Austrian pine)	4, 5, 6, 7, 8	Medium	Pyramidal-shaped. Prefers full sun. Grows in cities. Sensitive to salt, sulfur dioxide. Water heavily at first. Susceptible to pine needle scale.
Pinus ponderosa var. *scopulorium* (Rocky Mountain yellow pine)	6, 7, 8, 9	Medium	Pyramidal-shaped. Prefers full sun. Sensitive to sulfur dioxide, fluoride, ozone.
Pinus resinosa (red pine, Norway pine)	2, 3, 4, 5, 6, 7, 8	Medium	Pyramidal-shaped. Needs full sun. Tolerant of ozone. Susceptible to pine needle scale.
Pinus Strobus (eastern white pine)	3, 4, 5, 6, 7	Fast	Pyramidal-shaped with horizontal branching. Prefers full sun to medium shade. Sensitive to salt, ozone, sodium dioxide. Water heavily at first. Susceptible to white pine weevil.

Name	Hardiness Zones	Growth Rate	Comments
Pinus sylvestris (Scotch pine, Scots pine)	3, 4, 5, 6	Fast	Pyramidal-shaped. Prefers full sun. Sensitive to salt, ozone. Weak wood. Susceptible to pine needle scale. Red bark.
Pinus Thunbergiana (Japanese black pine)	to zone 5	Slow	Irregular-shaped. Good seashore evergreen. Low maintenance.
Pseudotsuga Menziesii, also known as *Pseudotsuga taxifolia, Pseudotsuga Douglasii* (Douglas fir)	to zone 4	Fast	Pyramidal-shaped. Prefers full sun. Tolerant of PAN, ozone. Sensitive to sulfur dioxide. Low maintenance. Weak wood. Cones.
Quercus agrifolia (California live oak, California field oak)	9	Slow to Medium	Horizontal branching. Sensitive to ozone. Prefers semiarid conditions.
Quercus Suber (cork oak)	8, 9, 10	Medium	Globe-shaped. Thick bark offers commercial cork. Sensitive to ozone.
Quercus virginiana (live oak, southern live oak)	7, 8, 9, 10	Rapid	Rounded in form. Prefers full sun. Sensitive to ozone. Tolerates salt spray. Low maintenance. Excellent shade or street tree.
Tsuga canadensis (Canadian hemlock)	3, 4, 5, 6, 7, 8	Medium	Pyramidal-shaped. Prefers medium shade. Does not thrive in city. Sensitive to salt. Must be watered. Susceptible to spruce mites.
Ulmus parvifolia, also known as *Ulmus sempervirens* (Chinese evergreen elm)	6, 7, 8	Fast	Globe-shaped. Sensitive ozone, sulfur dioxide, 2-4-D. Tolerant of salt. Less susceptible to Dutch elm disease.

EVERGREEN TREES UNDER THIRTY-FIVE FEET

Name	Hardiness Zones	Growth Rate	Comments
Agonis flexuosa (willow myrtle)	9, 10	Medium	White flowers.
Bauhinia Blakeana (Hong Kong orchid tree)	9, 10	Medium	Columnar-shaped. Showy pink flowers.
Brassaia actinophylla, also known as *Schefflera actinophylla* (Australia umbrella tree, Queensland umbrella tree, octopus tree)	9, 10	Medium	Prefers full sun. Red flowers.

Callistemon viminalis (weeping bottlebrush)	9, 10	Medium	Weeping habit. Needs pruning. Red flowers.
Cephalotaxus Harringtonia, also known as *Cephalotaxus drupacea* (Japanese plum yew, Harrington plum yew)	to zone 6	Medium	Male cones in clusters.
Cinnamomum Camphora (camphor tree)	8, 9, 10	Medium	Good for row plantings along street. Insect-resistant. Yellow flowers.
Citrus species (orange, lemon, lime, and grapefruit trees)	10	Variable	Globe-shaped. Prefers full sun. Sensitive to ozone, nitrous oxide, fluoride. Tolerant of sulfur dioxide. Fruit, fragrant flowers.
Litchi chinensis (lychee, litchi nut)	10	Medium	Requires abundant moisture. Edible fresh or dried fruit.
Magnolia virginiana also known as *Magnolia glauca* (sweet bay)	5, 6, 7, 8, 9	Slow to Medium	Globe-shaped. Grows in shade. Weak wood. White flowers.
Manilkara Zapota, also known as *Achras sapota* (saspodilla, nispero, chicozapote)	10	Medium	Attractive ornamental. Produces chicle original base for chewing gum. Fruit.
Olea europaea (common olive)	9, 10	Slow	Globe-shaped. Prefers full sun. Low maintenance. Fruit.
Picea abies cultivars (Norway spruce)	2, 3, 4, 5, 6	Fast	Pyramidal-shaped. Prefers medium shade. Semisensitive to salt. Susceptible to spruce gall aphids, mites.
Pinus halepensis (Aleppo pine)	8, 9, 10	Medium	Pyramidal-shaped. Resistant to salt. Yields turpentine.
Pittosporum phillyraeoides (weeping pittosporum, narrow-leafed pittosporum)	9, 10	Medium	Weeping. Sensitive to fluoride, nitrous oxide. Flowers.
Pittosporum rhombifolium (diamond leaf pittosporum, Queensland pittosporum)	9, 10	Medium	Oval-shaped. Sensitive to nitrous oxide, fluoride. Yellow fruits, ornamental flowers.
Podocarpus macrophyllus (Yew podocarpus, southern yew, Japanese yew)	8, 9, 10	Medium	Grows in shade.

Psidium littorale var. *longipes* (strawberry guava)	10	Medium	Sensitive to salt. White flowers, fruit.
Pyrus Kawakamii (evergreen pear)	9, 10	Medium	Semisensitive to salt. Flowers, distinctive foliage.
Schinus terebinthifolius (Brazilian pepper tree)	10	Fast	Weeping. Very ornamental. Much used for wreaths at Christmas. Red berries, flowers.
Sciadopitys verticillata (umbrella pine)	to zone 6	Slow	Horizontal branching, pyramidal-shaped. Prefers shade. Sensitive to pollution.
Tsuga canadensis (Canada hemlock)	3, 4, 5, 6, 7, 8	Medium	Pyramidal-shaped. Prefers shade. Sensitive to salt. Does not thrive in cities.
Tsuga caroliniana (Carolina hemlock)	to zone 4	Medium	Pyramidal-shaped. Prefers shade. Dense foliage. Grows in cities. Susceptible to spruce mites.
Yucca brevifolia (Joshua tree)	5, 6, 7, 8, 9	Slow to Medium	Irregular-shaped. Requires full sun. Good drainage, sandy loam, and open exposure are preferred. Flowers.

PALM TREES OVER THIRTY-FIVE FEET

Name	Hardiness Zones	Growth Rate	Comments
Arecastrum Romanzoffianum, also known as *Cocos plumosa* (Queen palm)	9, 10	Fast	Low maintenance.
Heterospathe elata (Sagisi palm)	10	Fast	Red-brown leaves.
Veitchia Winin	10	Fast	Leaves growing nine feet long.
Washingtonia filifera (Washington palm, desert fan, petticoat palm)	9, 10	Fast	"Petticoat" of hanging leaves at trunk. Must be watered.
Washingtonia robusta (Mexican Washington palm, thread palm.	9, 10	Fast	Trunk clothed in ragged shag. Tolerant of salt. Must be watered. Vulnerable to insects.

PALM TREES UNDER THIRTY-FIVE FEET

Name	Hardiness Zones	Growth Rate	Comments
Acoelorraphe Wrightii (Everglade palm)	9, 10	Slow	Useful cluster palm for landscapes in full sun or shade, with roots in water or in dry areas of sand or limestone with a high water table.
Brahea dulcis (rock palm)	10	Slow	Leaves grow to five feet. Susceptible to palm weevil.
Chamaerops humilis (European fan palm, Mediterranean fan palm)	9, 10	Slow	One of hardier palms. Forms clumps. Tolerant of salt. Must be watered. Weak wood.
Chrysalidocarpus lutescens, also known as *Areca lutescens* (butterfly palm, yellow palm, bamboo palm, Areca palm, cane palm)	9, 10	Medium to Fast	Globe-shaped. White fragrant flowers.
Livistona chinensis (Chinese fountain palm, Chinese fan palm)	9, 10	Fast	Globe-shaped. One of hardier palms.
Phoenix reclinata (Senegal date palm)	9, 10	Medium to Slow	Useful for large hedges and screens because of attractive clustering habit. Tolerant of salt.
Phoenix Roebelenii (dwarf date palm, pigmy date palm)	9, 10	Slow	Elegant pot plant. Prefers medium shade. Tolerant of salt.
Ptychosperma Macarthurii (Macarthur palm)	10	Fast	Columnar-shaped. Prefers medium shade. Suited to small garden or tub culture. White flowers.
Rhapidophyllum hystrix (needle palm, porcupine palm, blue palmetto)	7, 8, 9, 10	Slow	Hardiest of palms, withstanding −6°F. Prefers full shade to medium sun. Must be watered.
Rhapis excelsa, also known as *Rhapis flabelliformis* (lady palm)	9, 10	Slow	Grows in clumps or hedges. Prefers full sun to medium shade.
Sabal Etonia (scrub palmetto)	9, 10	Slow	Trunk mostly subterranean. Tolerant of salt.
Sabel Palmetto (cabbage palmetto, blue palmetto)	9, 10	Slow	Tolerant of salt. Low maintenance.

| *Trachycarpus Fortunei,* also known as *Trachycarpus excelsus, Chamaerops excelsa* (windmill palm, hemp palm) | 8, 9, 10 | Slow | High, globe-shaped. Trunk covered with black, hairlike fiber. Tolerant of salt. Pest-free. White to yellow flowers. |

DECIDUOUS WINDBREAKS, HEDGES, OR BORDERS

Name	Hardiness Zones	Growth Rate	Comments
Berberis Thunbergii (Japanese barberry)	5, 6, 7, 8, 9	Fast	Grows in shade. Tolerant of 2-4-D. Should be pruned. Bright-red berries, fall color.
Calycanthus floridus (strawberry shrub, Carolina allspice)	5, 6, 7	Medium	Large, fragrant flowers.
Caragana arborescens (Siberian pea tree)	2, 3, 4, 5	Medium	Requires full sun, sandy soil. Tolerant of salt. Showy, yellow flowers.
Caryopteris species (bluebeard)	3, 4, 5, 6, 7, 8	Medium	Prefers sun. Needs pruning. Attractive flowers.
Chaenomeles species, also known as *Cydonia* (flowering quince)	4, 5, 6, 7, 8, 9	Medium	Attractive ornamental. Sensitive to salt. Needs pruning. Susceptible to fire blight, borers, scale. Flowers.
Cotoneaster divaricatus (spreading cotoneaster)	5, 6, 7, 8	Medium	Pink flowers, red fruit.
Elaeagnus angustifolia (wild olive, Russian olive, silverberry)	3, 4, 5, 6, 7, 8, 9	Fast	Prefers full sun. Tolerant of fluoride, chloride, salt. Grows in cities. Pest-free. Distinctive foliage.
Elaeagnus commutata (silverberry)	to zone 2	Medium	Fragrant flowers, fruit.
Elaeagnus multiflora, also known as *Elaeagnus longipes* (cherry elaeagnus)	to zone 5	Medium	Prefers well-drained soil and sunny location. Fragrant flowers, orange fruit.
Euonymus alata cv. 'Compacta' (dwarf winged bush, dwarf burning bush)	5, 6, 7, 8	Fast	Prefers full sun. Grows in cities. Red fall foliage.

Forsythia species (forsythia, golden bells)	5, 6, 7, 8	Fast	Requires full sun. Grows in cities. Needs pruning. Yellow flowers.
Hydrangea macrophylla, also known as *Hydrangea hortensis* (common big leaf hydrangea, house hydrangea, French hydrangea, hortensia)	6, 7, 8, 9, 10	Medium	Blooms in full sun or partial shade. Needs pruning.
Kolkwitzia amabilis (beauty bush)	6, 7, 8, 9	Medium	Needs full sun. Sensitive to salt. Flowers.
Ligustrum amurense (Amur privet)	4, 5, 6, 7, 8, 9, 10	Fast	Sensitive to salt, fluoride, nitrous oxide. Tolerant of ozone.
Ligustrum ovalifolium (California privet)	6, 7, 8, 9, 10	Fast	Sensitive to salt, fluoride, nitrous oxide.
Ligustrum vulgare (prim privet, common privet)	5, 6	Fast	Sensitive to salt, fluoride, nitrous oxide.
Lonicera species (honeysuckle)	4, 5, 6, 7, 8, 9	Fast	Prefers sun to medium shade. Tolerant of ozone, salt. Fragrant flowers.
Prunus tomentosa (Manchu or Nanking cherry)	3, 4, 5	Medium	Semisensitive to fluoride. One of earliest flowering shrubs. Susceptible to borers, blight scale. Red tasty fruit, white flowers.
Salix discolor (pussy willow)	to zone 2	Fast	Sensitive to sulfur dioxide, ozone. Tolerant of salt.
Spiraea species (spirea, bridal wreath)	5, 6, 7, 8, 9	Fast	Thrives in sun or shade. Requires plenty moisture. Sensitive to salt. White flowers.
Symphoricarpos albus var. *laevigatus,* also known as *Symphoricarpos racemosus* (snowberry)	to zone 3	Medium	Prefers full sun. Tolerant of ozone. Susceptible to disease. Ornamental fruits, pink flowers.
Symphoricarpos orbiculatus (Indian current, coralberry)	to zone 3	Medium	White flowers. Coral red fruit.
Syringa vulgaris cultivars (lilacs)	3, 4, 5, 6, 7	Medium	Prefers full sun. Tolerant of salt, 2-4-D. Sensitive to ozone. Susceptible to lilac borer. Fragrant flowers.
Tamarix parviflora (Tamarisk, salt cedar)	8, 9, 10	Medium	Prefers sun. Tolerant of salt. Pink flowers.
Vitex Agnus-castus (chaste tree, hemptree, wild pepper)	7, 8, 9, 10	Medium	Prefers sun. Aromatic shrub. Must be pruned. Lavender flowers.

| Weigela species (weigela) | 6, 7 | Medium | Thrives in sun to medium shade. Sensitive to 2-4-D. Low maintenance. Showy flowers. |

EVERGREEN WINDBREAKS, HEDGES, OR BORDERS

Name	Hardiness Zones	Growth Rate	Comments
Berberis Julianae (wintergreen barberry)	5, 6, 7, 8	Medium	Thrives in medium sun to medium shade. Sensitive to salt. Yellow flowers.
Berberis X mentorensis (Mentor barberry)	5, 6, 7, 8	Medium	Sensitive to salt. Red berries
Buxus microphylla japonica (Japanese littleleaf boxwood)	6, 7, 8, 9	Slow	Thrives in medium shade. Yellow flowers.
Buxus sempervirens (common boxwood)	6, 7, 8, 9	Slow	Grows in shade. Needs special care. Susceptible to leaf miner.
Camellia japonica (common camellia)	7, 8, 9, 10	Slow	Grows in medium shade. Sensitive to fluoride. Must be fertilized. More than 2,000 cultivars. Beautiful flowers.
Camellia Sasanqua (sasanqua camellia)	7, 8, 9, 10	Medium	Needs full sun. Sensitive to fluoride. Must be fertilized. White to red flowers.
Coccoloba Uvifera (sea grape, shore grape)	9, 10	Slow	Does best in rich, sandy soil. Tolerant of salt. Fruit and flowers.
Codiaeum, variegatum cultivars (croton)	9, 10	Medium	Grows best in full sun. Tolerant of fluoride, nitrous oxide. White flowers, bright foliage.
Cotoneaster lacteus (Parney's red clusterberry)	to zone 6	Medium	Prefers full sun.
Elaeagnus pungens (thorny elaeagnus, silverberry)	7, 8, 9, 10	Medium	Grows in shade. Silvery foliage.
Eriobotrya japonica (loquat, Japanese plum)	8, 9, 10	Medium	Sensitive to salt. Bronze foliage, flowers, fruit.
Eugenia foetida (Spanish stopper)	9, 10	Medium	Easily propagated. White flowers.
Euonymus japonica (evergreen euonymus, spindle tree)	6, 7, 8, 9	Medium	Many cultivars. Fruit, flowers.

Feijoa Sellowiana (pineapple guava)	9, 10	Medium	Needs pruning. Edible fruit.
Gardenia jasminoides (gardenia, cape jasmine)	8, 9, 10	Medium	Needs medium shade. Sensitive to fluoride, nitrous oxide. Fragrant flowers.
Hibiscus Rosa-sinensis (Chinese hibiscus, rose of China)	9, 10	Fast	Sensitive to fluoride, nitrous oxide. Flowers.
Ilex opaca cultivars (American holly)	6, 7, 8, 9	Variable	Sensitive to salt. Tolerant of ozone. Red fruit.
Ilex vomitoria (yaupon, cassina)	7, 8, 9	Medium	Stiffly branched. Dried leaves give bitter tea.
Ixora coccinea (flame-of-the-woods, jungle geranium, ixora)	9, 10	Medium	Sensitive to fluoride, nitrous oxide. Bright colored flowers, attractive foliage.
Jasminum humile cv. 'Revolutum' (Italian jasmine)	to zone 7	Fast	Needs sun. Large and fragrant flowers.
Juniperus chinensis cultivars (Chinese juniper)	4, 5, 6, 7, 8, 9, 10	Slow	Needs full sun. Tolerant of fluoride, sulfur dioxide. Susceptible to juniper scale, mites. Fruits.
Juniperus scopulorum cultivars (Rocky Mountain juniper, western red cedar)	to zone 4	Medium	Needs full sun. Tolerant of fluoride, sulfur dioxide. Susceptible to red spider mites. Fruit.
Juniperus virginiana cultivars (eastern red cedar)	to zone 3	Variable	Needs full sun. Tolerant of fluoride, sulfur dioxide. Susceptible to red spider mites. Fruit.
Kalmia latifolia (mountain laurel, calico bush)	4, 5, 6, 7, 8, 9, 10	Medium	Thrives in full shade. Tolerant of ozone. Susceptible to lace bug. Pink and white flowers.
Ligustrum japonicum cultivars (Japanese privet, wax leaf privet)	7, 8, 9, 10	Medium	Semisensitive to fluoride, nitrous oxide.
Lonicera nitida (box honeysuckle)	to zone 7	Medium	Thrives in sun to medium shade. Tolerant of ozone, salt. Flowers.
Myrtus communis cultivars (myrtle, Greek myrtle)	9, 10	Medium	Needs pruning. Berries, fragrant, white flowers.
Nerium Oleander (oleander, rose bay)	7, 8, 9, 10	Fast	Needs full sun. Sensitive to fluoride, nitrous oxide. Needs some watering. All plant parts are very poisonous. Many colors, flowers.

Opuntia littoralis (prickly pear, tuna cactus)	6, 7, 8, 9, 10	Medium	Needs sun. Easily propagated from cuttings placed directly in sandy, well-drained soil. Requires little water. Showy flowers.
Osmanthus heterophyllus, also known as *Osmanthus ilicifolius* (holly osmanthus, holly olive, false holly)	7, 8, 9, 10	Slow to Medium	Thrives in medium shade.
Photinia serrulata (Chinese photinia)	7, 8, 9, 10	Medium	Needs sun. Bronze foliage, red fruit.
Pieris japonica (Japanese andromeda, lily-of-the-valley bush)	6, 7, 8, 9	Slow	Needs medium shade. White flowers.
Pittosporum Tobira (Japanese pittosporum)	8, 9, 10	Medium	Semisensitive to fluoride, nitrous oxide. Susceptible to lace bug, leaf spot. Fragrant flowers. Useful for seaside plantings.
Prunus caroliniana (Carolina cherry laurel, wild orange, mock orange)	7, 8, 9, 10	Medium	Semisensitive to fluoride. Attractive foliage.
Prunus Laurocerasus cultivars (cherry laurel, English laurel)	7, 8, 9	variable	Thrives in medium shade. Susceptible to blight, borer, scale. Orange fruit.
Pyracantha coccinea (fire thorn)	6, 7, 8, 9, 10	Medium	Tolerant of salt. Susceptible to borers, scale. Berries, flowers.
Taxus cuspidata (Japanese yew)	5, 6, 7, 8, 9	Slow	Thrives in sun or shade. Semisensitive to 2-4-D. Susceptible to taxus weevil. Many cultivars.
Taxus X media cultivars (yew)	to zone 5	Slow	Branches olive green and spreading. Otherwise similar to *T. cuspidata.*
Thevetia peruviana, also known as *Thevetia nereifolia* (yellow oleander, bestill tree)	9, 10	Medium	Thrives in rich, sandy soil. Yellow fragrant flowers.
Thuja occidentalis (American arborvitae, Douglas arborvitae, white cedar)	3, 4, 5, 6, 7, 8, 9	Medium	Tolerant of sulfur dioxide, ozone, chloride. Sensitive to ethylene. Susceptible to leaf miner, bagworm. Gold fall foliage.
Viburnum odoratissimum (sweet viburnum)	8, 9, 10	Variable	White, fragrant flowers.
Viburnum rhytidophyllum (leatherleaf viburnum)	6, 7, 8	Slow	Unusual foliage. Fruits.

Name	Hardiness Zones	Growth Rate	Comments
Viburnum Tinus (laurustinus)	to zone 7	Medium	White flowers.

DECIDUOUS SHRUBS

Name	Hardiness Zones	Growth Rate	Comments
Buddleia Davidii (orange eye butterfly bush, summer lilac)	5, 6, 7	Medium	Thrives in sun. Needs some pruning. Orange, fragrant flowers.
Calycanthus floridus (Carolina allspice, pineapple shrub, strawberry shrub)	to zone 5	Medium	Large, fragrant, reddish-brown flowers.
Cornus alba cv. 'Sibirica' (Siberian dogwood)	3, 4	Medium to Fast	Sensitive to 2-4-D. Must be pruned. Flowers, red stems
Cornus mas (cornelian cherry, sorbet)	to zone 5	Medium	Thrives in full sun or full shade. Tolerant of fluoride. Sensitive to 2-4-D. Yellow flowers, red fruit.
Cotinus Coggygria (smokebush)	to zone 5	Medium	Leaves purplish. Pest-resistant.
Cotoneaster apiculatus (cranberry cotoneaster)	to zone 5	Medium	Prefers sunny location in well-drained soil. Pink flowers, red fruit.
Cotoneaster divaricatus (spreading cotoneaster)	5, 6, 7, 8	Medium	Pink flowers, red fruit.
Crataegus monogyna (English hawthorn)	4, 5, 6, 7, 8	Slow	Sensitive to salt. Flowers.
Cytisus species (broom)	5, 6, 7, 8, 9, 10	Slow	Needs sun. Grows in cities. Good fall color, flowers.
Daphne Mezereum (February daphne)	4, 5, 6, 7, 8	Slow	Thrives in medium shade. Susceptible to twig blight. Pink fragrant flowers.
Deutzia species (deutzia)	5, 6, 7, 8	Medium	Needs sun. Sensitive to fluoride. White flowers.
Enkianthus campanulatus (redvein enkianthus, Chinese bellflower)	5, 6, 7	Medium	Thrives in full sun to medium shade. Member of heath family. Yellow flowers, good fall color.
Fuchsia species (lady's eardrops)	to zone 6	Medium	Pendulous, colorful summer flowers.
Fouquieria splendens (Ocotillo, coach whip, vine cactus)	7, 8, 9, 10	Medium	Needs sun. Protected by law. Scarlet flowers.

Hamamelis virginiana (witch hazel)	to zone 5	Fast	Grows in shade. Tolerant of salt. Susceptible to horned gall. Yellow, fragrant flowers.
Hibiscus syriacus (rose of Sharon, shrub althea)	5, 6, 7, 8, 9, 10	Medium	Needs full sun. Hardy species. Should not be pruned. Small pinkish, mauve flowers.
Hydrangea macrophylla, also called *Hydrangea hortensis* (common big leaf hydrangea, house hydrangea)	to zone 6	Medium to Fast	Showy flowers. Requires rich, porous soil. Prefers full sun.
Hydrangea paniculata cv. 'Grandiflora' (peegee hydrangea)	4, 5, 6, 7	Medium	White flowers.
Paeonia suffruticosa (tree peony)	to zone 5	Medium	Needs full sun to medium shade. Showy flowers.
Parkinsonia aculeata (Jerusalem thorn, Mexican palo verde)	10	Medium	Yellow flowers.
Philadelphus species (mock orange)	4, 5, 6, 7, 8, 9	Fast	Thrives in sun or shade. Tolerant of salt. Sensitive to ozone. Needs some pruning. Susceptible to leaf miner. White flowers.
Potentilla fruticosa (bush cinquefoil)	2, 3, 4, 5, 6, 7, 8, 9	Fast	Grows in shade. Yellow flowers, good fall color.
Prunus glandulosa (flowering almond)	to zone 4	Medium	Sensitive to salt. Susceptible to borers, tent caterpillars. White or pink flowers.
Rhododendron calendulaceum, also known as *Azalea calendulacea* (flame azalea)	5, 6, 7, 8, 9	Medium	Needs sun to medium shade. Sensitive to salt, ozone. Flowers.
Rhododendron mucronulatum (Korean rhododendron)	5, 6, 7, 8, 9	Medium	Needs sun to medium shade. Sensitive to salt, ozone. Flowers.
Rhododendron Schlippenbachii, also known as *Azalea schlippenbachii* (Royal azalea)	5, 6, 7, 8, 9	Medium	Needs sun to medium shade. Sensitive to salt, ozone. Flowers.
Rosa rugosa (rugosa rose, Japanese rose)	2, 3, 4, 5, 6, 7, 8	Medium	Sensitive to fluoride, salt. Tolerant of sulfur dioxide. Needs pruning. Pink or white flowers.
Spiraea latifolia (meadowsweet)	5, 6, 7, 8, 9	Fast	Thrives in sun or shade. Sensitive to salt.

Tamarix ramosissima, also known as *Tamarix odessana* (Odessa tamarisk, five stamen tamarisk)	8, 9, 10	Medium	Tolerant of salt. Useful along coast and in arid Southwest.
Viburnum X carcephalum (fragrant snowball, autumn foliage brilliant)	5, 6, 7, 8	Medium	Grows in medium shade. Good fall color, fragrant flowers.
Viburnum plicatum, also known as *Viburnum tomentosum* (Japanese snowball)	5, 6, 7, 8	Medium	Red fall foliage, white flowers.
Viburnum trilobum, also known as *Viburnum americanum* (American cranberry bush)	to zone 2	Medium	White flowers, scarlet fruit.

EVERGREEN SHRUBS

Name	Hardiness Zones	Growth Rate	Comments
Abelia X grandiflora (glossy abelia)	6, 7, 8, 9, 10	Medium	Grows in shade. Flowers.
Agave attenuata (foxtail agave, century plant)	9, 10	Slow	Needs sun. Flowers bloom every seven to fifteen years.
Agave Vilmoriniania (century plant)	9, 10	Slow	Needs sun. Erect twenty-foot column of flowers. Dies after flowering, producing hundreds of young plants.
Atriplex species (saltbush, orach)	to zone 6	Variable	Often occur in saline soils. Grown as ornamentals or for forage in desert regions.
Aucuba japonica (Japanese aucuba, Japanese laurel)	8, 9, 10	Medium	Thrives in partly shaded location in moist, well-drained soil. Fruit.
Brunfelsia pauciflora calycina (yesterday, today, and tomorrow)	9, 10	Medium	Needs full sun to medium shade. Flowers.
Callistemon citrinus, also known as *Callistemon lanceolatus* (crimson bottlebrush)	9, 10	Medium	Needs sun. Needs heavy pruning. Crimson flowers.

Carissa grandiflora (natal plum)	9, 10	Fast	Needs full sun. Tolerant of salt. Edible fruit.
Ceanothus species (deciduous or evergreen) (ceanothus, California lilac, wild lilac)	8, 9, 10	Medium to Fast	Needs full sun. Low maintenance. Blue or white flowers.
Chamaecyparis obtusa (Hinoki false cypress)	5, 6, 7	Slow	Needs medium shade.
Chamaecyparis pisifera (Sawara false cypress)	to zone 5	Slow	Needs medium shade.
Cotoneaster dammeri, also known as *Cotoneaster* *humifusus* (bearberry cotoneaster)	5, 6, 7, 8, 9, 10	Slow to Medium	Thrives in full sun or full shade. Susceptible to borers, scale. White flowers, scarlet berries.
Cotoneaster horizontalis (rock spray, rock cotoneaster)	4, 5, 6, 7, 8	Medium	Needs full sun to full shade. Susceptible to borers, scale. Scarlet berries.
Cotoneaster lacteus (cotoneaster)	to zone 6	Medium	White flowers in large clusters. Showy fruits.
Eriogonum giganteum St. Catherine's lace	9, 10	Medium	Leaves in rosettes. White-woolly flowers. Requires sun and well-drained soil.
Euonymus Fortunei (winter creeper)	5, 6, 7, 8, 9	Slow to Medium	Thrives in full sun or full shade. Needs some trimming and weeding.
Euphorbia pulcherrima (poinsettia)	8, 9, 10	Fast	Needs sun to partial shade. Sensitive to 2-4-D, ozone, sulfur dioxide. Attractive flowers. Many cultivars.
Fatsia japonica, also known as *Aralia* *japonica, Aralia sieboldii* (Japanese fatsia, paper plant)	8, 9, 10	Medium	Bold foliage.
Ilex X altaclarensis cv. 'Wilsonii' (Wilson holly)	6, 7, 8, 9	Medium to Fast	Vigorous tree with leathery leaves. Attractive fruit.
Ilex Aquifolium cultivars (English holly)	6, 7, 8, 9	Slow	Prefers medium shade. Sensitive to sulfur dioxide. Semisensitive to fluoride. Red fruit.
Ilex Cassine (dahoon, dahoon holly)	7, 8, 9, 10	Medium	Flowers, fruit.
Ilex cornuta (Chinese holly)	7, 8, 9, 10	Medium	Tolerant of chloride, mercury.

Ilex crenata cultivars (Japanese holly)	6, 7, 8, 9	Medium	Needs medium shade. Sensitive to ethylene.
Juniperus communis (common juniper)	to zone 2	Slow	Prefers full sun. Tolerant of fluoride, sulfur dioxide. Susceptible to insect pests. Fruit.
Juniperus conferta (shore juniper)	5, 6, 7, 8, 9, 10	Medium	Thrives in full sun or medium shade. Tolerant of salt.
Juniperus procumbens (Japanese garden juniper)	to zone 2	Slow	Prefers full sun. Tolerant of fluoride, sulfur dioxide.
Juniperus sabina (savin juniper)	5, 6, 7, 8, 9, 10	Medium	Thrives in full sun or medium shade. Tolerant of fluoride, sulfur dioxide. Must remove dead branches. Susceptible to juniper twig blight.
Justicia Brandegeana, also known as *Beloperone guttata* (shrimp plant)	8, 9, 10	Fast	Prefers medium shade. Must be pruned. Attractive, abundant flowers.
Laurus nobilis (sweet bay)	8, 9, 10	Medium	Aromatic.
Lemaireocereus Thurberi (organpipe cactus)	8, 9, 10	Medium	Needs sun. White flowers, red fruit.
Leptospermum scoparium (tea tree)	9, 10	Medium to Fast	Needs medium shade. White, pink flowers.
Leucothoe Fontanesiana, also known as *Leucothoe Catesbaei* (drooping leucothoe)	5, 6, 7, 8, 9	Medium to Slow	Prefers medium shade. Needs some pruning. White flowers, red fall color.
Mahonia Aquifolium (Oregon holly grape)	5, 6, 7, 8, 9	Medium	Prefers medium shade. Susceptible to foliar burn. Flowers, edible fruit.
Myrtis communis (Greek myrtle)	9	Medium	Dense foliage, strongly scented when crushed.
Nandina domestica (nandina, Chinese sacred bamboo)	7, 8, 9, 10	Medium	Thrives in sun or medium shade. Red fall and winter foliage.
Nolina Parryi (beargrass)	8, 9, 10	Medium	Needs sun. Should be watered. Flowers.
Pieris floribunda (mountain andromeda)	4, 5, 6, 7, 8, 9	Medium	Requires moist peaty or sandy soil and partial shade. Flowers.
Pinus aristata (bristlecone pine, hickory pine)	to zone 5	Medium	Prefers full sun. Sensitive to smog.
Pinus Mugo, also known as *Pinus montana* (mugo pine, Swiss mountain pine)	3, 4, 5, 6, 7, 8	Slow	Thrives in full sun to medium shade. Tolerant of sulphur dioxide. Sensitive to fluoride. Susceptible to pine needle scale.

Platycladus orientalis (Oriental arborvitae)	to zone 5	Slow	Tolerant of ozone. Susceptible to leaf miner, bugworm.
Rhododendron carolinanum (carolina rhododendron)	5, 6, 7, 8, 9	Medium	Prefers medium shade. Sensitive to salt, ozone. Pink flowers.
Rhododendrum indicum cultivars (Indian azalea)	5, 6, 7, 8, 9	Medium	Thrives in sun or medium shade. Sensitive to ozone, salt. Flowers.
Rhododendron maximum (rosebay rhododendron, great laurel)	5, 6, 7, 8, 9	Medium	Thrives in sun to medium shade. Sensitive to ozone, salt. Flowers.
Skimmia japonica (Japanese skimmia)	8, 9	Medium	Thrives in sun or shade. Fragrant flowers, attractive fruit.
Spartium junceum (Spanish broom)	8, 9, 10	Fast	Needs full sun. Tolerates salt. Needs pruning. Fragrant yellow flowers.
Taxus baccata (English yew)	4, 5, 6, 7	Slow	Thrives in sun or shade. Sensitive to salt. Susceptible to taxus weevil.
Tetrapanax papyriferus, also known as Fatsia papyrifera (rice paper plant)	8, 9, 10	Medium	Source of rice paper.
Tibouchina Urvilleana, also known as Tibouchina semidecandra and Pleroma grandiflora (glory bush, princess flower)	8, 9, 10	Medium	Thrives in full sun or medium shade. Purple flowers.
Yucca Whipplei (candle of the Lord)	8, 9, 10	Slow	Requires sun. Extremely persistent after fires, sprouts leaves. Spectacular blooms.

DECIDUOUS VINES

Name	Hardiness Zones	Growth Rate	Comments
Actinidia arguta (bower actinidia, tara vine)	5, 6, 7, 8, 9, 10	Fast	Thrives in full sun or medium shade. Fruits, fragrant flowers.
Actinidia chinensis (chinese actinidia, kiwi fruit)	7, 8, 9, 10	Fast	Thrives in full sun or medium shade. Needs some support. Fruits.
Antigonon leptopus (coral vine)	9, 10	Fast	Needs full sun. Must prune dead sections. Flowers.
Campsis X Tagliabuana (trumpet vine)	5, 6, 7, 8, 9, 10	Fast	Needs full sun. Flowers.

Celastrus scandens (American bittersweet)	3, 4, 5, 6, 7, 8	Fast	Thrives in full sun or medium shade. Needs pruning. Fruits.
Clematis hybrids (hybrid clematis)	6, 7, 8, 9, 10	Fast to Medium	Thrives in full sun or medium shade. Needs some pruning. Showy flowers.
Clematis montana (pink anenome clematis)	6, 7, 8, 9, 10	Fast to Medium	Needs full sun to medium shade. Needs some pruning. Flowers.
Dolichos Lablab (hyacinth bean)	7, 8	Fast	Thrives in full sun to medium shade. Pest-free. Flowers.
Humulus japonicus, also known as *Humulus scandens* (Japanese hop)	3, 4, 5, 6, 7, 8, 9, 10	Fast	Thrives in full sun to medium shade.
Hydrangea anomala subsp. *petiolaris,* also known as *Hydrangea petiolaris* or *Hydrangea scandens* (climbing hydrangea)	5, 6, 7, 8, 9, 10	Fast	Needs full sun to medium shade. Flowers.
Ipomoea alba, also known as *Ipomoea bona-nox* and *Calonyction aculeatum* (moonflower)	6, 7, 8, 9, 10	Fast	Thrives in full sun to medium shade. Flowers.
Lonicera Heckrottii (goldflame honeysuckle)	5, 6, 7, 8, 9, 10	Fast	Thrives in full sun to medium shade. Needs trimming. White to yellow fragrant flowers.
Lonicera japonica cv. 'Halliana' (Hall's honeysuckle)	4, 5, 6, 7, 8, 9, 10	Fast	Thrives in full sun to medium shade. Tolerant of ozone, salt. Needs trimming. White to yellow fragrant flowers.
Lonicera sempervirens cultivars (trumpet honeysuckle)	4, 5, 6, 7, 8, 9, 10	Fast	Thrives in full sun to medium shade. Tolerant of ozone, salt. Needs trimming. Flowers, fruits.
Lycium halimifolium (matrimony vine)	6, 7, 8, 9, 10	Fast	Prefers full sun. Fruits. Useful for dry, poor soils.
Macfadyena unguis-cati, also known as *Bignonia tweediana* (cat's claw vine)	8, 9, 10	Fast	Needs full sun to medium shade. Needs watering. Flowers.
Parthenocissus quinquefolia, also known as *Ampelopsis quinquefolia* (Virginia creeper)	3, 4, 5, 6, 7, 8, 9, 10	Fast	Thrives in full sun to medium shade. Tolerant of salt. Sensitive to ozone. Colored, fall foliage.
Parthenocissus tricuspidata, also known as *Ampelopsis tricuspidata* (Boston ivy, Japanese creeper)	5, 6, 7, 8, 9, 10	Fast	Thrives in full sun to medium shade. Sensitive to ozone. Needs heavy trimming. Colored fall foliage.

Polygonum Aubertii (silver fleece vine, silver lace vine)	5, 6, 7	Fast	Needs full sun. Flowers, fruits.
Pueraria lobata, also known as *Pueraria Thunbergiana* (kudzu)	3, 4, 5, 6, 7, 8, 9, 10	Very Fast	Needs full sun. Grows extremely fast. Flowers.
Vitis coignetiae (glory vine)	5, 6, 7, 8, 9	Fast	Needs full sun. Fruits.
Vitis riparia (riverbank grape)	3, 4, 5, 6, 7, 8, 9	Fast	Needs full sun. Sensitive to ozone, fluoride, sulfur dioxide. Needs pruning, fertilization. Fruits.
Vitis species (grapevine species)	3, 4, 5, 6, 7, 8, 9	Fast	Prefers full sun. Sensitive to ozone, fluoride, sulfur dioxide. Needs pruning, fertilization. Fruits.
Wisteria floribunda cultivars (Japanese wisteria)	6, 7, 8, 9, 10	Fast	Needs full sun. Needs pruning. Pendant clusters of flowers.
Wisteria sinensis, also known as *Wisteria chinensis* (Chinese wisteria)	6, 7, 8, 9, 10	Fast	Needs full sun. Needs pruning. Flowers.

EVERGREEN VINES

Name	Hardiness Zones	Growth Rate	Comments
Akebia quinata (five-leaf akebia)	4, 5, 6, 7, 8, 9, 10	Fast	Thrives in full sun to medium shade. Fragrant flowers (not showy). Half-evergreen.
Bignonia capreolata, also known as *Anisostichus capreolatus, Doxantha capreolata* (cross vine)	to zone 6	Fast	Needs sun. flowers.
Bougainvillea hybrids (bougainvillea)	9, 10	Fast	Needs sun. Sensitive to fluoride, nitrous oxide, ozone. Tolerant of salt. Scarlet or purple flowers.
Euonymus Fortunei (common winter creeper)	6, 7, 8, 9	Medium	Thrives in full sun or full shade. Needs trimming and weeding.
Ficus pumila (creeping fig)	9, 10	Fast to Medium	Thrives in full sun to medium shade.

Gelsemium sempervirens (evening trumpet flower, Carolina jasmine)	9, 10	Medium	Thrives in full sun or medium shade. Must be watered, thinned. Disease free. Flowers. Poisonous.
Hedera canariensis (Algerian ivy)	8, 9, 10	Fast	Needs full sun to medium shade. Trim annually. Water.
Hedera Helix (English ivy)	5, 6, 7, 8, 9, 10	Fast	Thrives in full sun or full shade. Sensitive to salt. Trim annually. Water.
Justicia Brandegeana, also known as *Beloperone guttata* (shrimp plant)	8, 9, 10	Fast	Thrives in full sun or medium shade. Must be pruned. Flowers.
Lantana montevidensis (lantana)	9, 10	Fast	Needs full sun. Needs cutting and thinning. Fragrant lavender flowers.
Lonicera sempervirens (trumpet honeysuckle)	5, 6, 7, 8, 9, 10	Fast	Thrives in full sun to medium shade. Tolerant of ozone, sale. Needs cutting. Flowers, fruits.
Thunbergia grandiflora (skyflower, blue trumpet vine, clock vine)	8, 9, 10	Fast	Needs full sun. Needs pruning. Susceptible to yellowing. Flowers.
Trachelospermum jasminoides, also known as *Rhynchospermum jasminoides* (star jasmine, Confederate jasmine)	6, 7, 8, 9, 10	Slow	Needs full sun or medium shade. Sensitive to salt. Needs cutting, feeding, weeding. Fragrant, small white flowers.

GROUND COVERS

Name	Hardiness Zones	Growth Rate	Comments
Aegopodium Podagraria (silver-edge bishop's weed, silver-edge goutweed)	to zone 3	Fast	Thrives in sun or medium shade. Flowers.
Ajuga reptans (bugleweed, carpet bugle)	4, 5, 6, 7, 8, 9, 10	Fast	Thrives in full sun or medium shade. Some feeding, trimming, watering needed. Blue flowers.
Androsace sarmentosa (rock jasmine)	to zone 2	Medium	Must be watered. Flowers.
Antennaria dioica (everlasting, pussy's toes)	2, 3, 4, 5, 6, 7, 8, 9, 10	Medium	Adapted to poor soil. Flowers.

Arctostaphylos uva-ursi (bearberry, kinnikinnick)	3, 4, 5, 6, 7, 8, 9, 10	Slow	Thrives in full sun to medium shade. Needs watering, needs good drainage.
Asparagus Sprengeri (Sprenger asparagus)	9, 10	Slow to Medium	Thrives in full sun or medium shade. Needs feeding, trimming. Fragrant pink flowers, fruits.
Baccharis pilularis (dwarf coyote bush, chaparral broom)	to zone 7	Fast	Thrives in full sun to medium shade. Needs little water, some feeding. Profuse flowers.
Bougainvillea species (bougainvillea)	9, 10	Fast	Needs sun. Sensitive to fluoride, nitrous oxide, ozone. Tolerant of salt. Needs minimal watering. Scarlet, purple, yellow flowers.
Ceanothus gloriosus (Point Reyes ceanothus)	7, 8, 9, 10	Fast to Medium	Needs full sun. Low maintenance. Lavender-blue flowers.
Ceanothus griseus var. *horizontalis* (Carmel creeper)	7, 8, 9, 10	Medium to Fast	Needs full sun. Low maintenance. Blue flowers.
Ceanothus thyrsiflorus var. *repens* (creeping blue blossom)	7, 8, 9, 10	Medium to Fast	Needs full sun. Low maintenance. Blue flowers.
Convolvulus mauritanicus (ground morning glory)	6, 7, 8, 9, 10	Medium to Fast	Needs full sun. Needs light trimming. Lavender-blue flowers.
Dichondra micrantha (dichondra)	10	Medium to Fast	Cultivated as substitute for lawn grass. Creeping herb.
Echinocereus Engelmannii (Hedgehog cactus)	9, 10	Slow	Thrives in sun or medium shade. Plants are not long-lasting. Hot pink flowers.
Euonymus Fortunei (winter creeper)	5, 6, 7, 8	Slow to Medium	Thrives in full sun or full shade. Needs trimming and weeding. Purple foliage in winter.
Hedera Helix (English ivy)	5, 6, 7, 8, 9, 10	Fast	Thrives in full sun or full shade. Sensitive to salt. Trim annually, water. Many cultivars. Berries.
Juniperus chinensis cultivars (Chinese juniper)	4, 5, 6, 7, 8, 9, 10	Slow	Needs full sun. Tolerant of fluoride, sulfur dioxide. Susceptible to juniper scale, mites. Fruit.
Juniperus horizontalis cv. 'Wiltonii' (Wilton carpet juniper)	5, 6, 7, 8, 9, 10	Medium	Needs full sun. Semisensitive to salt. Susceptible to mites. Purple fall foliage.
Juniperus prostrata (creeping juniper)	5, 6, 7, 8, 9, 10	Medium	Prefers full sun. Semisensitive to salt.
Mahonia repens (creeping mahonia, dwarf holly grape, Oregon grape)	3, 4, 5, 6, 7, 8, 9	Slow to Medium	Thrives in medium to full shade. Small yellow flowers, blackfruits.

Ophiopogon japonicus (mondo grass)	7, 8, 9, 10	Slow	Thrives in full sun or full shade. Light-lavender flowers.
Osteospermum fruticosum (trailing African daisy)	9, 10	Medium	Needs full sun. Colorful flowers.
Pachysandra terminalis (Japanese pachysandra)	5, 6, 7, 8	Fast	Thrives in medium or full shade. Keep weeded and watered. Small white flowers, white berries.
Paxistima Canbyi (canby paxistima)	4, 5, 6, 7	Slow to Medium	Thrives in full sun or medium shade.
Pilea microphylla (artillery fern)	8, 9, 10	Medium	Prefers medium shade. Must be watered.
Rosmarinus officinalis cv. 'Prostratus' (dwarf rosemary)	6, 7, 8, 9	Slow	Needs full sun. Tolerant of salt. Needs feeding and thinning out. Light-blue flowers.
Saxifraga species (rock foil)	to zone 2	Fast	Thrives in sun to medium shade. Needs watering. Good for rock gardens.
Sedum species (stonecrop, live-forever)	to zone 2	Fast	Thrives in full sun to medium shade. Succulents found from North Temperate Zone through Tropics.
Thymus praecox subsp. *arcticus* (mother-of-thyme)	to zone 2	Fast	Thrives in sun to medium shade. Low maintenance. Flowers.
Thymus serpyllum (creeping thyme)	to zone 2	Fast	Thrives in full sun to medium shade. Small, purplish-white flowers.
Vinca minor (common periwinkle, trailing myrtle, creeping myrtle)	4, 5, 6, 7, 8, 9, 10	Fast	Thrives in medium to full shade. Needs feeding, watering, cutting. Susceptible to twig blight. Small flowers.
Wedelia trilobata (wedelia)	10	Medium	Yellow flowers.
Zebrina pendula (wandering Jew)	10	Fast	Thrives in sun to medium shade. Purple underside to leaves.

BIBLIOGRAPHY

CHAPTER 1

Aronin, Jeffrey. *Climate and Architecture.* New York: Reinhold, 1953.

Calvert, Floyd. *Energy Utilization in Buildings.* Washington, D.C.: University Press of America, 1977.

Federer, C. A. "Trees and Forests in Urbanized Environment." Effects of trees in modifying urban microclimate, published by Cooperative Extension Service, University of Massachusetts, U.S. Department of Agriculture, Amherst, Massachusetts, March 1971.

Fitch, James Marston. *American Building: Historical forces that Shaped It.* New York: Houghton Mifflin, 1948.

———"Primitive Architecture and Climate." *Scientific American*, Vol. 203, #6, 1960.

Flemer, William III. "The Role of Plants in Today's Energy Conservation." *American Nurseryman*, Vol. 139, LXXXIX (9), 1974.

Goodland, Robert. "Buildings and the Environment," published by the Carey Arboretum of the New York Botanical Garden, 1976.

Molen, Ronald. *House Plus Environment.* Olympus Press, 1974.

Schiler, Marc. "Foliage Effects on Computer Simulation of Building Energy Load Calculations." Thesis, Cornell University, 1979.

Watson, Donald, and Bertrand, Alain. "Indigenous Architecture as a Basis of House Design in Developing Countries." *Habitat*, Vol. 1, # 3/4, 1976.

CHAPTER 2

American Society of Heating, Refrigerating and Air-Conditioning Engineers: *Handbook of Fundamentals*. Menasha, Wisconsin: George Banta and Company, 1974.

Aronin, Jeffrey E. *Climate and Architecture*. New York: Reinhold, 1953.

Deering, Robert B. "Effect of Living Shade on House Temperatures." *Journal of Forestry*, Vol. 54, 1956.

Flemer, William III. "The Role of Plants in Today's Energy Conservation." *American Nurseryman*, Vol. 139, LXXXIX (9), 1974.

Geiger, Rudolph. *The Climate Near the Ground*. Cambridge, Massachusetts: Harvard University Press, 1965.

Givoni, B. *Man, Climate and Architecture*. London: Building Research Station, Technion, (&) Applied Science Publishers, Ltd.

Hammond, J., Hunt, M., Cramer, R., and Neubauer, L. *A Strategy for Energy Conservation*. Energy Conservation Ordinance Project, Davis, California, 1974.

Kramer, Paul J., and Kozlowski, Theodore T. *Physiology of Trees*. New York: McGraw-Hill, 1960.

Olgyay, Victor. *Design with Climate: Bioclimatic Approach to Architectural Regionalism*. Princeton: Princeton University Press, 1963.

"Regional Guidelines for Building Passive Energy Conserving Homes," published by the U.S. Department of Housing and Urban Development in cooperation with the U.S. Department of Energy, 1978.

Robinette, Gary. *Plants, People and Environmental Quality: A Study of Plants and Their Environmental Function*. Washington, D.C.: U.S. Department of Interior, National Park Service, 1972.

University of Minnesota. *Earth Sheltered Housing Design*. Van Nostrand Reinhold Co., 1978.

Walsh, J. W. T. *The Science of Daylight*. London: Pitman Publishing Corp., 1961.

Woodruff, N. P. "Shelterbelt and Surface Barrier Effects on Wind Velocities, Evaporation, House Heating, Snowdrifting." Kansas Agricultural Experimental Station, Technical Bulletin 77, Manhattan, Kansas.

CHAPTER 3

Culjat, Boris. *Climate and the Built Environment in the North*. Stockholm: Avdelningen for Arkitektur, KTH, 1975.

Erskine, Ralph. "The Challenge of the High Latitudes." *RAIC Journal*, January 1964.

Griffin, C. W. *Energy Conservation in Buildings*. Construction Specifications Institute, Washington, D.C., 1974.

National Bureau of Standards. *Window Design Strategies to Conserve Energy*. 003-003-01794-9, Government Printing Office, Washington, D.C.

Shurcliff, William A. *Solar Heated Buildings of North America*. Church Hill, Harrisville, New Hampshire. Brick Publishing Co.

Stites, J., and Mower, R. G. "Rock Gardens." New York State College of Agriculture and Life Sciences, Cornell University, Ithaca, N. Y., 1979.

University of Minnesota. *Earth Sheltered Housing Design*. Van Nostrand Reinhold Co., 1978.

CHAPTER 4

AIA Research Corporation. *Regional Guidelines for Building Passive Energy Conserving Homes*. U.S. Department of Housing and Urban Development in cooperation with the U.S. Department of Energy, November 1978.

American Horticultural Society. *Cultivated Palms.* January 1961.

Benson, L. *The Cacti of Arizona.* Tucscon: University of Arizona Press, 1969.

Cravens, R. H. *Vines.* Alexandria, Virginia: Time-Life Books, 1979.

Crockett, J. U. *Landscape Gardening.* Alexandria, Virginia: Time-Life Books, 1971.

Crowther, Richard. *Sun, Earth: How to Use Solar and Climatic Energies.* New York: Charles Scribner's Sons, 1978.

Fry, Maxwell, and Drew, Jane. *Tropical Architecture in the Dry and Humid Zones.* New York: Reinhold, 1964.

Givoni, B. *Man, Climate and Architecture.* London: Building Research Station, Technion, (&) Applied Science Publishers.

Hammond, J., et al. *A Strategy for Energy Conservation prepared for the City of Davis, Cal.,* 1974, published by Living Systems, Winters, California.

Innes, Clive. *Cacti and Succulents.* London: Ward Lock Limited, 1977.

Mathias, H. E. (ed.). *Color for the Landscape.* California Arboretum Foundation, 1964.

Mathias, M. (ed.). *Color for the Landscape.* California Arboretum Foundation, Inc., 1973.

McClenon, C., and Robinette, G. O. *Landscape Planning for Energy Conservation.* Environmental Design Press, 1977.

Moore, Jr., Harold. *The Major Groups of Palms and Their Distribution.* Bailey Hortorium, 1973.

Polunin, O., and Huxley, A. *Flowers of the Mediterranean.* Boston: Houghton Mifflin Co., 1966.

Progressive Architecture. *Energy Conscious Design.* April 1979, April 1980. Stamford, Connecticut, Cleveland, Ohio: Reinhold Publishing.

Rudofsky, Bernard. *Architecture Without Architects.* New York: Doubleday, 1969.

Sandia Laboratories. *Passive Solar Buildings: A Compilation of Data and Results.* Albuquerque, New Mexico 87185, 1978.

Soil Conservation Society of America. Natural Vegetation Committee, Arizona Chapter; *Landscaping with Native Arizona Plants.* Tucson: University of Arizona Press, 1973.

U.S. Department of Energy. *Options for Passive Energy Conservation in Site Design.* U.S. Department of Commerce, 5285 Port Royal Road, Springfield, Virginia 22161.

Weniger, Del. *Cacti of the Southwest.* University of Texas Press Bruder Hartman, Berlin, 1970.

Williamson, J. F. *Lawns and Groundcovers.* Menlo Park: Sunset Books, 1975.

CHAPTER 5

AIA Research Corporation. *Regional Guidelines for Building Passive Energy Conserving Homes.* U.S. Department of Housing and Urban Development in cooperation with the U.S. Department of Energy, November 1978.

Cravens, R. H. *Vines.* Alexandria, Virginia: Time-Life Books, 1979.

Crockett, J. U. *Landscape Gardening.* Alexandria, Virginia: Time-Life Books, 1971.

Fry, Maxwell, and Drew, Jane. *Tropical Architecture in the Dry and Humid Zones*. New York: Reinhold, 1964.

Ledin, B. (ed). *Cultivated Palms*. American Horticultural Society, Amer. Hort. Mag 40 (1) : i January 1961.

Mathias, M. (ed.). *Color for the Landscape*. California Arboretum Foundation, Inc., 1973.

McClenon, C., and Robinette, G. O. *Landscape Planning for Energy Conservation*. Environmental Design Press, 1977.

Polunin, O., and Huxley, A. *Flowers of the Mediterranean*. Boston: Houghton Mifflin Co., 1966.

Ransom, W. H. *Solar Radiation: Thermal Effects on Building Materials*. Tropical Building Studies No. 3, Building Research Station, London, 1962.

Symposium on Design for Tropical Living; *Proceedings*, Durban, South Africa, 1957.

Williamson, J. F. *Lawns and Groundcovers*. Menlo Park: Sunset Books, 1975.

CHAPTER 6

AIA Research Corporation. *Regional Guidelines for Building Passive Energy Conserving Homes*. U.S. Department of Housing and Urban Development in cooperation with the U.S. Department of Energy, November 1978.

Cravens, Richard H. *Vines*. Alexandria, Virginia: Time-Life Books, 1979.

Crockett, James Underwood. *Landscape Gardening*. Alexandria, Virginia: Time-Life Books, 1971.

Erley, Duncan, and Jaffe, Martin. *Site Planning for Solar Access: A Guidebook for Residential Developers*. American Planning Association, 1313 East Sixtieth St., Chicago.

Leckie, Masters, Whitehouse, Young. *Other Homes and Garbage: Designs for Self Sufficient Living*. San Francisco: Sierra Club Books, 1975.

Mass Design, Architects and Planners. *Solar Heated Houses for New England and Other North Temperate Climates*.

Mathews, F. Schuyler. *Field Book of American Trees and Shrubs*. New York: G. P. Putnam's Sons, eighteenth impression.

McClenon, Charles, and Robinette, Gary. *Landscape Planning for Energy Conservation*. Environmental Design Press, 1977.

Williamson, Joseph F. *Lawns and Groundcovers*. Menlo Park: Sunset Books, 1975.

CHAPTER 7

Argue, R., et al. "The Sun Builders." *Renewable Energy in Canada*, 1978.

Aylor, Donald. "Sound Transmission through Vegetation in Relation to Leaf Area Density, Leaf Width, and Breadth of Canopy," Acoustical Society of America, Journal, 1972, Vol. 51.

———. "Noise Reduction by Vegetation and Ground." Acoustical Society of America, Journal, 1972, Vol. 51.

Bennett, H. H. *Elements of Soil Conservation*. New York: McGraw-Hill, 1955.

Bethlehem Steel Company. "Your Land— A handbook of practical methods for preventing and curing soil erosion." 1942.

Blumenfeld, Dennis E., and Weiss,

George H. "Attenuation Effects in the Propagation of Traffic Noise." *Transportation Research*, Vol. 9, 1975.

Embleton, T. F. W. "Sound Propagation in Deciduous and Evergreen Woods." Acoustical Society of America, Journal, Vol. 35, 1963.

Franklin Research Center. "The First Passive Solar Home Awards." U.S. Department of Housing and Urban Development, January 1979.

Hindawi, I. J. "Air Pollution Injury to Vegetation." U.S. Department of HEW, 1970.

Illinois Institute for Environmental Quality—Southern Illinois University. "Determination of Maximum Permissible Levels of Selected Chemicals that Exert Toxic Effects on Plants of Economic Importance in Illinois." August 1974.

Jacobson, J. S., and Hill, A. C. "Recognition of Air Pollution Injury to Vegetation: A Pictorial Atlas." Air Pollution Control Association, Pittsburgh, 1970.

Naegele, J. A. (ed.). "Air Pollution Damage to Vegetation." The American Chemical Society, 1973.

The Pennsylvania State College. "Preventing Soil Erosion." 1945.

Rundel, Philip. "Fire and Nature." University of California, Irvine (in press).

Stanford Research Institute. "Economic Impact of Air Pollutants in the United States." November 1971.

Webster, A. D. *Town Planting*. George Routledge & Sons, Ltd., 1910.

Solar Energy in America. Washington, D.C., American Association for the Advancement of Science, 1978.

Powell, Jeanne W. *An Economic Model for Passive Solar Designs in Commercial Environments*. U.S. Department of Commerce, National Bureau of Standards, Washington, D.C., 1980.

Progressive Architecture (entire issue). April 1979.

Progressive Architecture (entire issue). April 1980.

Schiler, M., and Greenberg, D. "The Calculation of Translucent and Opaque Shadow Effects in Building Energy Simulation." *Proceedings: CAD 80 the 4th International Conference on Computers in Architecture and Engineering, Brighton 1980*, Guildford, Surrey, IPC Science and Technology, Ltd. 1980.

Schiler, M., and Greenberg, D.: "The Calculation of Foliage Shading Effects in Computer Simulation of Building Energy Loads." *Proceedings: 16th Annual Design Automation Conference, San Diego 1979*. New York, Association for Computing Machinery, 1979.

Scientific American (entire issue, "Energy and Power"). September 1971, Vol. 224, ab.3.

U.S. Department of Energy, *Building Energy Performance Standards* and *Technical Support Documents*. Washington, D.C., 1979 (see also *Federal Register* for continuing information).

CHAPTER 8

AIA Journal (entire issue). December 1977.

Hammond, Allen, and Metz, William.

INDEX

Adaptation, human, 29–30
Air conditioners, sunscreens for, 88
Air-conditioning: in hot, humid regions, 98, 101; vs. landscaping, 19, 80, 117–118
Air flow: measurement in hot, humid regions, 102; plants and, 163; in urban environment, 64f
Air locks and vestibules, 114
Air movements: comfort and, 29; determination of direction of, 44; offshore and onshore breezes, 46–47, 48f. See also Air flow; Breezes; Winds
Air pollution, 139–142
Air purification system of plants, 140
Altitude angle, 31f, 33, 34f
Apartment dwellers, 12. See also Balcony gardens
Architects: computer graphics and, 161–163. See also Home designs
Artificial building materials, 52, 54
Asphalt and concrete, absorption of radiant energy by, 87
Atmosphere, density and thickness of, solar radiation and, 35, 36f
Atriums, enclosed, 86f, 87, 88, 89f
Attics and crawl spaces, 55, 58

Balcony gardens: in hot, humid regions, 104, 105f, 107; in temperate regions, 129f, 130
Bearing angle, 31f, 33, 34f

Berms: around structures in cool regions, 71f, 72; climatic effects of, 50; deflection of breezes by, 50f; as insulator for building, 51; noise control and, 144, 145f; with plants, 50–51, 65; and wind control, 124
Blacktop, 52
Borders. See Deciduous windbreaks, hedges, and borders; Evergreen windbreaks, hedges, and borders
Breezes: channeling, 102, 103f, 123–124, 125; deflection by berm, 50
Breezeways, 43–44, 45f
Building and Energy Performance Standards (BEPS), 158–159
Building materials, 51–54; artificial, 52; classifications of, 51; damaged by vines, 101, 127; glass, 52–53; in hot, arid regions, 80; in hot, humid regions, 95; natural, inorganic, 52; natural, organic, 51–52; natural vs. synthetic, 54; in primitive societies, 15; synthetic, 53–54; in temperate regions, 114
Buildings. See Home designs
Bushes. See Shrubs

Canopies, 85
Carbon dioxide, oxygen needs and, 141
Change of state. See Latent heat
Cities: air flow in, 64f; balcony

gardens in, 129–130; pollution-resistant plants in, 140–142; radiational cooling in, 26
Climate: and berms, 50–51; comfort and, 25–59; home designs for, 15–16, 54–59; human adaptability to, 29–30. See also Sun; Water; Winds
Clouds: climate and, 47; solar radiation and, 35
Cold, human response to, 29–30. See also Temperatures
Color: and response of materials to radiant energy, 52; of roofs, 59
Comfort, human, 25–59; building materials and, 51–54; home design and, 25, 54–59; landforms and, 50; perception of, 25; physical characteristics of, 25–29; physiological ability to adapt and, 29–30; plants for sun control and, 36–38; sun and, 30–36; water and, 45–47; winds and, 38–40; wind-chill factor and, 29–30
Computer graphics, 161–163; and computer simulation of landscape, 162f; drawing board used in, 161f
Conduction, 26, 27f; and heat loss from body, 30
Construction materials. See Building materials
Convection, 27, 28f; and heat loss from body, 30; and heat loss from winds, 40, 67

Cool regions, 63–76; clear areas in, 65, 66f; description of, 63–64; home designs for, 55, 56f; landforms in, 71–72; landscape design for, 65, 74f; plant species for, 75–76; special landscaping strategies for, 72–73; sun in, 65–66; water in, 70–71; windbreaks in, 67f, 68f, 69–70; winds in, 66–70

Costs: of development of new energy sources vs. passive systems, 157–158; and energy-efficient landscape design, 17–20; of landscape maintenance, 20, 21; of shading, 18–19

Deciduous shrubs: for hot, arid regions, 91; for hot, humid regions, 109; list of, 202–204; shading and, 125; for temperate regions, 135

Deciduous trees. See Short and medium deciduous trees; Tall deciduous trees

Deciduous vines: for cool regions, 76; for hot, arid regions, 92; for hot, humid regions, 110; list of, 207–209; for temperate regions, 135–136

Deciduous windbreaks, hedges, and borders: for hot, arid regions, 91; for hot, humid regions, 109; list of, 197–199

Desert regions: temperature fluctuations in, 46. See also Hot, arid regions

Downwind, 39–40, 68b

Drainage, in hot, humid regions, 104

Driveways and walkways, position of windbreaks and, 41

Earth-sheltered homes, 59. See also Underground homes

Energy crisis, status of, 157–163

Erosion control, landscaping for, 147, 148f, 149f

Evaporation: and dense trees, 117–118; and garden pools and fountains, 49; in hot, arid regions, 84; in hot, humid regions, 95; and plants for control of solar radiation, 37; and transfer of radiant energy into latent heat, 46

Evergreen bushes, snow insulation and, 125–126

Evergreen shrubs: for cool regions, 76; for hot, arid regions, 91–92; for hot, humid regions, 109–110; list of, 204–207; for temperate regions, 135

Evergreen trees: over thirty-five feet tall, list of, 191–193; under thirty-five feet tall, list of, 193–195. See also Tall evergreen trees

Evergreen vines: for hot, arid regions, 92; for hot, humid regions, 110; list of, 209–210; for temperate regions, 136

Evergreen windbreaks, hedges, and borders: for cool regions, 76; list of, 199–202; for temperate regions, 134

"Eyebrow" trellises, 101

Fire-resistant plants, 146–147

Forests: ground and tree canopy temperatures in, 38; rain in, 49

Foundation plantings, 125–126

Fountains. See Pools and ponds

Fuel shortages: impact on housing design, 16; and life styles, 11

Galleries around building, 96

Gardens: enclosed, in hot, arid regions, 86f, 87, 88, 89f; fire-resistant, 146–147. See also Balcony gardens

Gazebo, 50

Glare: control of, 142f, 143; in hot, humid regions, 101, 102f, 103; plants and, 82

Glass, 52–53. See also Windows

Government energy program, 157–161

Grasses: and control of solar radiation, 36, 38; in hot, arid areas, 82; and latent heat transfer, 28; maintenance of, 129; temperatures above, compared with artificial groundcovers, 54

Greenhouse effect, 52, 53f

Greenhouses, energy-efficient design for, 148–149, 150f, 151

Groundcovers: artificial and natural, 54; in checkerboard pattern, 84f; and control of solar radiation, 36, 38; for cool regions, 72, 76; drought-resistant, 82, 83; for erosion control, 148; for hot, arid regions, 92; for hot, humid regions, 101, 110; list of, 210–212; shrubs as, 107; and sound control, 146; for temperate regions, 127, 128f, 129, 136

Heat: absorption, synthetic materials and, 54; convection by trees, 117–118; distinguished from temperature, 26; human response to, 30; reradiation of, 26, 38, 47, 83; and shade trees, see Shade; solar radiation and,

35; transfer, 26–28. See also Heat gain and loss

Heat gain and loss, 17–21, 40; and airlocks, vestibules, and porches, 114; and exposed foundation, 125–126; greenhouses and, 149, 151; plants adjacent to building, and 43, 44f; snow as insulator and, 47; window glass and, 53

Heating costs, winds in urban environments and, 64

Hedges: for hot, arid regions, 85, 87–88; of trees, 118, 119f; for wind funnel, 123–124. See also Deciduous windbreaks, hedges, and borders; Evergreen windbreaks, hedges, and borders

Hemisphere home design, 55

Hollows, 50

Home designs, 54–59; for cool regions, 55, 64, 71–72; early, 15–16; early American, 114; greenhouse and, 149, 151; in hot, arid regions, 57f, 58–59, 80; in hot, humid regions, 96, 98f, 99f, 104f; in temperate regions, 55, 58, 113–114

Hot, arid regions, 79–92; description of, 79; home design in, 57f, 58–59, 80; plants for, 80; radiational cooling in, 26; special planting strategies in, 86–89; sun in, 81–83; water in, 84–86; wind control in, 84

Hot, humid regions, 95–110; description of, 95–96; home design in, 57f, 58; landforms in, 104; plant species for, 96, 107–110; special landscape strategies in, 104–107; sun control in, 98–101; water in, 103–104; wind control in, 102, 103f

Houseplants: in hot, arid regions, 36; in hot, humid regions, 104

Humidity: in cool regions, 63; creation in hot, arid regions, 84–85; and garden pools and fountains, 47, 49; houseplants and, 86, 104; latent heat transfer and, 28; plants and, 49–50. See also Relative humidity

Hurricanes, 95

Insulators: berms as, 51; double-row plant screens as, 126; snow as, 126f; vines as, 72

Irrigation: and drought-resistant plants, 87; in hot, humid regions, 104

Jalousies, 96

Landforms: in cool regions, 71–72; in hot, humid regions, 104; negative, 50; with plants, 50–51. *See also* Berms

Landscape: desert, 81*f*; use by early builders, 15–16. *See also* Landscape design, energy-saving

Landscape design, energy-saving: advantages over mechanical devices, 21, 157–163; benefits of, 11; bibliography on, 213–217; computer graphics and, 161–163; for cool regions, *see* Cool regions; economic benefits of, 12, 17–21; future of, 157–163; for hot, arid regions, *see* Hot, arid regions; for hot, humid regions, *see* Hot, humid regions; and landforms with plants, 50–51; planning and, 21; psychological benefits of, 152–154; rationale for, 15–21; research on, 161–163; and sun control by plants, 36–38; for temperate regions, *see* Temperate regions; theory of, 16–21; and wind control by plants, *see* Windbreaks, Winds. *See also* Landscape strategies, special

Landscape maintenance: cost of, 20, 21; ground covers and, 128–129

Landscape strategies, special: in cool regions, 72–73; in hot, arid regions, 86–89; in hot, humid regions, 104–107; selection of, 21; in temperate regions, 125–132

Latent heat: body loss of, 30; conversion of solar radiation to, 37; for temperature control in hot, arid areas, 80; transfer of, 28*f*, 46

Latitudes: of North America, 32*f*, and solar path, 31, 33, 34

Leeward, 39–40

Local persistent winds, 38–39

Mechanical shading methods, 19

Metals, 114

Microclimate: and pools and ponds in cool regions, 71; primitive builders and, 15–16; water and plants, 47, 49–50. *See also* Sun; Water; Winds

Moisture: conservation, home design for, 58; loss in hot, arid regions, 84; retention, plants and, 49–50. *See also* Humidity; Water

Mountains, climatic effects of, 50

National Solar Heating and Cooling Information Center, 161

Native plants, 21

Natural, inorganic building materials, 52

Natural, organic building materials, 51–52

Noise control: berms and, 50, 51, 144, 145*f*; plants and, 143, 144*f*, 145*f*, 146, 153–154

Nuclear power plants, 157–158

Offshore breezes, 124; convection and, 48*f*; and water and ground temperatures, 46–47

Onshore breezes, convection and, 48*f*

Outbuildings: position of, 55; as windbreaks, 55

Outdoor living areas: berms and hollows and, 50; in hot, humid regions, 96–97; landforms with plants and, 50–51; in temperate regions, 114

Overhangs, 55, 118. *See also* Trellises

Oxygen requirements, 141

Ozone, 142

Palm trees, 81; disadvantages of, 99, 101; in hot, humid regions, 98*f*, 99*f*, 101; over thirty-five feet tall, list of, 195; shading atrium, 86*f*; shading in hot, humid regions and, 99, 100*f*, 101; under thirty-five feet tall, list of, 196–197. *See also* Short palm trees; Tall palm trees

Passive cooling, 114

Patio, landscaped, in hot, humid regions, 97*f*

Pavements: gravel, glare and, 102*f*; in hot, humid regions, 104

Pavilions, 50

Pergola, vine-covered, 118

Permafrost regions, underground homes in, 71–72

Pesticides, 142

Plant species: for city gardens, 130; for cool regions, 75–76; for erosion control, 148; for fire-resistant, 146; for hot, arid regions, 87, 90–92; for hot, humid regions, 96, 107–110; pollution-resistant, 140–142; for privacy, 153; by size and form, 183–212; sun-blocking activity of, 163; for temperate regions, 125, 132–136. *See also* Plants

Planting plan: for balcony garden, 130; for rock garden, 73. *See also* Landscape strategies, special

Plants: acoustical effects of, 143–146; air pollution and, 139–142; compared with mechanical cooling devices, 80; control of solar radiation with, 36–38; double-row screen of, 126; for eastern exposure in temperate regions, 115*f*; for erosion control, 147, 148*f*; flame-resistant, 146–147; glare and reflection control with, 142*f*, 143, 144*f*; landforms with, 50–51; latent heat transfer and, 28; for northern exposures of hot, arid regions, 83; oxygen needs and, 141; prevention of water erosion with, 148, 149*f*; privacy and, 153; removal of, 20; for screening, 152*f*, 153*f*; shading with, *see* Shade; sound control with, 153–154; water and, 49–50; wind control with, 40–45; zones of hardiness for, 167–169. *See also* Plant species *and under individual types of, i.e.,* Shrubs; Trees; Vines

Pollutants, plants and, 139–142

Ponds. *See* Pools and ponds

Pools and ponds, 47, 49; in cool regions, 71; in enclosed atriums, 87; in hot, arid regions, 84, 85*f*; in hot, humid regions, 103; in temperate regions, 124–125

Porches, 114

Precipitation: in cool regions, 63; in hot, humid regions, 96; in temperate regions, 113. *See also* Snow

Privacy: berms and, 50; plants and, 153

Radiant solar energy, 27*f*, 30–31; absorbed by asphalt and concrete, 87; and color of building materials, 52; storage in greenhouse, 151; wind and, 120. *See also* Reradiation

Radiational cooling, 26

Rain. *See* Precipitation

Reflection, control of, 142*f*, 143, 144*f*

Relative humidity, 29; plants for control of solar radiation and, 37

Reradiation: bushes and, 83; clouds and, 47; in forests, 38

Road salt, 142

Rock gardens, 72, 73*f*

Roof gardens. *See* Balcony gardens

Sea breezes, 47; formation of, 48*f*

Seasons: in cool climates, 63–64; and solar path, 34; in temperate zone, 113

Shade, 37; and calculation of placement of plants, 118, 119*f*; in hot, arid regions, 80*f*; 81–82, 88; in hot, humid regions, 96–97, 98, 99, 100*f*; and overhangs, 118; and spacing of homes, 59; and species' shape, 38; in summer in cool climates, 66; tall narrow trees *vs.* short wide trees for, 116*f*; in temperate regions, 114; and vines in terrace gardens, 105, 107; vines and trellises for, 117*f*, 118. *See also* Shade trees

Shade trees, 17–19, 20–21; placement of, 118; tall narrow *vs.* short wide, 116*f*; for temperate regions, 115

Shadow calculations, 118, 119*f*

Shelterbelt. *See* Windbreaks

Short and medium deciduous trees: for cool regions, 75; for hot, arid regions, 90; for hot, humid regions, 107–108; list of, 187–190; for temperate regions, 133

Short and medium evergreen trees: for cool regions, 75–76; for hot, humid regions, 108; for temperate regions, 134

Short palm trees, for hot, humid regions, 108–109

Shrubs: between water and structures in cool climates, 71; and control of solar radiation, 36; in cool regions, 72; as ground covers, 107; and snow as insulator, 47; in temperate regions, 125; as underplantings, 126. *See also* Evergreen shrubs

Slopes, protection from wind, 40

Small evergreen trees, planted next to homes, 125

Smog: and radiational cooling, 26; and solar radiation, 35

Snow: and direction of air movements, 44; and foundation plantings, 125–126; as insulator, 47, 72, 126*f*; and windbreaks, 41, 42*f*

Softwoods: as precipitation barriers, 49; and windbreaks, 45

Solar angle table for North America, 171–175

"Solar bank act," 160

Solar collectors, 158; in hot, humid regions, 101; trees and, 118

Solar energy, and water, 46

Solar energy panels, in hot, humid regions, 99–100

Solar greenhouses. *See* Greenhouses

Solar path, 34*f*; and balcony gardens, 130; determination of, 31, 34–35; planting in harmony with, 115, 117–118

Solar path charts, 31, 33, 34*f*

Solar projection maps, 35*f*

Solar radiation, 35–36; absorbed and reflected, 36; and berms, 50; capture and storage by water body, 46*f*; and clouds, 47; control by plants, 36–38; in cool climates, 65–66; earth's atmosphere and, 35, 36*f*; reflection, absorption, and transmission by plants of, 37*f*; shortwave and longwave, glass and, 52*f*; and windbreaks in cool climates, 68–70

Sound attenuation methods, 144*f*. *See also* Noise control

Specific heat, 26; of water, 45

Spring perennials, planted beneath windbreaks, 41

Sulfur-dioxide-resistant trees, 140–141

Sun, 30–36; in cool climates, 63–64, 65–66; in hot, arid regions, 81–83; in hot, humid regions, 98–101; in temperate regions, 114–120. *See also* Solar path; Solar radiation

Sunscreens, 143; for air-conditioners, 88; in hot, arid regions, 81; in hot, humid regions, 99, 101; trees as, 162–163

Synthetic building materials, 53–54

Tall deciduous trees: for cool regions, 75; for hot, arid regions, 90; for hot, humid regions, 107; list of, 183–187; for temperate regions, 132–133

Tall evergreen trees: for cool regions, 75; for hot, arid regions, 90–91; for hot, humid regions, 108; for temperate regions, 133–134

Tall palm trees, for hot, humid regions, 108

Tax credits for residential energy conservation, 160

Temperate regions, 113–136; description of, 113; home designs for, 55, 56*f*, 58; plant species for, 132–136; shade trees in, 17, 18*f*, 19; shading in, 20–21; special planting strategies for, 125–132; sun control in, 114–120; water in, 124–125;

wind in, 120–124

Temperatures: above artificial and natural grass, 54; in cool regions, 63, 70–71; distinguished from heat, 26; fluctuations in desert regions, 46; in forests, 15; in hot, arid regions, 79; in hot, humid regions, 95–96; and humidity, 29; over grassy surfaces *vs.* soil, 28; and solar radiation and reradiation, 38; of water and ground, offshore breezes and, 46–47; of zones of plant hardiness, 167

Thermopane windows, 53

Topsoil, formation of, 147

Trees: adjacent to building, 43, 44*f*; "air-conditioning" by, 43–44, 117–118; and control of solar radiation, 36, 37; in cool regions, 65, 66*f*, 73; densities, table of, 181–182; drought-resistant, 80; for hot, arid regions, 80, 83; shading function, 17–19, 20–21, 81, 97; by size and form, 183–197; solar collectors and, 118; and sound control, 145; sulfur dioxide-resistant, 140–141; as sunscreens, 162–163; for temperate regions, 115, 119–120; as windbreaks, 19–20, 40, 43, 67–68, 70. *See also* Short and medium deciduous trees; Tall deciduous trees; Tall evergreen trees

Trellises, 55; and channeling breezes in hot, arid regions, 85; in hot, humid regions, 102; shading function, 19, 81, 82*f*; with slats at solar control angle, 82*f*. *See also* Overhangs; Vines and trellises

Underground homes, 51, 65, 71–72;

U.S. Department of Agriculture, 160–161

Ventilation, in hot, arid regions, 58

Venturi effect, 42, 43*f*, 84, 102; and designing wind funnels, 123–124

Vertical shading devices, 58

Vines: and control of solar radiation, 37, 38; cooling effect of, 126–127; and insulation in cool climates, 72; problems with, 127; for shading, 19; in temperate regions, 125; in terrace gardens, 104, 105*f*, 107. *See also* Deciduous vines; Vines and trellises

Vines and trellises, 50; and blocking of radiated heat, 26; for hot, arid regions, 82; for hot, humid regions, 100*f*, 101; for shading, 117, 118

Warm regions, breezeway in, 43–44, 45*f*

Water: capture and storage of solar radiation by, 46*f*; in cool regions, 70–71; erosion and, 148; in hot, arid regions, 84–86; in hot, humid regions, 103–104; and offshore breezes, 46–47; plants and, 47, 49–50; recirculation of, 84, 85; specific heat of, 26; storage of solar energy by, 46; in temperate regions, 124–125

Windbreaks, 40; buildings as, 55; calculation of height and distance from structure, 68, 69*f*, 70; in cool regions, 65, 67*f*, 68*f*, 69–70; double-row plant screen as, 126; effect on wind velocity, 41*f*, erosion control and, 147–148; heat loss and, 20; for hot, arid regions, 84; for hot, humid regions, 102; loose and dense, 70; on north, 123*f*; and reduction of wind velocity, 40; selection of species for, 45; snowdrifts and, 41, 42*f*; for temperate regions, 114, 121*f*, 122, 123*f*, 124; and Venturi effect, 42, 43*f*, 44. *See also* Deciduous windbreaks, hedges,

and borders; Evergreen windbreaks, hedges, and borders

Wind-chill factor, 29, 30*f*

Wind funnels, designing, 124

Windows, 52–53; in cool regions, 65; in hot, arid regions, 80

Winds, 38–40; and berms, 124; categories of, 38; and city gardens, 130; control by plants, 40–45; in cool regions, 64, 66–70; determination of direction of, 121; of drought, 79; in hot, arid regions, 79, 84; in hot, humid regions, 102, 103*f*; sea breezes, 47; in temperate regions, 113, 120–124; velocity, 19–20, 40

Wood chips, 83